McMindfulness

**How Mindfulness Became the
New Capitalist Spirituality**

McMindfulness

How Mindfulness Became the
New Capitalist Spirituality

RONALD E. PURSER

Published by Repeater Books

An imprint of Watkins Media Ltd

Unit 11Shepperton House
89-93 Shepperton Road
London
N1 3DF
United Kingdom
www.repeaterbooks.com
A Repeater Books paperback original 2019
4

Distributed in the United States by Random House, Inc., New York.

Cover design: Johnny Bull
Typography and typesetting: Frederik Jehle
Typefaces: Meriden LT Std, Libre Bodoni, Helvetica Neue

ISBN: 9781912248315
Ebook ISBN: 9781912248490

Printed and bound in the United Kingdom by TJ International Ltd

CONTENTS

chapter one
What Mindfulness Revolution?

Mindfulness is mainstream, endorsed by celebrities like Oprah Winfrey, Goldie Hawn and Ruby Wax. While meditation coaches, monks and neuroscientists rub shoulders with CEOs at the World Economic Forum in Davos, the founders of this movement have grown evangelical. Prophesying that its hybrid of science and meditative discipline "has the potential to ignite a universal or global renaissance," the inventor of Mindfulness-Based Stress Reduction (MBSR), Jon Kabat-Zinn, has bigger ambitions than conquering stress. Mindfulness, he proclaims, "may actually be the only promise the species and the planet have for making it through the next couple hundred years."[1]

So, what exactly is this magic panacea? In 2014, *Time* magazine put a youthful blonde woman on its cover, blissing out above the words: "The Mindful Revolution." The accompanying feature described a signature scene from the standardized course teaching MBSR: eating a raisin very slowly indeed. "The ability to focus for a few minutes on a single raisin isn't silly if the skills it requires are the keys to surviving and succeeding in the 21st century," the author explained.[2]

I am skeptical. Anything that offers success in our unjust society without trying to change it is not revolutionary — it just helps people cope. However, it could also be making things worse. Instead of encouraging radical action, it says

7

the causes of suffering are disproportionately inside us, not in the political and economic frameworks that shape how we live. And yet mindfulness zealots believe that paying closer attention to the present moment without passing judgment has the revolutionary power to transform the whole world. It's magical thinking on steroids.

Don't get me wrong. There are certainly worthy dimensions to mindfulness practice. Tuning out mental rumination does help reduce stress, as well as chronic anxiety and many other maladies. Becoming more aware of automatic reactions can make people calmer and potentially kinder. Most of the promoters of mindfulness are nice, and having personally met many of them, including the leaders of the movement, I have no doubt that their hearts are in the right place. But that isn't the issue here. The problem is the product they're selling, and how it's been packaged. Mindfulness is nothing more than basic concentration training. Although derived from Buddhism, it's been stripped of the teachings on ethics that accompanied it, as well as the liberating aim of dissolving attachment to a false sense of self while enacting compassion for all other beings.

What remains is a tool of self-discipline, disguised as self-help. Instead of setting practitioners free, it helps them adjust to the very conditions that caused their problems. A truly revolutionary movement would seek to overturn this dysfunctional system, but mindfulness only serves to reinforce its destructive logic. The neoliberal order has imposed itself by stealth in the past few decades, widening inequality in pursuit of corporate wealth. People are expected to adapt to what this model demands of them. Stress has been pathologized and privatized, and the burden of managing it outsourced to individuals. Hence the peddlers of mindfulness step in to save the day.

But none of this means that mindfulness ought to be banned, or that anyone who finds it useful is deluded. Its proponents tend to cast critics who hold such views as malevolent cranks. Reducing suffering is a noble aim and it should be encouraged. But to do this effectively, teachers of mindfulness need to acknowledge that personal stress also has societal causes. By failing to address collective suffering, and systemic change that might remove it, they rob mindfulness of its real revolutionary potential, reducing it to something banal that keeps people focused on themselves.

A Private Freedom

The fundamental message of the mindfulness movement is that the underlying cause of dissatisfaction and distress is in our heads. By failing to pay attention to what actually happens in each moment, we get lost in regrets about the past and fears for the future, which make us unhappy. The man often labeled the father of modern mindfulness, Jon Kabat-Zinn, calls this a "thinking disease."[3] Learning to focus turns down the volume on circular thought, so Kabat-Zinn's diagnosis is that our "entire society is suffering from attention deficit disorder — big time."[4] Other sources of cultural malaise are not discussed. The only mention of the word "capitalist" in Kabat-Zinn's book *Coming to Our Senses: Healing Ourselves and the World Through Mindfulness* occurs in an anecdote about a stressed investor who says:

"We all suffer a kind of A.D.D."[5]

Mindfulness advocates, perhaps unwittingly, are providing support for the status quo. Rather than discussing how attention is monetized and manipulated by corporations such as Google, Facebook, Twitter and Apple, they locate the crisis in our minds. It is not the nature of the capitalist system that is inherently problematic; rather, it is the failure of individuals to be mindful and resilient in a precarious and uncertain economy. Then they sell us solutions that make us contented mindful capitalists.

The political naiveté involved is stunning. The revolution being touted occurs not through protests and collective struggle but in the heads of atomized individuals. "It is not the revolution of the desperate or disenfranchised in society," notes Chris Goto-Jones, a scholarly critic of the movement's ideas, "but rather a 'peaceful revolution' being led by white, middle class Americans."[6] The goals are unclear, beyond peace of mind in our own private worlds.

By practicing mindfulness, individual freedom is supposedly found within "pure awareness," undistracted by external corrupting influences. All we need to do is to close our eyes and watch our breath. And that's the crux of the supposed revolution: the world is slowly changed — one mindful individual at a time. This political philosophy is oddly reminiscent of George W. Bush's "compassionate conservatism." With the retreat to the private sphere, mindfulness becomes a religion of the self. The idea of a public sphere is being eroded, and any trickle-down effect of compassion is by chance. As a result, notes the political theorist Wendy Brown, "the body politic ceases to be a body, but is, rather, a group of individual entrepreneurs and consumers."[7]

Mindfulness, like positive psychology and the broader happiness industry, has depoliticized and privatized stress. If we are unhappy about being unemployed, losing our health insurance, and seeing our children incur massive debt through college loans, it is our responsibility to learn to be more mindful. Jon Kabat-Zinn assures us that "happiness is an inside job" that simply requires us to attend to the present moment mindfully and purposely without judgment.[8] Another vocal promoter of meditative practice, the neuroscientist Richard Davidson, contends that "wellbeing is a skill" that can be trained, like working out one's biceps at the gym.[9] The so-called mindfulness revolution meekly accepts the dictates of the marketplace. Guided by a therapeutic ethos aimed at enhancing the mental and emotional resilience of individuals, it endorses neoliberal assumptions that everyone is free to choose their responses, manage negative emotions, and "flourish" through various modes of self-care. Framing what they offer in this way, most teachers of mindfulness rule out a curriculum that critically engages with causes of suffering in the structures of power and economic systems of capitalist society.

If this version of mindfulness had a mantra, its adherents would be chanting "I, me and mine." As my colleague C.W. Huntington observes, the first question most Westerners ask when considering the practice is: "What is in it for me?"[10] Mindfulness is sold and marketed as a vehicle for personal gain and gratification. Self-optimization is the name of the game. I want to reduce *my* stress. I want to enhance *my* concentration. I want to improve *my* productivity and performance. One invests in mindfulness as one would invest in a stock hoping to receive a handsome dividend. Another fellow skeptic, David Forbes, sums this up in his book *Mindfulness and Its Discontents*:

> Which self wants to be de-stressed and happy? Mine! The Minefulness Industrial Complex wants to help your self be happy, promote your personal brand — and of course make and take some bucks (yours and mine) along the way. The simple premise is that by practicing mindfulness, by being more mindful, you will be happy, regardless of what thoughts and feelings you have, or your actions in the world.[11]

Of course, this is a reflection of capitalist norms, which distort many things in the modern world. However, the mindfulness movement actively embraces them, dismissing critics who ask if it really needs to be this way.

The Commodification of Mindfulness

Mindfulness is such a well-known commodity that it has even been used by the fast-food giant KFC to sell chicken pot pies. Developed by a high-powered ad agency, KFC's "Comfort Zone: A Pot Pie-Based Meditation System" uses a soothing voiceover and mystical images of a rotating Col Sanders sitting in the lotus posture with a pot pie head. The video "takes listeners on a journey," says the narrator: "The Comfort Zone is a groundbreaking system of personal meditation, mindfulness and affirmation based on the incredible power of KFC's signature pot pie."[12]

Mindfulness is now said to be a $4 billion industry, propped up by media hype and slick marketing by the movement's elites. More than 100,000 books for sale on Amazon have a variant of "mindfulness" in their title, touting the benefits of *Mindful Parenting, Mindful Eating, Mindful Teaching, Mindful Therapy, Mindful Leadership, Mindful Finance, a Mindful Nation,* and *Mindful Dog Owners,* to name just a few. There is also *The Mindfulness Coloring Book,* a bestselling subgenre in itself. Besides books, there are workshops, online courses, glossy magazines, documentary films, smartphone apps, bells, cushions, bracelets, beauty products and other paraphernalia, as well as a lucrative and burgeoning conference circuit. Mindfulness programs have made their way into public schools, Wall Street and Silicon Valley corporations, law firms, and government agencies including the US military. Almost daily, the media cite scientific studies reporting the numerous health benefits of mindfulness and the transformative effects of this simple practice on the brain.

Branding mindfulness with the veneer of hard science is a surefire way to get public attention. A key selling and marketing point for mindfulness programs is that it has been *proven* that meditation "works" based on the "latest neuroscience." But this is far from the case. As many prominent contemplative neuroscientists admit, the science of mindfulness and other forms of meditative practice is in its infancy and understanding of brain changes due to meditation has been characterized as trivial.[13] "Public enthusiasm is outpacing scientific evidence," says Brown

University researcher Willoughby Britton. "People are finding support for what they believe rather than what the data is actually saying."[14] The guiding ethos of scientific research is to be disinterested and cautious, yet when studies are employed for advocacy, their trustworthiness becomes suspect. "Experimenter allegiance," Britton worries, "can count for a larger effect than the treatment itself." There is a great deal of momentum in the mindfulness movement to override the caution that is the hallmark of good science. Together, researchers seeking grant money, authors seeking book contracts, mindfulness instructors seeking clients, and workshop entrepreneurs seeking audiences have talked up an industry built on dubious claims of scientific legitimacy.

Another marketing hook is the distant connection to Buddhist teachings, from which mindfulness is excised. Modern pundits have no qualms about flaunting this link for its cultural cachet — capitalizing on the exoticness of Buddhism and the appeal of such icons as the Dalai Lama — while at the same time dismissing Buddhist religion as foreign "cultural baggage" that needs to be purged. Their talking points frequently claim that they offer "Buddhist meditation without the Buddhism," or "the benefits of Buddhism without all the mumbo jumbo." Leaving aside the insulting tone, to which most seem oblivious (although it's the same as saying: "I really like secular Jews without all the Jewishness... you know, all the beliefs, rituals, institutions, and cultural heritage of Judaism — all that mumbo jumbo..."), they are stuck in a colonial mode of discourse. They lay claim to the authentic essence of Buddhism for branding prestige, while declaring that science now supersedes Buddhism, providing access to a universal understanding of mindfulness.

Some Buddhist responses make challenging points. To quote Bhikkhu Bodhi, an outspoken American monk, the power of meditative teachings might enslave us: "Absent a sharp social critique," he warns, "Buddhist practices could easily be used to justify and stabilize the status quo, becoming a reinforcement of consumer capitalism."[15] While I could argue whether mindfulness is a Buddhist practice or not (spoiler alert: it's not), that would only distract from what is really at stake.

As a management professor and a longstanding Buddhist practitioner, I felt a moral duty to start speaking out when large corporations with questionable ethics and dismal track records in corporate social responsibility began introducing mindfulness programs as a method of performance enhancement. In 2013, I published an article with David Loy in the *Huffington Post* that called into question the efficacy, ethics and narrow interests of mindfulness programs.[16] To our surprise, what we wrote went viral, perhaps helped by the title: "Beyond McMindfulness."

The term "McMindfulness" was coined by Miles Neale, a Buddhist teacher and psychotherapist, who described "a feeding frenzy of spiritual practices that provide immediate nutrition but no long-term sustenance."[17] Although this label is apt, it has deeper connotations. The contemporary mindfulness fad is the entrepreneurial equal of McDonald's. The founder of the latter, Ray Kroc, created the fast food industry. Like the mindfulness maestro Jon Kabat-Zinn, a spiritual salesman on par with Eckhart Tolle and Deepak Chopra, Kroc was a visionary. Very early on, when selling milkshakes, Kroc saw the franchising potential of a restaurant chain in San Bernadino, California. He made a deal to serve as the franchising agent for the McDonald brothers. Soon afterwards, he bought them out, and grew the chain into a global empire. Inspiration struck Kabat-Zinn after earning his doctorate in molecular biology at MIT. A dedicated meditator, he had a sudden vision in the midst of a retreat: he could adapt Buddhist teachings and practices to help hospital patients deal with physical pain, stress and anxiety. His masterstroke was the branding of mindfulness as a secular crypto-Buddhist spirituality.

Both Kroc and Kabat-Zinn had a remarkable capacity for opportunity recognition: the ability to perceive an untapped market need, create new openings for business, and perceive innovative ways of delivering products and services. Kroc saw his chance to provide busy Americans instant access to food that would be delivered consistently through automation, standardization and discipline. He recruited ambitious and driven franchise owners, sending them to his training course at "Hamburger University" in Elk Grove, Illinois. Franchisees would earn certificates in "Hamburgerology with a Minor in French Fries." Kroc continued to expand the reach of McDonald's by identifying new markets that would be drawn to fast food at bargain prices.

Similarly, Kabat-Zinn perceived the opportunity to give stressed-out Americans easy access to MBSR through a short eight-week mindfulness course for stress reduction that would be taught consistently using a standardized curriculum. MBSR teachers would gain certification by attending programs at Kabat-Zinn's Center for Mindfulness in Worcester, Massachusetts. He continued to expand the reach of MBSR by identifying new markets such as corporations, schools, government and the military, and endorsing other forms of "mindfulness-based interventions" (MBIs). As entrepreneurs, both men took measures to ensure that their products would not vary in quality or content across franchises. Burgers and fries at McDonald's are predictably the same whether one is eating them in Dubai or in Dubuque. Similarly, there is little variation in the content, structuring and curriculum of MBSR courses around the world.

Since the publication of "Beyond McMindfulness," I have observed with great trepidation how mindfulness has been oversold and commodified, reduced to a technique for just about any instrumental purpose. It can give inner-city kids a calming time-out, or hedge fund traders a mental edge, or reduce the stress of military drone pilots. Void of a moral compass or ethical commitments, unmoored from a vision of the social good, the commodification of mindfulness keeps it anchored in the ethos of the market.

A Capitalist Spirituality

This has come about partly because proponents of mindfulness believe that the practice is apolitical, and so the avoidance of moral inquiry and the reluctance to consider a vision of the social good are intertwined. Laissez-faire mindfulness lets dominant systems decide such questions as "the good." It is simply assumed that ethical behavior will arise "naturally" from practice and the teacher's "embodiment" of soft-spoken niceness, or through the happenstance of inductive self-discovery. However, the claim that major ethical changes intrinsically follow from "paying attention to the present moment, non-judgmentally" is patently flawed. The emphasis on "nonjudgmental awareness" can just as easily disable one's moral intelligence. It is unlikely that the Pentagon would invest in mindfulness if more mindful soldiers refused en masse to go to war.

Mindfulness is the latest iteration of a capitalist spirituality whose lineage dates back to the privatization of religion in Western societies. This began a few hundred years ago as a way of reconciling faith with modern scientific knowledge. Private experience could not be measured by science, so religion was internalized. Important figures in this process include the nineteenth-century psychologist William James, who was instrumental in psychologizing religion, as well as Abraham Maslow, whose humanistic psychology provided the impetus for the New Age movement. In *Selling Spirituality: The Silent Takeover of Religion*, Jeremy Carrette and Richard King argue that Asian wisdom traditions have been subject to colonization and commodification since the eighteenth century, producing a highly individualistic spirituality, perfectly accommodated to dominant cultural values and requiring no substantive change in lifestyle.[18] Such an individualistic spirituality is clearly linked with the neoliberal agenda of privatization, especially when masked by the ambiguous language used in mindfulness. Market forces are already exploiting the momentum of the mindfulness movement, reorienting its goals to a highly circumscribed individual realm.

Privatized mindfulness practice is easily coopted and confined to what Carrette and King describe as an "accommodationist" orientation that seeks to "pacify feelings of anxiety and disquiet at the individual level rather than seeking to challenge the social, political and economic inequalities that cause such distress."[19] However, a commitment to a privatized and psychologized mindfulness *is* political. It amounts to what Byung-Chul Han calls "psycho-politics," in which contemporary capitalism seeks to harness the psyche as a productive force.[20] Mindfulness-based interventions fulfill this purpose by therapeutically optimizing individuals to make them "mentally fit," attentive and resilient so they may keep functioning within the system. Such capitulation seems like the farthest thing from a revolution and more like a quietist surrender.

Mindfulness is positioned as a force that can help us cope with the noxious influences of capitalism. But because what it offers is so easily assimilated by the market, its potential for social and political transformation is neutered. Leaders in the mindfulness movement believe that capitalism and spirituality can be reconciled; they want to relieve the stress of individuals without having to look deeper and more broadly at its social, political and economic causes.

Some might wonder what is wrong with offering mindfulness to corporate executives and the rest of society's dominant 1%? Aren't they entitled to the benefits of mindfulness like anyone else? The more relevant question is what sort of mindfulness is actually on offer. Corporate executives get the same product as anyone else, and what it provides is an expedient tool for assuaging stress without wisdom and insight about where it comes from.

A truly revolutionary mindfulness would challenge the Western sense of entitlement to happiness irrespective of ethical conduct. However, mindfulness programs do not ask executives to examine how their managerial decisions and corporate policies have institutionalized greed, ill will and delusion, which Buddhist mindfulness seeks to eradicate. Instead, the practice is being sold to executives as a way to de-stress, improve productivity and focus, and bounce back from working eighty-hour weeks. They may well be "meditating," but it works like taking an aspirin for a headache. Once the pain goes away, it is business as usual. Even if individuals become nicer people, the corporate agenda of maximizing profits does not change. Trickle-down mindfulness, like trickle-down economics, is a cover for the maintenance of power.

Mindfulness is hostage to the neoliberal mindset: it must be put to use, it must be proved that it "works," it must deliver the desired results. This prevents it being offered as a tool of resistance, restricting it instead to a technique for "self-care." It becomes a therapeutic solvent — *a universal elixir* — for dissolving the mental and emotional obstacles to better performance and increased efficiency.[21] This logic pervades most institutions, from public services to large corporations, and the quest for resilience is driven by the dictum: "Adapt — or perish."[22] The result is an obsessive self-monitoring of inner states, inducing social myopia. Self-absorption trumps concerns about the outside world. As Byung-Chul Han observes, this reinvents the Puritan work ethic:

Endlessly working at self-improvement resembles the self-examination and self-monitoring of Protestanism, which represents a technology of subjectivation and domination in its own right. Now, instead of searching out sins, one hunts down negative thoughts.[23]

The marketing success of mindfulness often makes it seem seductively innocuous. Besides, it appears to be helpful, so why pick holes? Isn't a little bit of mindfulness better than none? What's wrong with an employee listening to a three-minute breathing practice on an app before a stressful meeting? On the surface, not much, but we should also think about the cost. If mindfulness just helps people cope with the toxic conditions that make them stressed in the first place, then perhaps we could aim a bit higher. Why should we allow a regime to usurp mindfulness for nefarious corporate purposes? Should we celebrate the fact that this perversion is helping people to "auto-exploit" themselves? This is the core of the problem. The internalization of focus for mindfulness practice also leads to other things being internalized, from corporate requirements to structures of dominance in society. Perhaps worst of all, this submissive position is framed as freedom. Indeed, mindfulness thrives on freedom doublespeak, celebrating self-centered "freedoms" while paying no attention to civic responsibility, or the cultivation of a collective mindfulness that finds genuine freedom within a cooperative and just society.

Of course, reductions in stress and increases in personal happiness and wellbeing are much easier to sell than seriously questioning causes of injustice, inequity and environmental devastation. The latter involves a challenge to the social order, while the former plays directly to its priorities, sharpening people's focus, improving their performance at work and in exams, and even promising better sex lives. Pick up any issue of *Mindful*, a new mass-market magazine, and one finds a plethora of articles touting the practical and worldly benefits of mindfulness. This inevitably appeals to consumers who value spirituality as a way of enhancing their mental and physical health. Not only has mindfulness been repackaged as a novel technique of psychotherapy, but its utility is commercially marketed as self-help. This branding reinforces the notion that spiritual practices are indeed an individual's private concern. And once privatized, these practices are easily coopted for social, economic and political control.

As originally argued in "Beyond McMindfulness," this is only the case because of how modern teachers frame the practice:

Decontextualizing mindfulness from its original liberative and transformative purpose, as well as its foundation in social ethics, amounts to a Faustian bargain. Rather than applying mindfulness as a means to awaken individuals and organizations from the unwholesome roots of greed, ill will and delusion, it is usually being refashioned into a banal, therapeutic, self-help technique that can actually reinforce those roots.[24]

This book explores how that occurs, and what might be done about it. There is no need for mindfulness to be so complicit in social injustice. It can also be taught in ways that unwind that entanglement. This requires us to see what is actually happening, and commit ourselves to trying to reduce collective suffering. The focus needs to shift from "me" to "we," liberating mindfulness from neoliberal thinking.

To that end, the critique that I offer is uncompromising, intolerant of unfairness, selfishness, greed, and the delusions of empire. It seeks to bring to light the unmindful allegiances in the mindfulness movement that obscure the relationship between personal stress and social oppression. It provides a much-needed critical counterbalance to the celebratory and self-congratulatory presentation of mindfulness by its boosters. I seek to illuminate, and thereby bring to mind, a shadow side that has been buried under the hype and anti-intellectual sentiment of much of the mindfulness movement. This process combats the social amnesia that leads to mindful servants of neoliberalism. The true meaning of mindfulness is an act of re-membering, not only in terms of recalling and being attentively present to our situation, but also of putting our lives back together, collectively.

chapter two
Neoliberal Mindfulness

For a couple of years, the *New York Times* business reporter David Gelles had a regular column on "Meditation for Real Life." Having written a book about *Mindful Work*, he dished out Hallmark card-like platitudes, covering "How to Be Mindful When Doing Your Taxes," "How to Be Mindful at the Gym" and "How to Be Mindful at the Doctor's Office." One such offering, "How to Be Mindful on the Subway," is too much fun to pass up. Imagine a New Yorker in a crowded subway following Gelles' advice:

> Take a few deep breaths, turn your lips up into a half-smile, softly gaze at another person on the subway car. Notice the thoughts or feelings that arise as you consider this person. Try to adopt a gaze of warmth and kindness, perhaps by imagining that this person is a friend of yours.[1]

This version of mindfulness is stoic self-pacification. Never mind what might cause your anxiety, just be mindful of what's in front of your face, and do your best to feel fuzzily warm (presumably hoping that the person you stare at does the same)!

The aim, says mindfulness guru Jon Kabat-Zinn, is to get better at "living in harmony with oneself and with the world."[2] By practicing mindfulness, people can learn to manage their emotional reactions and impulses, racing thoughts, stresses and worries, providing an oasis of relief.

Beneficial as this may sound, it has hidden consequences. Firstly, it promotes a focus on oneself and the mind's inner workings, deflecting attention from sources of stress in modern society's massive inequalities, austerities, and injustices. As a result, it reinforces some causes of suffering. Secondly, and more specifically, living in harmony with the world means accepting capitalism as a given. No radical critique or vision of social change is needed. With a breezy shrug from his well-paid position at the *New York Times*, Gelles assures us: "We live in a capitalist economy, and mindfulness can't change that."[3]

Well, it certainly won't if sold in those terms. Its presentation as a market-friendly palliative explains its warm reception in popular culture. It slots so neatly into the mindset of the workplace that its only real threat to the status quo is to offer people ways to become more skillful at the rat race. Modern society's neoliberal consensus argues that those who enjoy power and wealth should be given free rein to accumulate more. Those mindfulness merchants who accept market logic are an unsurprising hit with CEOs at the World Economic Forum in Davos, where Kabat-Zinn has no qualms about preaching the gospel of competitive advantage from meditative practice.[4]

Over the past few decades, neoliberalism has outgrown its conservative roots. It has hijacked public discourse to the extent that even self-professed progressives, such as Kabat-Zinn, think in neoliberal terms. Market values have invaded every corner of human life, defining how most of us are forced to interpret and live in the world.

The mindfulness movement took shape under neoliberal leadership. It began in 1979 with the founding of Kabat-

Zinn's Stress Reduction Clinic at the University of Massachusetts Medical School. This was the same year that Margaret Thatcher became the prime minister of the UK, to be joined soon after by Ronald Reagan as US president. Both advanced a neoliberal program — "Economics are the method; the object is to change the heart and soul," Thatcher said.[5] Could mindfulness be doing something similar, rewiring us to serve the requirements of neoliberalism? The mindfulness industry's market-friendliness should make us suspicious.

Me, Inc.

Perhaps the most straightforward definition of neoliberalism comes from the French sociologist Pierre Bourdieu, who calls it: "A program for destroying collective structures which may impede the pure market logic."[6] That goes further than a set of policies doled out by governments, central banks or global elites at the IMF. Rather, neoliberalism is a complex form of cultural hegemony. In its insidious worldview, human beings are best understood as entrepreneurs running their own private personal enterprise — the business of Me, Inc. — in competition with others. Textbooks talk about rational economic actors, but the effects of this in practice are stark, remaking the species as a dollar-hunting animal: *homo economicus*. The marketing mentality is easy to see on modern social media, where profiles on Facebook, Twitter, Instagram and LinkedIn promote a curated personal image. We are generally conditioned to think that a market-based society provides us with ample (if not equal) opportunities for increasing the value of our "human capital" and self-worth. And in order to fully actualize personal freedom and potential, we need to maximize our own welfare, freedom, and happiness by deftly managing internal resources.

Since competition is so central, neoliberal ideology holds that all decisions about how society is run should be left to the workings of the marketplace, the most efficient mechanism for allowing competitors to maximize their own good. Other social actors — including the state, voluntary associations, and the like — are just obstacles to the smooth operation of market logic, and they ought to be dismantled or disregarded. In theory, at least, neoliberalism promotes entrepreneurship by providing the defense of private property rights and upholding market freedoms. In practice, some economic actors — such as banks deemed "too big to fail" — get to game the system, while others — such as people on welfare — are demonized as scroungers.

Let's see how this plays out. Suppose your instincts lean vaguely leftwards, and that you therefore reject most neoliberal policies, but unwittingly share the basic outlook behind them. Suppose that at the same time you are firmly convinced of the value of mindfulness and making it widely available. These two orientations line up closely, supporting the promotion of a capitalist practice. For an actor in neoliberal society, mindfulness is a skill to be cultivated, or a resource to be put to use. When mastered, it helps you to navigate the capitalist ocean's tricky currents, keeping your attention "present-centered and non-judgmental" to deal with the inevitable stress and anxiety from competition. Mindfulness helps you to maximize your personal wellbeing.

All of this may help you to sleep better at night. But the consequences for society are potentially dire. The Slovenian philosopher Slavoj Žižek has analyzed this trend with great acuity. As he sees it, mindfulness is "establishing itself as the hegemonic ideology of global capitalism," by helping people "to fully participate in the capitalist dynamic while retaining the appearance of mental sanity."[7] No wonder Wall Street traders and hedge fund managers now use the practice to fine-tune their brains, up their game and gain an edge.

By deflecting attention from social, political and economic structures — that is, material conditions in a capitalist culture — mindfulness is easily coopted. Celebrity role models bless and endorse it, while "cool" Californian companies — including Google, Facebook, Twitter, Yahoo, Salesforce, Apple, and Zynga — have embraced it as an adjunct to their brand. Google's former in-house mindfulness czar Chade-Meng Tan had the actual job title Jolly Good Fellow. "Search inside yourself," he counseled colleagues (as well as readers of his bestselling book), for there — not in corporate culture — lies the source of your problems. Applied in this way, mindfulness becomes a form of capitalist spirituality, perfectly attuned to maintaining the neoliberal self.

A Technology of the Self

How is mindfulness presented to the public? Googling a wide range of terms — such as mindfulness in schools, corporations, hospitals, government, prisons, and even the military — typically leads to the same generic image:

a lone individual in a meditative posture with their eyes closed, blissfully detached from the outside world. This subjective activity effectively internalizes neoliberal edicts: each individual should take charge of their own "self-care" to remain employable. The dismantling of social protections along with market deregulation leaves people reliant on self-governance to manage their stress and help them thrive. Mindfulness delivers the message with a velvet glove, but it still contains the iron fist.

Around the same time as Jon Kabat-Zinn invented MBSR, and Margaret Thatcher won power vowing to "liberate those who create wealth,"[8] Michel Foucault identified the "neoliberal turn." In this cultural shift, the French thinker explained, there is a dual style of government, extending far beyond political activity. Foucault refers to this concept as "governmentality," which links power relations to processes of subjectification — or what he described as the "conduct of conduct." In other words, neoliberal institutions exercise micro-levels of power, reformulating what it means to be a person, self and identity. Foucault's critique and historical account, described in his 1978-79 Collège de France lectures, focused on exposing how this works. Governmentality explores how knowledge, expertise, and practices are developed to guide voluntary conduct.

Foucault distinguishes between two different modes of power: "techniques of domination," administered from outside, and "techniques of the self," by which the individual acts upon itself. Both are instrumental for the formation of selfhood as a neoliberal subject. They also influence each other. As Foucault explains: "The contact point, where the way individuals are driven by others is tied to the way they conduct themselves, is what we can call government."[9]

Unlike previous ways of exercising power, which used harsh punishment to restrict forbidden behaviors, neoliberal "disciplinary power" reaches into people's psyches through professions and institutions. It thereby induces free and enterprising people to govern themselves. According to Foucault, it is this link between enterprise culture and individual wellbeing that is most instructive: economic activity is said to be optimized by promoting entrepreneurship, while individuals are persuaded that their lives will be improved if they are free to conduct themselves entrepreneurially.

This is very different from early forms of institution-alization that derived their authority from organized religions, where the clergy served as intermediaries between church doctrine and cultural codes of conduct. Despite the influence of secularization, remnants of the Catholic confessional remain intact, administered by the scientifically authorized priests of mindfulness. As Foucault points out, "the obligation to confess is now relayed through so many different points, is so deeply ingrained in us, that we no longer perceive it as the effect of a power that constrains us."[10]

In a typical mindfulness course, the teacher-cum-expert provides the instructions for various practices, such as watching the breath, scanning body sensations, paying attention to the moment without judgment, and so on. After the conduct of an exercise there is often a period of "inquiry" and didactic interaction between teacher and participants. Instead of confessing their cardinal sins, participants confess how their mind was wandering, or how they got lost in their thoughts and ruminations, or how they were carried away by an emotional reaction. In this respect, confession does not operate as a coercive, top-down power structure. Rather, mindful confessions work by presupposing a bandwidth of acceptable affects and styles of thought, from which a deviation must be confessed, revealing what participants "noticed" about their wayward attention. These subtle power relations give those in authority a means of imparting their requirements. Through confessions, people learn to shape themselves into dutiful mindful subjects who can monitor, care and govern themselves.

The Mindfulness-Academic-Science Complex

As a technique of the self, mindfulness draws heavily upon diverse forms of institutional expertise to govern and manage behaviors instrumentally. There are now numerous university centers studying mindfulness and related fields, in Massachusetts, Wisconsin, California and the United Kingdom, along with the pioneering Mind & Life Institute, which facilitates discussions between scientists and meditators, overseen by the Dalai Lama. These academic centers are not only the sites for the conduct of scientific studies of mindfulness interventions, but also include academic programs for the training and certification of mindfulness teachers. The burgeoning "science of mindfulness" has provided new technologies of subjectivity, new vocabularies for the self-regulation of individuals, and new means for normalizing and calibrating individual affects that are aligned with enterprise culture. As the latest addition to the psy-disciplines, this new mindfulness-academic-science complex disseminates expert knowledge and practices promising individual psychological freedom, wellbeing and happiness.

These centers rely on, and compete for, large sums of government funding and grants for their existence. This inevitably encourages an entrepreneurial mentality, in which scholars try to spin multiple projects from each piece of research, maximizing returns by publishing and speaking about their work in the best shopwindows. The main aim of exposure is the chance to raise money, with little concern for where it comes from.

In *America the Anxious: How Our Pursuit of Happiness Is Creating a Nation of Wrecks*, Ruth Whippman points out that the positive psychology movement, which is also led by academic centers, has been funded by some of the most right-wing conservative organizations.[11] The John Templeton Foundation, founded by an evangelical Christian billionaire, has the ambitious mission of putting religion and science on an equal footing. It says on its website that it "aims to advance human wellbeing by supporting research on the Big Questions, and by promoting character development, individual freedom, and free markets."[12] This leads to funding for research that promotes the individual as the primary fulcrum for change and wellbeing. With an endowment of over $1.1 billion, the foundation has doled out tens of millions of dollars in grants and prizes to positive psychology professors. The Mind & Life Institute, one of the leading organizations promoting the scientific study of mindfulness, has also received over $1.2 million.

By producing an organized body of knowledge, and institutionally transmitting scientific studies, practices, discourses and professional expertise, university mindfulness centers have forged a regime of truth that harnesses micro-fields of power to shape the mindful subject. Margaret Thatcher would be proud. They have become "engineers of the human soul," to quote the British sociologist Nikolas Rose, playing an instrumental role in the neoliberal management of subjectivity, yet mindfulness is made to sound benignly therapeutic. In *Governing the Soul: The Shaping of the Private Self,* Rose shows how the psy-disciplines have shaped the "self-directing propensities of subjects to bring them into alliance with the aspirations of authorities."[13]

Similar to the self-help genre, much of mindfulness discourse, both in scientific journals and in the popular media, valorizes individual autonomy, freedom, choice, and authenticity. The penetration of dominating power is well disguised, but it is not a mere coincidence that neoliberalism and the mindfulness movement both conceive of social wellbeing in individualistic and psychologized terms.

The rhetoric of "self-mastery," "resilience" and "happiness" assumes wellbeing is simply a matter of developing a skill. Mindfulness cheerleaders are particularly fond of this trope, saying we can train our brains to be happy, like exercising muscles. Happiness, freedom and wellbeing become the products of individual effort. Such so-called "skills" can be developed without reliance on external factors, relationships, or social conditions. Underneath its therapeutic discourse, mindfulness subtly reframes problems as the outcomes of choices. Personal troubles are never attributed to political or socio-economic conditions, but are always psychological in nature and diagnosed as pathologies. Society therefore needs therapy, not radical change. This is perhaps why mindfulness initiatives have become so attractive to government policy-makers. Societal problems rooted in inequality, racism, poverty, addiction and substance abuse and deteriorating mental health, can be reframed in terms of individual psychology, requiring therapeutic help. Vulnerable subjects can even be told to provide this themselves.

Mindfulness as a Disimagination Machine

Neoliberalism divides the world into winners and losers. It accomplishes this task through its ideological linchpin: the individualization of all social phenomena. Since the autonomous (and free) individual is the primary focal point for society, social change is achieved not through political protest, organizing and collective action, but via the free market and atomized actions of individuals. Any effort to change this through collective structures is generally troublesome to the neoliberal order. It is therefore discouraged.

An illustrative example is the practice of recycling. The real problem is the mass production of plastics by corporations, and their over-use in retail. However, consumers are led to believe that being personally wasteful is the under-lying issue, which can be fixed if they change their habits. As a recent essay in *Scientific American* scoffs: "Recycling plastic is to saving the Earth what hammering a nail is to halting a falling skyscraper."[14] Yet the neoliberal doctrine of individual responsibility has performed its sleight-of-hand, distracting us from the real culprit. This is far from new. In the 1950s, the "Keep America Beautiful" campaign urged individuals to pick up their trash. The project was bankrolled by corporations such as Coca-Cola, Anheuser-Busch, and Phillip Morris, in partnership with the public service announcement Ad Council, which coined the term "litterbug" to shame miscreants. Two decades later, a famous TV ad featured a Native American man weeping at the sight of a motorist dumping garbage. "People Start Pollution. People Can Stop It," was the slogan. The essay in *Scientific American*, by Matt Wilkins, sees through such charades:

> At face value, these efforts seem benevolent, but they obscure the real problem, which is the role that corporate polluters play in the plastic problem. This clever misdirection has led journalist and author Heather Rogers to describe Keep America Beautiful as the first corporate greenwashing front, as it has helped shift the public focus to consumer recycling behavior and actively thwarted legislation that would increase extended producer responsibility for waste management.[15]

We are repeatedly sold the same message: that individual action is the only real way to solve social problems, so we should take responsibility. We are trapped in a neoliberal trance by what the education scholar Henry Giroux calls a "disimagination machine," because it stifles critical and radical thinking.[16] We are admonished to look inward, and to manage ourselves. Disimagination impels us to abandon creative ideas about new possibilities. Instead of seeking to dismantle capitalism, or rein in its excesses, we should accept its demands and use self-discipline to be more effective in the market.

The depoliticized nature of mindfulness means its therapeutic ethos of individual action supports neoliberalism. When the individualized self bears sole responsibility for its happiness and emotional wellbeing, failure is synonymous with failure of the self, not external conditions. To change the world, we are told to work on ourselves — to change our minds by being more mindful, nonjudgmental, and accepting of circumstances. In this way, neoliberal mindfulness functions as a machine of disimagination. The self is interpellated to make (or make-over) a project out of its own identity, constantly monitoring its conduct, and refashioning it in ways that feed fantasies of unfettered agency, aspiring to be free from the constraints of social conditioning. Yet this is never quite possible. Fully "being in the moment" is always elusive when one is a neoliberal actor, since part of one's attention is monitoring the project of the self.

Many are therefore skeptical of unsubstantiated claims that mindfulness courses will transform society. The Buddhist studies scholar Richard Payne notes that neoliberal imperatives mean modern meditators often get preoccupied with emotional states, and their duty to manage them in search of a hazy conception of happiness. Yet the practice of looking inside oneself is heralded as a daily "bold and heroic act" that creates peace and harmony, one individual at a time. The fantasy that this will create a mindful world rests on the assumption that social action is merely the sum of individual actions, which involves what Payne describes as "ignoring the massively entrenched power of capitalist institutions in favor of a mystical notion of all wisdom being inside oneself."[17]

This brings us to a fundamental tenet of neoliberal mindfulness, that the source of people's problems is found in their heads. This has been accentuated by the pathologizing and medicalization of stress, which then requires a remedy and expert treatment — in the form of mindfulness interventions. The ideological message is that if you cannot alter the circumstances causing distress, you can change your reactions to your circumstances. In some ways, this can be helpful, since many things are not in our control. But to abandon all efforts to fix them seems excessive. The notion that "as long as I am mindful, I'm OK," is in itself a form of magical thinking. It hypnotizes people into submission by presenting stress as a maladaptive psycho-physiological reaction. Hence, there is no need for critical inquiry into its systemic, institutional and structural causes. But the question of how we explain and respond to suffering — individually and socially — is ultimately both ethical and political. Mindfulness practices, as currently conceived and taught, do not permit critique or debate of what might be unjust, culturally toxic or environmentally destructive. Rather, the mindful imperative to "accept things as they are" while practicing "nonjudgmental, present moment awareness" acts as a social anesthesia, preserving the status quo.

Privatizing the causes of stress dovetails nicely with neoliberal priorities, undermining the concepts of a public sphere and body politic. In neoliberalism, public discourse gives way to private gain. Depoliticized practices of self-care can diminish our capacities for political citizenship, collective action and civic virtues. The mindfulness movement's promise of "human flourishing" (which is also the rallying cry of positive psychology) is the closest it comes to defining a vision of social change. However, this vision remains individualized and depends on the personal choice to be more mindful. Mindfulness practitioners may of course have a very different political agenda to that of neoliberalism, but the risk is that they start to retreat into their own private worlds and particular identities — which is just where the neoliberal power structures want them.

A Therapeutic Turn Inward

The rhetorical strategies of mindfulness missionaries are seductive. Like self-help authors, they are adept at luring people in by sounding critical of modern society while offering solutions. In *The Therapeutic Turn: How Psychology Altered Western Culture*, Ole Jacob Madsen uses the example of the popular TV show host and author Dr Phil, who often prefaces his books with dire warnings that "society is going downhill," while citing a litany of problems.[18] The same scare tactics are used by Jon Kabat-Zinn, who is fond of telling acolytes that our whole society suffers from Attention Deficit Disorder, that we are addicted to our smartphones, disconnected from each other, and losing touch with the natural world. As a leading figure of the mindfulness movement, Kabat-Zinn has framed and presented mindfulness as individualistic, not collective. Even his chapter "World Stress" in *Full Catastrophe Living* defines both the problem and a "solution" in such terms. "To have a positive effect on the problems of the larger environment," Kabat-Zinn writes, "we will need continually to tune and retune to our own center, cultivating awareness and harmony in our individual lives."[19]

The diagnosis is really quite simple: our thoughts are the culprit, every time! We undermine ourselves by being mindless, emotionally reactive and lost in rumination. We have therefore implicitly failed and been morally judged. Critical thinking is pathologized in mindfulness. It is seen as a diversion from the practice. Yet repeating this message has political outcomes. As the philosophy professor Chris Goto-Jones observes, the dominant narrative of mindfulness has reached an odd conclusion: "It is the majority in society that is somehow muddled-headed and sick."[20]

Rather than actually talking about ways of addressing social problems, or even suggesting this might be required, promoters of mindfulness stick to their mantra. For Kabat-Zinn, like Dr Phil, the answer is to turn inward, to work on the self, and personal growth — whether as a means to improve self-esteem or become more mindful. Through mindfulness, we are told, we can "reperceive" our conditions and miserable lot in life. Whatever the merits of this as a step in crisis management, it is wholly inadequate as a bigger-picture answer. Kabat-Zinn's expert prognosis of our cultural malaise is that we simply need to shift from a "doing" mode to "being," all together. Yet there is never a suggestion of altering the framework within which "being" has to function.

Mindfulness might sound like a buffer against life's challenges — a return to a more noble state, not unlike Rousseau's romantic notions of a natural self that social conditioning tends to corrupt. But there is a high political cost to this dreamy vision. By valorizing "pure awareness" in the "being" mode, mindfulness displaces the practice of public debate on which democracy depends. "Doing" is effectively demonized as a distraction. Yet this is cloaked in descriptions of mindfulness as our "natural birthright," a universal state to which we all have access. That of course sounds more appealing than capitulating daily to neoliberal needs.

The implicit political vision is one of retreat into the "authentic" private self. The autonomous individual is free to seek elusive happiness alone. The neoliberal self is always being encouraged to "go a little deeper" into the interior, to take better care of itself. As this self-management moves to the foreground, collective lives become less important. Mindfulness therefore squares nicely with political stories that keep us attached to competition. As described by Julie Wilson in *Neoliberalism*, these narratives "prompt us to turn our disaffected consent inwards toward ourselves, to double down on the present in order to protect and secure ourselves against others."[21]

Mindful Correctness

In an essay on "structures of feeling" in the 1970s, Raymond Williams explained how broader historical, political and economic forces shape the "affective elements of consciousness and relationships."[22] With the flattening of the political landscape under neoliberalism, a certain neoliberal affect is engendered by mindfulness practice. Since stress is pathologized, mindfulness programs step in with an individualized focus on a subject's inner life. Emotional reactions are problematized, and subjected to mindful scrutiny. According to mindfulness science, certain emotions — such as anger, disgust, sadness, contempt, frustration and aggression — are "destructive," negative affects requiring emotional self-regulation. But what if one is angry, even enraged, about injustice? Just let it go. Focus on your breath. Bring your attention back to the present moment. Of course, mindfulness practitioners still have thoughts outside of practice, but they are conditioned to see these as problems if strong emotions get involved. This has a disempowering impact on political thinking. Even if it helps not to act with anger, we still need to act if we want things to change outside our heads. Instead, as Joshua Eisen notes, the platitudinous instructions of mindfulness programs treat emotions as "free floating" and "cut loose from any kind of ideological grounding," except of course for the dictates of the prevailing social order:

This kind of desocializing logic is a central part of neoliberal formulations of subjectivity. It is also a central element in many popular forms of mindfulness. When negative emotions are seen as things that must be acknowledged and let go of, but never engaged, they lose their significance. This has the effect of neutering the politically generative potential of emotions by consigning feelings of anger, sadness, or disappointment to the realm of personal pathology.[23]

Teachers tend to model this behavior with slow and deliberate speech in gentle tones, expecting others to copy it. In many respects, the pursuit of "mindful correctness" resembles the acquisition of manners and social etiquette among the courtly class in medieval Europe. In *The Civilizing Process*, Norbert Elias chronicled how a once barbarous Middle Age gradually became affectively transformed and civilized through changes in feelings of delicacy, shame, refinement, and repugnance.[24] If one wanted to climb the social hierarchy, one needed to move, gesture, and speak with civility. Should there be any doubt about the link to modern mindfulness, the "Manners and Mindfulness" website offers "an etiquette program designed to provide the necessary and foundational training to help children and teens navigate the social skills in life."[25] Meanwhile, the Protocol School of Washington's blog has a module on "How to be 'Manners Mindful' at Work."[26] The blog gives a number of tips on mindful correctness. You should "control your temper," and "refrain from using offensive or demeaning language to colleagues and subordinates," while "showing gratitude," and so on. Attending a mindfulness conference reveals the pretentious facades of the holier than thou. Speaking loudly or showing any signs of strong emotions or criticism tends to elicit incredulous looks. Yet admitting that one doesn't practice mindfulness will certainly provoke people's inner evangelists.

Mindfulness practice is embedded in what Jennifer Silva calls the "mood economy." In *Coming Up Short: Working-*

Class Adulthood in the Age of Uncertainty, Silva explains that, like the privatization of risk, a mood economy makes "individuals solely responsible for their emotional fates."[27] In such a political economy of affect, emotions are regulated as a means to enhance one's "emotional capital." At Google's "Search Inside Yourself" mindfulness program, emotional intelligence (EI) figures prominently in the curriculum. The program is marketed to Google engineers as instrumental to their career success — by engaging in mindfulness practice, managing emotions generates surplus economic value, equivalent to the acquisition of capital. The mood economy also demands an affective resilience, the ability to bounce back from setbacks to stay productive in a precarious economic context. Like positive psychology, the mindfulness movement has merged with the "science of happiness." Once packaged in this way, it can be sold as a technique for personal life-hacking optimization, disembedding individuals from social worlds.

A Cruel Optimism

All the promises of mindfulness resonate with what Lauren Berlant calls "cruel optimism," a defining neoliberal characteristic.[28] It is cruel in that one makes affective investments in what amount to fantasies. We are told that if we practice mindfulness, and get our individual lives in order, we can be happy and secure. It is therefore implied that stable employment, home ownership, social mobility, career success and equality will naturally follow. We are also promised that we can gain self-mastery, controlling our minds and emotions so we can thrive and flourish amidst the vagaries of capitalism. As Joshua Eisen puts it, "Like kale, acai berries, gym memberships, vitamin water, and other new year's resolutions, mindfulness indexes a profound desire to change, but one premised on a fundamental reassertion of neoliberal fantasies of self-control and unfettered agency."[29] We just have to sit in silence, watching our breath, and wait. It is doubly cruel because these normative fantasies of the "good life" are already crumbling under neoliberalism, and we make it worse if we focus individually on our feelings. Neglecting shared vulnerabilities and interdependence, we disimagine the collective ways we might protect ourselves. And despite the emptiness of nurturing fantasies, we continue to cling to them.

Mindfulness isn't cruel in and of itself. It's only cruel when fetishized and attached to inflated promises. It is then, as Berlant points out, that "the object that draws your attachment actively impedes the aim that brought you to it initially."[30] The cruelty lies in supporting the status quo while using the language of transformation. This is how neoliberal mindfulness promotes an individualistic vision of human flourishing, enticing us to accept things as they are, mindfully enduring the ravages of capitalism.

chapter three
The Mantra of Stress

Mindfulness would not be where it is without the problem of stress. The two phenomena are opposite sides of the same modern coin. So pervasive is the discourse of stress, and such is the drain on profits due to stress-related work leave, that a professor of psychology has claimed that "stress is the 21st-century equivalent of the Black Death."[1]

Similar hyperbole is used to sell mindfulness. Take, for example, the inside jacket of Kabat-Zinn's *Full Catastrophe Living*: "Stress. It can sap our energy, undermine our health if we let it, even shorten our lives. It makes us more vulnerable to anxiety and depression, disconnection and disease."[2]

Although people clearly get anxious and depressed, what is far from clear is that the cause of this suffering lies solely in their minds. However, this is Kabat-Zinn's diagnosis, saying that we are "so caught up in our heads and in what we think is important, that it is easy to fall into a state of chronic tension and anxiety that continually drives our lives."[3] As a leading spokesperson for the mindfulness movement, his message is one of fear and uncertainty, with a distant prospect of relief. Stress is a noxious influence, he says, and it is up to us, as individuals, to mindful up. Nothing else can help:

> There are no drugs that will make you immune to stress or to pain or that will by themselves magically solve your life's problems or promote healing. It will take

conscious effort on your part to move in a direction of healing and inner peace.[4]

It's a seductive proposition, with potent side effects. Mindfulness helps people face pain with equanimity. But it also conditions us to think about stress in unhelpful ways. First, it says we face an epidemic, which is simply an inevitable part of modern life. Second, since stress is endemic, it is up to us all to get it under control and adapt to these conditions as best we can. It sounds like an empowering tool, but it ignores any source of pain outside our heads, such as the capitalist system, which exerts so much pressure in everyday life. The result is to pathologize stress, while offering a treatment that fails to address its broader causes.

The Stress Discourse

Like mindfulness itself, the concept of stress can be hard to define. Its very ambiguity makes it ubiquitous, but it should also make us wary of accepting some assumptions in popular discourse, particularly those that relate to inevitability. The discourse of stress has ideological components, and the mindfulness movement adopts these to build a whole industry around the stressed subject. However, this subject is also an object of outside forces. Professionals — including academics, practitioners and journalists — help to create it, observes Tim Newton in *Managing Stress*, "by telling us about ourselves and our world through, say, the discourses of psychiatry, psychology, biology, medicine, economics which reveal the secret of our selves."[5]

Most of us know about stress through the discourse of science, whose biomedical descriptions make the problem individual, with no historical, social or political context.

Leaders of the mindfulness movement have rarely questioned this discourse of stress. As purveyors of a therapy sold as the only way to treat it, they have significant investments in this way of understanding it. Of course, one is free to decide if one wants to learn mindfulness or not, and it is this emphasis on individual agency that makes the discourses on stress and mindfulness appealing.

The problem is what gets obscured. By individualizing social problems, the practice of mindfulness disadvantages those who suffer the most under the status quo. Critiquing definitions of stress in such limiting ways, Dana Becker has coined the term "stressism" to describe

the current belief that the tensions of contemporary life are primarily individual lifestyle problems to be solved through managing stress, as opposed to the belief that these tensions are linked to social forces and need to be resolved primarily through social and political means.[6]

The mindfulness movement has adopted a doctrine of stressism, promoting itself as the remedy for a wide range of "stress-related" conditions. The focus is squarely on the individual, who is expected to heal what Kabat-Zinn likes to label the "thinking disease." By practicing mindfulness, he says, we can switch from a frantic fixation on "doing" — and our accompanying hopes and fears — to a more harmonious mode of "being," in which we learn to let go of and flow with stressful situations. To use the scientific framing of mindfulness, it becomes a mental vaccine that helps us to "thrive."

American Nervousness

How did we arrive at this stress-filled moment in our history? Before World War II, psychological stress wasn't really discussed. Little attention was paid to the word or the underlying concept, even in scientific circles. However, there are earlier versions of a similar idea. In the mid-to-late nineteenth century, American life was prone to "nervousness." As the engines of industrialization and urbanization gathered steam, this was the fashionable diagnosis for the anxieties associated with modernizing lifestyles — adjusting to railroads, the telegraph, stock market tickers, daily news and a proliferation of watches and clocks.

In 1869, George M. Beard, a New York neurologist, published an article in the *Boston Medical and Surgical Journal* diagnosing a condition called "neurasthenia." Its debilitating symptoms included physical and mental fatigue, lethargy, headaches, heart palpitations, depression, anxiety, insomnia, an inability to concentrate, a lack of ambition, and even tooth decay — all qualified for the same diagnosis. It was a blanket description of discomfort in the face of rapid change.

Neurasthenia, from the Greek, denotes a "lack of nerve energy." Lacking a clear physical pathology, neurasthenia was conceived as a condition brought about by a finite amount of nerve energy. One could only expend so much, or one's nerves would malfunction. This theory was often compared to how electric current flows through a wire to power light bulbs and motors.

The majority of those diagnosed with neurasthenia were from the middle and upper classes, primarily women. In addition to the impact of social and technological change, Beard thought women were more vulnerable because of their increasing participation in society, putting them under greater strain. Late-nineteenth-century physicians generally agreed with him. In accordance with the social Darwinism of the time, the upper classes viewed themselves as more highly evolved, with more sensitive nervous systems. And due to the belief that women were especially delicate, they were considered more susceptible to neurasthenia than men. Beard, like other neurologists, portrayed neurasthenia as a disease of civilization, a medical testament to the challenges of adapting to the pressures of modern society.

By the turn of the century, neurasthenia was a household word in American culture.[7] Many public figures fell victim to the disease, including William James, Jane Adams, and Charlotte Perkins Gilman. The press often called the condition nervous exhaustion, or simply "nerves." Rather than being stigmatized, a neurasthenia diagnosis was often viewed as a badge of honor among middle- and upper-class men and women. It medically explained their symptoms and linked them to sacrifices made in pursuit of American competitiveness. Beard later contended in his book *American Nervousness* that neurasthenia was not only uniquely American, but a testament to the nation's greatness as an advanced civilization, characterized by citizens (especially the upper class) possessing active minds, competitive characters, and a love of liberty.

This rationalization of the "brain work" performed by the upper classes served to make them feel better about their struggles to adapt to the demands of capitalism. A little discomfort seemed a small price to pay, in Beard's analysis, for fine achievements. His social Darwinian leanings excluded laborers from the same diagnosis. They did not have to bear the same burden as the elite, whose more mentally taxing obligations supposedly made them more prone to nervous exhaustion. Those on the lower rungs of society — including non-whites and non-Protestants — had to resort to tonic and pills from "snake-oil" salesmen, as well as other dubious patent-medicine remedies for "bad nerves."

What was the cure for this mysterious disorder? Treatments for men and women differed considerably. Showing signs of "nerves," or missing work, was socially unacceptable for men in the nineteenth century. Their treatments often included rugged outdoor activities, strenuous physical exercise, and retreats in the wilderness. Many men were sent to the American West to live and work on cattle ranches. Theodore Roosevelt, the "conservationist president," was one prominent figure diagnosed with neurasthenia.

For women, physicians usually prescribed the "rest cure." Depending on the severity of the diagnosis, this often involved staying in bed for six to eight weeks in isolation from their family and children. Because mental activities were considered to drain and deplete a woman's nervous energy, patients were denied access to books and periodicals. Nervous women were also considered to be too thin and their blood too weak. Silas Weir Mitchell, a prominent Philadelphia physician, was well known for trademarking the rest cure. His variant recommended a modicum of mental activity.

Beard supplemented these treatments by administering electrotherapy, thinking human nerves could be recharged like a battery. Applying a mild electric current to patients, he placed one electrode on the scalp and then moved his hand with the other over parts of the body. Many said they felt refreshed after electrotherapy, even in cases where the battery had died without their knowing. Similar to a placebo effect, Beard called this "mental therapeutics."

Eventually, neurasthenia faded into the annals of history, only to be replaced with something almost as nebulous: stress.

The Caveman Theory

Most modern explanations of stress — and therefore mindfulness — invoke the idea that we are maladapted cavemen inhabiting twenty-first-century lifestyles. If we can learn to rewire a few default responses, our brains can be optimized to cope with the present. If we don't, we fall victim to stress. This biological account can be summed up as follows. Our ancestors had to be ready to face fearsome predators like saber-toothed tigers. As a result, they evolved the capacity to draw quickly on vast amounts of energy so they could respond to potential threats. For Stone Age man, the adrenalin-fueled "fight-or-flight" instinct was a survival mechanism, which became "hard-wired" into human biology. And since our brains have evolved very little in the intervening centuries, we still fall back on this overreaction to things that unsettle us.

However, unlike a relatively leisurely hunter-gatherer, we do not retreat to a cave and take time out so our systems recover from pumping adrenalin. If we did, we'd have no problem. Instead, we get on with our lives and stress accumulates. We are so stressed out (a phrase which only became popular in the 1980s) because our fight-or-fight alarm gets pushed so often, throwing our homeostatic systems out of whack. This wears down our bodies and immune systems, whittling away at our natural resilience. However, mindfulness can teach us the skill of self-regulation, and by paying attention to present experience we learn to unwind. Or so the basic theory goes.

Although it gets jazzed up with the latest neuroscience, much of what it says is a century old. And while it clearly has some relevance — particularly to the treatment of post-traumatic stress — it is all too often used as a general explanation, obscuring other causes of modern discomfort. The original ideas date from 1914, when the Harvard medical professor Walter B. Cannon first used the word "stress" in a scientific paper. Cannon performed experiments on cats and dogs. The latter were placed in the cages of the former, which caused them distress. Cannon's interest was in how they recovered. The physiology of stress seemed less important than that of instincts and emotions, and biological mechanisms responsible for homeostasis. He wanted to know how animals could return to a state of equilibrium after facing a threat.

Cannon's theorizing mainly referred to biological conditions such as "cold, lack of oxygen, low blood sugar, loss of blood." Having observed how distressed cats in his laboratory experiments released the hormone adrenalin when exposed to barking dogs, he inferred that responses such as fear and rage were part of our biological evolution, and that instinctual reactions arose "for quick service in the struggle for existence."[8]

Cannon was heavily influenced by social Darwinism, eugenics, and the theory of instincts. To prevent the degeneration of the population, he advocated that our "fighting instinct" should be satisfied, especially if we wanted to avoid war. He concluded that aggression was biological in nature, rather than arising in a social context. He therefore planted the seed for the popular notion in mindfulness discourse that social problems are induced by biology. Regardless of the social complexity people now have to deal with, the root of their problems is reduced to outmoded caveman instincts.

Naturalizing Stress

There is a strange idea implicit in this oft-repeated tale about an ongoing battle between Stone Age physiology and modern lifestyles. Although no one quite says it this clearly in mindfulness literature, the underlying suggestion is that if only we had evolved further biologically, capitalist societies would have no stress or conflicts. Meanwhile, the practice of mindfulness can help change our brains so we can eradicate these antiquated problems.

In other words, there is nothing inherently wrong with our modern age. It's just our maladaptive responses that make us unhappy. Having inherited this flawed biology, it is up to us to compensate and self-correct. Biological reductionism, inherited from Cannon, puts the onus on individuals to monitor and manage unruly emotions. The capitalist economy is simply a given, to which all must adapt. It's a survival-of-the-fittest ideology that naturalizes stress, ignoring structural factors that cause the response.

It took another few decades after Cannon's research for the theory of stress to become fully formed. The trigger was World War II, which brought the ideas to public consciousness. The US military had a keen interest in methods for training soldiers in resilience, as well as treatments for veterans returning from war with emotional battle wounds. Seizing this opportunity, a physician and biochemist named Hans Selye began using terms such as the "stress response," the "stress syndrome" and "stressors" as a way to raise interest in his research.

Selye, a Czech who fled the Nazis in the 1930s, conducted experiments at the University of Montreal. An ambitious researcher, Selye set his sights on identifying new female sex hormones. Working as an assistant to endocrinologist James B. Collop, he would go to the slaughterhouse each morning and fill a bucket with cow ovaries, grind them into an extract with formaldehyde as a preservative, then inject these tissue extracts into female rats. The autopsies on the rats showed no change in their sex hormones.

However, Selye noticed something peculiar. Every rat he injected had three common responses: the enlargement of adrenal glands, shrinking of the thymuses, spleens and lymph nodes, and bleeding, peptic ulcers. Initially, Selye believed he had found his sex hormone. After several months, he tested extracts from bovine placentas, kidneys, spleens and pituitary glands, and the results were not as he had predicted. No matter which extract was injected in rats, they all showed the same symptoms. Almost on a whim, Selye tried something else, injecting a rat with the toxic formaldehyde solution. To his surprise, the same triad of symptoms presented even more strongly in this rat. He was baffled and deemed his work to be a failure.

A few days later, Selye snapped out of his funk and had a brainwave. What if the rats were not exhibiting a specific hormonal response to the extracts, but a non-specific, general response to noxious agents? To test this hypothesis, Selye performed numerous experiments on rats, essentially torturing them by various means. No matter if the rat was exposed to freezing or hot temperatures, noise, perpetual treadmills, or even bright light with their eyelids sewn open, Selye found the same three responses.

He postulated that these were a default reaction to anything that overwhelmed the rats' capacity to adapt, calling it General Adaptation Syndrome (GAS). Its initial *alarm* stage triggered the body's fight-or-flight system, with physiological arousal. Endocrine glands released hormones that produced a racing heart, perspiration, and blood sugar spikes. This was followed by the *resistance* stage, in which the body sought to repair itself and return to homeostasis. If that proved to be impossible, and the stressor persisted, the final *exhaustion* stage could result in disease, or even death.

The Father of Stress

In 1956, Selye published a popular book, *The Stress of Life*, which revamped his GAS theory into a psychosocial explanation.[9] His writings claimed to have found the missing link between stress and illness. He sounded warnings to the public and medical practitioners that managing stress — or rather, successfully adapting to the environment — was the key to good health and the ultimate prevention of disease and unhappiness. Selye's medicalization of stress, along with his emphasis on the relationship between stress and disease, drew widespread interest.

Over the course of his career, Selye would go on to publish some 1,700 academic papers, forty books, and establish a stress research library that contained 110,000 articles across many languages. As a tireless self-promoter for his ideas, Selye gave many public lectures, appeared on TV shows, and was even featured in *Time* magazine as the "father of stress." He was immensely successful in securing large amounts of funding for his laboratory research from both the private and public sectors. By the late 1950s and early 1960s, he was a public figure, and his notions of stress had become a popular cultural meme. The scientific community, however, was not entirely convinced.

Many of Selye's scientific colleagues found his conceptualization of stress too vague, while others questioned his research methods, and even the link between stress and disease. Although Selye's theory of stress was derived from laboratory experiments on rats, his popular writings took the liberty of generalizing findings to human beings, essentially psychologizing stress. Disputing Selye's conceptual leap in a journal article, the social anthropologist Kristian Pollock points out: "By some, no doubt, inadvertent, sleight of mind, a social-psychological theory has been substituted for a more concrete, but fundamentally non-comparable, physiological model, which, nevertheless, still serves as the basis of its legitimation."[10]

Despite these criticisms, Selye's evangelism continued unabated. His writings became more grandiose, utopian and politically prescriptive, going so far as to articulate a national and international policy for guiding society to a "better, healthy philosophy." By the 1980s, his theory of stress was taken for granted, despite being what Pollock called "a manufactured concept which has now become a 'social fact'."[11]

As with the underlying Caveman Theory, Selye's ideas have some validity in understanding the body's response to complex trauma. But they by no means explain all forms of mental tension, since they ignore cultural inputs. Nor do they clearly define what counts as stress, instead widening the net to psychologize many modern problems. This is important to remember, as Dana Becker notes in her book about the stress discourse:

Just as in the case of neurasthenia, the "truth" of the stress concept and the American embrace of it did not come about through scientific agreement or through medical cures for "stress-related" diseases. It was stress's popularity that *made* it true.[12]

Selye's promotion of stress played on public fears, and the contested link between stress and illness was an instrumental factor, keeping his theory alive in people's minds and inspiring new treatments. His ideas portrayed the stressed person as a victim: weak, vulnerable, and biologically ill-equipped for the daily pressures of modern life. Parroting Selye's message, the media hyped the dangers of stress, opening the floodgates for a new industry of stress management and anti-anxiety psychoactive pharmaceuticals.

Stress and Big Tobacco

There is a dark side to Selye's work, casting serious doubts on the credibility and scientific integrity of stress research, particularly its implications for public health policy. From the late 1950s to the 1970s, he was bankrolled by the tobacco industry. This was a little known fact until fourteen million internal documents from tobacco companies were published under court order in 2002. Mark Pettigrew and his colleagues at the London School of Hygiene and Tropical Medicine sifted through the files via an online archive at the University of California San Francisco. They discovered the extent of Big Tobacco's influence on Selye, whose research on stress and health helped serve their purposes.[13] "He had a very, very close working relationship with the tobacco industry," Pettigrew explains. "They helped him to shape his ideas, and he helped them to shape theirs."[14]

Cigarette manufacturers were interested in marketing smoking as a form of stress relief, while recruiting scientists to obfuscate and distort the links between tobacco and chronic illness. Seeing an opportunity to coopt the science of stress research by Selye, who was repeatedly nominated for Nobel Prizes, industry executives and lawyers sought to disseminate a rival narrative. Ignoring the epidemiological studies linking smoking to cardiovascular disease, cancer, chronic bronchitis and emphysema, the message they wished to convey was that it was stress, not cigarettes, that was the cause.

Selye first initiated contact, unsuccessfully seeking funding from the American Tobacco Company. However, lawyers for manufacturers and the Council for Tobacco Research (CTR) soon began soliciting him to serve as an expert witness. The CTR's mission was explicitly to fund research with significant "adversary value," or put simply: to mislead the public and regulatory bodies. Selye and other pro-industry scientists were not allowed to disclose that their research projects were commissioned for litigation. In addition, recipients of CTR funding were not allowed to reveal that their work had been reviewed by the industry before publication.

Selye initially wrote a memo that downplayed the links between smoking and cancer. Later, in 1967, he was paid $2000 to write about stress. Unsure what to say, he asked industry lawyers for guidance. William Shinn, counsel for Philip Morris and Lorillard, said: "Selye should comment on the unlikelihood of there being a mechanism by which smoking could cause cardiovascular disease."[15] Shinn also advised Selye to argue that public service anti-smoking messages were themselves "stressful."

Selye claimed smoking could have "prophylactic and curative" effects, since smoking was one of many useful "diversions" from the stress of life. Elaborating in a Tobacco

Institute pamphlet, he stated: "It is frightening that no-one mentions the benefits of tobacco. I am sure that often more damage is done by creating, through well-meaning crusades of enlightenment, innumerable hypochondriacs."[16] Five months later, Shinn composed a letter for his industry colleagues — known as the "ideas on Selye" letter — defining his mission. "The desirability of adjusting to a stressful life by seeking diversions," Shinn writes, "would be established as a general proposition." Moreover, "the theory should be promulgated through articles, books, TV appearances, etc."[17]

While never publicly declaring the funding he was receiving from the tobacco industry, Selye was a frequent expert witness in governmental hearings, testifying against anti-smoking legislation, advertising restrictions, and health warnings. Selye's collusion intensified in 1969 when CTR awarded him $50,000 annually for three years to conduct a "special project." A Canadian tobacco interest group also gave him a further $50,000. Soon thereafter, Selye was testifying to Canadian governmental committees, making frequent radio appearances advocating for the benefits of smoking, and even appearing in Tobacco Institute public relations films. He also attended an infamous 1972 conference in the French Antilles, convened and sponsored by Phillip Morris and attended by all six big tobacco companies. This meeting was eventually used as evidence against them in a US Justice Department antiracketeering case.

Although the tobacco industry eventually lost interest in Selye, it continued to focus on stress. The Tobacco Institute Research Committee (TIRC) took great interest in American cardiologists Meyer Friedman and Ray Roseman, whose work found a causal relationship between heart disease and the behavior patterns of what they would later call the "Type A personality." Focusing on men, they described the typical Type A subject as intense, driven, and "invariably punctual and greatly annoyed if kept waiting."[18] This very specific type of stress response was given the blame for chronic illness.

Phillip Morris was a major funder for this research. Over the course of a decade, it poured over $11 million into the Meyer Friedman Institute, including funding for an endowed chair at the University of California San Francisco Medical School. The ideas were widely challenged by researchers, and by the 1990s, systematic reviews found no significant correlation between Type A personalities and coronary heart disease. Yet despite the lack of evidence, this link lives on as a popular concept in the media.

Selling Stress

Mindfulness owes much of its popularity to ideas based on junk science. Although most of us have experienced stress to some degree, it is as vague as happiness in scientific terms. However, mindfulness trades on the former to sell a pathway to the latter, cashing in on people's stress-related fears. References to the damaging effects of stress have reinforced the notion that it causes physical maladies, but that much of our suffering is somehow our fault. Even if mindfulness helps to address this, its reduction of stress to biological factors stops us treating social ills. Capitalism's unpredictable cycles and crises, along with its gross disparities in wealth and power, generate stress — a fact rarely acknowledged by mindfulness advocates. And its activation of primitive fight-or-flight mechanisms makes people vulnerable to psychological domination.

Although MBSR was designed to help those who suffered from chronic illnesses, its target market has grown to be everyone. This wouldn't have been possible without uncritical acceptance of the stress discourse. Chanting its mantra helps mindfulness merchants to trade on anxieties. They have a vested interest in psychologizing, pathologizing and normalizing stress, promoting interventions that are said to provide magical keys to controlling the causes of our misery. However, sources of collective suffering in external conditions are left unchanged.

chapter four
Privatizing Mindfulness

The meditative practice used in mindfulness comes from Buddhism. However, it has been decontextualized to alter what it offers, presenting a pragmatic approach that is fully compatible with modern science and psychology. This is one of its selling points, according to Jon Kabat-Zinn. "From the beginning," he says, "I bent over backwards to find ways to speak about it that avoided as much as possible the risk of it being seen as Buddhist, 'New Age,' 'Eastern Mysticism' or just plain flakey."[1]

Kabat-Zinn's first course, in 1979, was called a "Stress Reduction and Relaxation Program." It took place in a basement at the University of Massachusetts Medical Center, and would not have been feasible without his credentials as a scientist. As he reflected in an interview with *Time* more than thirty years later:

> The idea of bringing Buddhist meditation without the Buddhism into the mainstream of medicine was tantamount to the Visigoths being at the gates about to tear down the citadel of Western civilization. Partly because I had a PhD from MIT in molecular biology and had studied in the lab of a Nobel Laureate, people projected onto me that "He must know what he's doing." So they let me do it.[2]

Locating his "Stress Reduction Clinic" within a university medical center gave Kabat-Zinn the cover that he needed to make mindfulness sound mainstream. Removing its religious connotations, he rebranded it as a universal and scientific method, which he said was detached from historical and cultural contingencies. Although he got the idea to open his clinic on a Buddhist retreat, all mentions of Buddhism and its vocabulary were replaced with biomedical terms. "If you want to be able to integrate into medicine," he explained at a conference on Buddhism in America in 1997, "you've got to be able to charge insurance companies for this."[3]

Fearing rejection by the medical establishment, Kabat-Zinn was initially careful to avoid using words such as mindfulness, or even meditation. Even once his clinic was established, he only spoke about mindfulness as a basic phenomenological technique of "moment-to-moment awareness." This echoed his scientific predecessor, Herbert Benson, whose research had provided explanations for the efficacy of Transcendental Meditation (TM) in biomedical terms. Like Kabat-Zinn's descriptions of MBSR, Benson framed the "relaxation response" as simply a "universal capacity of the body," having no special allegiance to any religious or spiritual tradition.[4]

Kabat-Zinn is married to the daughter of the late radical historian and social activist Howard Zinn. But although he joined anti-Vietnam War protests in the late 1960s, his attention soon turned inward. He discovered Zen Buddhism while still a student at MIT, when he attended a talk by Philip Kapleau, and continued his foray into meditation under Korean Zen Buddhist teacher Seon Sahn at the Cambridge Zen Center. Later, he practiced Theravada techniques at the Insight Meditation Society in Barre,

Massachusetts, which gave him first-hand experience of modernist ideas from the Buddhist tradition.

The Mindfulness-Only School

The technique that Kabat-Zinn learned at the Insight Meditation Society had been imported from revival movements in Burma, Thailand, and Sri Lanka. Under occupation by the British Empire, Theravada Buddhist monks had resisted conversion attempts by Christian missionaries by promoting *vipassana*, a form of "insight" meditation. Before the late nineteenth century, few laypeople meditated. However, led by reformers such as Ledi Sayadaw and Mahasi Sayadaw in Burma, a large movement developed, which was globalized by Western students and influential teachers like S.N. Goenka. These figures downplayed the importance of Buddhist doctrine as well as more difficult concentration practices. Instead, they emphasized mindfulness, which was construed in novel ways as "the heart of Buddhism," yet compatible with science and rational Western sensibilities.

This "mindfulness-only" school, as Richard King calls it, resisted colonialism by copying Western ways of seeing. Buddhism's meditative methods were presented as a "science of mind," decoupled from rituals and pre-modern ideas. This enabled reformers to claim — with some success — that it was Christian doctrine that was more super-stitious, while Asian culture contained ideas that could resonate strongly with Western priorities. The colonized were therefore not backward but deserved independence.

However, as King points out, "this was not a value-neutral de-contextualization of Buddhist ideas and practices, as is often claimed by modern secular proponents of mindfulness-based practices."[5] Instead, it was a cultural defense against colonial hegemony, which had the side-effect of promoting mindfulness as offering practical worldly benefits.

MBSR: The Birth of a New Lineage

The Theravada reform movement, like its Western insight meditation offshoot, became immensely popular while still appealing to Buddhist authority and tradition. Yet MBSR could not afford to do so if it wanted acceptance by non-Buddhists in clinical and medical settings. Explaining this rationale for ditching dharma — a collective term for the Buddha's teachings — Kabat-Zinn says he "never meant to exploit, fragment or decontextualize the dharma, but rather to recontextualize it." Describing this in "dharmic" terms as his "karmic assignment," he says he chose "the framework of science, medicine (including psychiatry and psychology), and healthcare so that it would be maximally useful to people who could not hear or enter into it through more traditional dharma gates."[6]

Successful branding stories are often characterized by disruption, which turns an established industry or experience upside down. The MBSR brand is one such disruptive force, with Kabat-Zinn's talking points including pithy quips such as: "The Buddha wasn't a Buddhist," or Buddhists "don't own mindfulness" because it is "an innate, universal human capacity." Potential customers are thereby assured that MBSR is a non-religious product, yet still offers the best bits of what the Buddha taught. In Kabat-Zinn's words, his version of mindfulness is "a place-holder for the entire dharma."[7]

This claim has a powerful branding story with emotional resonance: no less an authority than the Dalai Lama is said to have endorsed it, sanctioning MBSR as a form of "universal dharma." As Kabat-Zinn recalls:

> I specifically asked His Holiness the Dalai Lama at the Mind and Life XIII conference in Washington, D.C., in 2005 whether there was any fundamental difference between Buddhadharma and universal dharma and he said "no".[8]

However, a video recording of the exchange provides a different account. During a presentation to the Dalai Lama on the history and accomplishments of MBSR, one of Kabat-Zinn's slides posed his crucial question. The Dalai Lama's translator, Thupten Jinpa, relayed it: "Can we make a valid distinction between the Buddhadharma, on the one hand, and the universal dharma, on the other?" The response came with a chuckle. "Oh yes," the Dalai Lama replied. "Suppose we are trying to put universal dharma, this for scientists... [pause, laugh] ... we just can't apply to all dharma."[9] Clearly, this was not the resounding "no" that Kabat-Zinn implies. It seems to say that the so-called "universal dharma" may be useful in the scientific realm, but it is by no means equivalent to all of the teachings of the Buddha. Nonetheless, it still seems important to Kabat-Zinn to go out of his way to seek Buddhist validation for MBSR, while at the same time disavowing its connections to Buddhism for marketing purposes.

This strange contradiction pervades the whole movement. Margaret Cullen, a longtime teacher of MBSR, believes that mindfulness-based interventions are spawning a "new American Dharma," which is widely accessible, democratic, non-dogmatic, pragmatic and utilitarian. "The intention of MBSR is much greater than simple stress reduction," she says.[10] With such proclamations, Kabat-Zinn and his peers have positioned what they teach as a new Buddhist school in a manner consistent with tradition, whatever they think. Each variant of Buddhism grounds itself in a reading of scriptural sources, and a focus on certain selected practices, then claims this reading to be an appropriate interpretation of the Buddha's true intent. In Buddhist historical terms, Kabat-Zinn does nothing less than declare himself the founder of a new lineage.

If, as he claims, MBSR represents "a universal dharma that is co-extensive, if not identical, with the teachings of the Buddha," then it ought to be interrogated as such.[11] To busy Westerners, mindfulness offers a convenient "one-stop shop" of diluted Buddhism. Kabat-Zinn describes it as "mostly *vipassana* practice (in the Theravada sense as taught by people like Joseph Goldstein and Jack Kornfield) with a Zen attitude," informed by both the Soto and Rinzai traditions, plus ideas from Korean Seon and Chinese Chan.[12]

When pressed about connections to Buddhism, mindfulness teachers often say that their curriculum is just as robust as traditional forms of Buddhist training, missing nothing out. MBSR claims to be grounded in the four foundations of mindfulness as put forth by the Buddha in the *Satipatthana Sutta*. The "body scan" — in which practitioners rotate awareness from the head to the toes while observing sensations — claims to be an application of the first foundation of mindfulness ("watching the body"). A short seated meditation supposedly expands to include the other three (watching feelings, mental states and the constituent qualities of all things), although the fourth foundation is simply referred to as "mental contents." Even ethical foundations — which traditionally require training in restraint of the body, speech and mind — and the *brahma viharas* (promoting loving-kindness, compassion, sympathetic joy, and equanimity) are all "seamlessly integrated" into the practice. A little *hatha* yoga and poetry are also thrown in for good measure. Given that formal Buddhist teachings really have no place in a secular setting, what matters most for MBSR teachers, supposedly, is the mysterious capacity to embody and transmit the essence of the dharma in their conduct.

Without the fertile soil of Buddhist modernism, tilled earlier by the *vipassana* revival movements that trained some of Kabat-Zinn's teachers, it is hard to imagine that MBSR would have taken root. However, Kabat-Zinn is no traditionalist. Although he is fond of appealing to Buddhist sources and flaunting his earlier Buddhist experience, his mission has been to modernize mindfulness for the masses. Like other Western and secular Buddhists, Kabat-Zinn often speaks as if he has extracted the highest of the Buddha's insights and discarded the junk that religion wrapped around them. Manu Bazzano, a London-based Zen teacher and existential psychotherapist, recalls a four-hour chat with Kabat-Zinn at an academic conference:

> I told him that MBSR was all very well, but without the lineage and one-to-one transmission (from teacher to student) his was no real Dharma. His reply surprised me. "What I am creating with MBSR — he said — *is* a new lineage". I was disappointed: by his overconfidence, but also by the suggestion that his expedient technique could be compared to the sheer magnitude of the Dharma.[13]

Seeing himself as the founder of a lineage, Kabat-Zinn derives his authority not from the traditional Buddhist institutions, but from personal charisma. He essentially claims special access to the miracle of mindfulness, which he interprets and shares with the world. Charismatic leadership is a common feature of new religious movements. Kabat-Zinn's intentional retention of Buddhist-inflected language — such as "lineage" — signals his guru-like status in authorizing followers and transmitting mindfulness.

Coming Out of the Buddhist Closet: MBSR is the Dharma?

Now that MBSR has moved beyond its start-up phase to entrepreneurial maturity and widespread acceptance, the Center for Mindfulness (as the Stress Reduction Clinic is now known) is no longer in stealth mode. Deflecting accusations that MBSR is dumbed-down dharma, its website declares: "MBSR is a vehicle for embodying and transmitting the dharma in a wholly secular and universal idiom. It is a *recontextualizing* of dharma, not a decontextualizing of it." This statement is becoming a talking point. One of the most senior MBSR teachers told me: "I really feel MBSR is not secular, I actually don't like that word and don't like to see MBSR fall into that category. Secular implies not holy or sacred, that it is a separation from the 'church' and from my perspective MBSR is very spiritual and holy."

Whatever this teacher may "feel," a stripped-down and decontextualized model of mindfulness is problematic. It assumes that mindfulness has a context-free essence, and that by extracting this essence, it can be better understood, studied and practiced. Yet the mindfulness movement has a context of its own. It is distinctively American, priding itself on the narrative of scientific progress, the belief in the individual as the sole nexus of meaning, an entrepreneurial ethos, and other underlying and generally unexamined assumptions that are anything but universal, much less Buddhist, but are simply absorbed from its social environment. This narrative is also a radical break with the past, and is used to reinforce the view that mindfulness stands outside of, rather than within, social and historical contexts. In this respect, the mindfulness revolution is a typically American big-bang innovation myth.

Kabat-Zinn first came to public prominence in 1993, with an appearance on Bill Moyers' Public Broadcasting Station special, *Healing and the Mind*. By this time, Kabat-Zinn had been publishing extensively in scientific journals to document benefits from mindfulness practice. From the 1980s onwards, numerous medical studies (many of which are now considered poor quality) were conducted on MBSR, showing its efficacy in treating stress-related illnesses. Other positive outcomes ranged from improvements in recovery time for psoriasis patients to greater immune responses to the flu vaccine.

Emboldened by scientific legitimacy, Kabat-Zinn renamed his clinic and began calling its program Mindfulness-Based Stress Reduction. The standardized eight-week MBSR course is now offered in over six hundred clinics worldwide. In three decades, twenty thousand people have graduated from UMass's clinic alone, and nine thousand have attended MBSR teacher-training programs offered through the Center for Mindfulness. The widespread acceptance of MBSR by the scientific and medical communities has encouraged many clinicians and entrepreneurs to spin-off numerous mindfulness-based programs. This includes Mindfulness-Based Cognitive Therapy (MBCT), a group intervention that aims to prevent relapse in recurrent depression, which is now a treatment modality recognized by the UK's National Health Service.

Self-Help Mindfulness

Kabat-Zinn's charisma has played a big part in popularizing mindfulness. He is the author of three best-selling books, the first of which — *Full Catastrophe Living* — has sold over four hundred thousand copies and is now in its fifteenth edition. He has also spread the mindfulness gospel through audio courses, international lectures, and frequent media appearances. Kabat-Zinn's self-help enterprise has now reached millions of people — way beyond the thousands who have taken the MBSR course at his center. The majority of people come across his mindfulness products through books and CDs, opening the doors to a "do-it-yourself" medicalized version of practice. As with most other self-help tools and techniques, their creator promoted the notion that mindfulness could be learned and practiced on one's own. A little bit of mindfulness is better than none. The promise and allure of this easily accessible technique also meant that it was no longer bound to the standards and requirements of institution-alized medicine.

A key discursive element of privatized mindfulness, wherever one learns it, is this self-help narrative. Throughout Kabat-Zinn's writings and audio courses, we are told that health and happiness are contingent on turning inward to recover our "inner resources" for healing. The sociologist Kirstin Barker has analyzed Kabat-Zinn's most popular books and recordings to see how mindfulness is medicalized. Many human problems and experiences have now been pathologized in terms that require interventions to treat them. Identifying stress as a personal pathology was the first step, but as Barker points out, mindfulness medical-ization now applies the labels "healthy" and "illness" to "an ever increasing part of human existence."[14] Disorder becomes an ever-present risk, and mindfulness serves therapeutic order in response, defining us all as poten-tially unwell unless we practice. As Barker puts it: "the common malaise of everyday life is a diseased state" and "mindfulness portrays our failure to pay attention as the principal reason."[15]

Kabat-Zinn repeatedly expounds the idea that stress is omnipresent and inevitable, because we have lost touch with innate capabilities to be mindful. Paying attention to the present moment is the medical way to treat a disease of inattentiveness. Indeed, the whole premise of MBSR is that we suffer on account of letting our emotions get the better of us. Like other self-help techniques, mindfulness targets individuals and seems insensitive to social, political and economic dimensions of suffering. Kabat-Zinn's publisher categorizes his bestseller *Wherever You Go, There You Are* in the "self-help/spirituality" genre. More telling still is a back-cover endorsement that exclaims: "Want to meet the most interesting, exciting person you will ever know? Let Jon Kabat-Zinn introduce you to YOU. Nowhere else in the literature on meditation can you find so simple and commonsensical a path to yourself."

Far from being a countercultural force (remember the promised "revolution"), the mindfulness movement's reinforcement of Western individualism seems more like an entitled, self-centered, and myopic path to happiness. A stress-free life is ours for the taking, within a protective bubble that screens out the cries of the world. The products are marketed as providing more fulfilling and sensual experiences, not the development of virtue, ethical behavior, moral courage, and compassion.

Self-Centered Mindfulness

The privatizing of mindfulness is disconcerting given the epidemic of social isolation in America and other capitalist societies. Despite relative affluence, significant numbers of people report being very lonely, without meaningful relationships, notes Ruth Whippman in *America the Anxious*. Skeptical of this trend towards privatized self-help, Whippman laments that "in the midst of this social isolation, we are getting the message that the key to happiness is everyone sitting in the room in total silence, with each individual plodding his or her own solitary path to inward bliss."[16] She underscores the irony of this situation — people complain of being too stressed, busy and lonely, lacking time to spend with their children or nurture friendships, but they seem to have plenty of time to attend long silent retreats or practice mindfulness meditation by themselves.

The mindfulness movement is an example of an ideological shift, in which an obsessive focus on wellness and happiness becomes a moral imperative. In *The Wellness Syndrome*, Carl Cederström and André Spicer call this development "healthism," a form of bio-morality that tells individuals to make themselves flexible and more marketable in a precarious economy by making the "right" life choices — whether it's exercise, food, or meditation.[17] Buddhist teachings on impermanence are often coopted by mindfulness advocates to celebrate the acceptance of change in the face of late-capitalist insecurities, including serial unemployment (the traditional focus on eradicating greed is conveniently omitted). In addition, with the onus of responsibility placed on individuals to manage their own bodies, emotions, and health, the ideological subtext of modern mindfulness is that changing the world starts with changing oneself. And this change is seen primarily as a personal lifestyle choice, rather than directly engaging with society and politics.

The injunction to "be mindful" includes implicit assumptions that individuals lack self-control, discipline, and willpower. In many respects, the imposed self-management of "the wellness syndrome" is like the continual failure and episodic guilt associated with diets; both forms of self-discipline internalize the punitive commands of the superego. The individual is forever vigilant, wary of slipping from their regimen and fearful of becoming tormented by feelings of shame.

As MBSR moves outside of the medical-clinical setting, its tone becomes increasingly hedonic, promising greater wellbeing and happiness. This is offered without any need to challenge or change one's beliefs and assumptions, values and priorities or lifestyle (apart from anything that gets in the way of being mindful). It seems to be of no importance whether one's worldview or choices are dysfunctional, because mindfulness allows one to reduce unwanted symptoms — stress, depression and anxiety — even if one's way of life is out of balance with reality. Think Wall Street traders.

Kabat-Zinn seems to agree. When asked if reducing stress entails making changes to one's lifestyle, he told an interviewer:

> I don't think that it means giving up anything. I think it means embracing the whole of experience and discerning what has merit in terms of your own heart and your own intuition. That will be different for different people. Some thrive on Wall Street while

others thrive in the wilderness. In many ways, stress is in the eye of the beholder.[18]

For the most part, MBSR and the mindfulness movement have downplayed and even ignored the importance of ethics. They also neglect the role played by a path of cultivation, not only as a foundational support for the development of mindfulness, but also in terms of the practice's meaning, purpose and aims. This raises the ultimate question: what is mindfulness for? Is it merely to attain better health, higher exam scores, focused concentration at work, or "self-compassion?" Is it a medical form of self-improvement? In a way, posing the question is tantamount to asking what constitutes "the good life," the traditional basis of philosophy.

Mindfulness training, at least as understood within the Buddhist tradition, is inseparable from ethical development. The cultivation of "right mindfulness" is only one part of the Buddha's Eightfold Path, along with "right" understanding, intention, speech, action, livelihood, effort and concentration. This list has no Western equivalent. Each of the factors is interrelated, and none of them correlates directly to Judeo-Christian edicts, or Western ideas about prescriptive duties that people "should" perform to be morally upright. However, the other dimensions that support "right mindfulness" — which leads to wisdom by cultivating wholesome mental states — are left out of MBSR, suggesting its teachers have misconstrued Buddhist ethics.

In light of their secular commitments, Kabat-Zinn and a number of his senior teachers have argued that an ethical framework would be an inappropriate imposition. To fill this void, some MSBR apologists make weak appeals to the Hippocratic Oath. This is a limited concept: it only covers professionals teaching MBSR in healthcare settings, not in other contexts, for example in corporations or the military. More importantly, the Hippocratic Oath has no bearing on the participants in MBSR courses. When pushed on this issue, the last line of defense from mindfulness merchants is the dubious claim that an ethical path is somehow implicitly integrated into the practice, because it involves being kinder to oneself by stepping out of stressful thought patterns.

It could of course be argued, as Kabat-Zinn does, that recontextualizing dharma for modern Western needs is to be celebrated. After all, the history of Buddhism has been one of transformation since its migration from the Indian subcontinent, often undergoing major changes to adapt to new host cultures. One could therefore claim, with some foundation, that modern mindfulness isn't really all that different from how Chinese translators needed to strip away Indian scholasticism, its pantheon of deities and cosmology, and other cultural overlays, resulting in Chan's (Chinese Zen) earthy emphasis on meditative practice.

What is unique at this juncture of history is that the transformation of the dharma within capitalist societies involves big risks as well as opportunities. The risk today is not whether mindfulness will be accepted by modern science, as was the case in the early years of MBSR, but that it is becoming psychologized in harmful ways. Reduced for the most part to a "privatized spirituality," its scope is limited to helping individuals to cope, adapt and function more effectively despite the ever-increasing strains of life in neoliberal societies.

Historically, Buddhism has been a prophetic force for personal transformation *and* radical social change only when it has been able to maintain its marginality from what was considered the "normal" functioning of society. As Erich Fromm eloquently observes in his essay "The Pathology of Normalcy," society could itself be a disturbing pattern of collective pathology. For the ancient Greeks, the true love of wisdom meant that the philosopher was *atopos*, "out of place," an untimely critic intent on going against the stream of normalcy. The Buddhist monastic community (the *sangha*) has not only served as the corporate vehicle of the Buddhist teachings, but its communal space has provided the crucible for a radical questioning of the normal and conventional modes of living that lead to suffering and social disharmony.

In Jon Kabat-Zinn's view, mindfulness "has nothing to do with Buddhism. It has to do with freedom."[19] However, this so-called freedom is not conceived in social terms. Rather than be burdened by the civic responsibilities of a community or the normative expectations of the public sphere, one can mindfully retreat with a smartphone meditation app. After all, mindfulness is simply a matter of pumping neurons — an exercise in mental fitness — without having to go to the gym. The privatized spirituality of the mindfulness movement has lost sight of collective endeavor embedded in dharma, and the very idea that communal wellbeing is a prerequisite for authentic happiness and *eudaimonia*, the Greek word for "flourishing" often deployed by positive psychologists.

The conspicuous absence of a path for ethical development in the secularized mindfulness movement creates a moral vacuum. A belabored form of self-surveillance — being in the present moment — displaces ethical reflection, severing the chain from past to future. Forethought and care, vigilant awareness of the consequentiality of one's actions, and striving to eradicate unwholesome mental qualities (all basic Buddhist aims) take a back seat to just "being mindful," "being present," and other platitudinous edicts like "radical acceptance." Lacking a noble vision and purpose, the mindfulness movement seems adrift, resigned to a do-it-yourself, make-it-up-as-you-go-along mentality. The ambiguity of Kabat-Zinn's umbrella term "mindfulness" has become a new "Brand X," inviting commodification and pilfering. The lowest common denominators of mainstream Western consumerist culture — corporate capitalism, crass instrumentalism, and scientific materialism — are sadly becoming the new "place-holder for the entire dharma."

chapter five
Colonizing Mindfulness

Let me start by making one thing clear: I do not question the value of adapting mindfulness for therapeutic use, nor do I deny that it can help people. What bothers me is how its promoters want things both ways: one minute, mindfulness is science, since that's what sells; the next, it stands for everything in Buddhism, since that makes it sound deep. Switching "Buddhist" branding on and off for one's own convenience is contradictory and misleading. There is also a related problem in claiming that mindfulness is somehow universal: the underlying essence of human experience, or its transcendent core. Mystical terms shield promoters of mindfulness from engaging with critics. If what they sell is a thing beyond words, anyone who argues should learn to be mindful and keep quiet.

The rhetoric of MBSR, amplified by the media, is anti-intellectual. Although much has been gained from making mindfulness treatments more widely accessible, the pursuit of scientific legitimacy comes at a cost, which is rarely discussed. Buddhism is borrowed and exploited in ways that date back to colonialism, which distorts modern Western understanding of Buddhist traditions. My objection is not that Buddhists have exclusive rights to mindfulness. I am critiquing how people have used it to serve their own goals, while pretending that their adaptations of mindfulness are the equivalent of Buddhism.

The discursive habits of mindfulness cheerleaders are often downright offensive to actual Buddhists, whose traditions are dismissed as outdated accretions. The author Sam Harris is a case in point, deriding the "spooky metaphysics and unjustified claims within Buddhism" while praising its practices, and telling fellow meditators "we have to get out of the religion business."[1] Dan Harris, a TV news anchor and the author of the best-selling book *10% Happier*, decries "meditation's massive PR problem," which is basically code for links to Buddhism, plus New Age tropes that Harris thinks it includes. "I always thought meditation — also known as mindfulness practice — was for people who live in a yurt or collect crystals," he says. "As it turns out, there is all this science that says it can boost your immune system, reduce your blood pressure, and rewire key parts of your brain."[2] Mindfulness needs these media-savvy entrepreneurs like Sam and Dan Harris.

Another news anchor took a subtler approach on *60 Minutes*, which screened a special report on mindfulness in 2014. CNN's Anderson Cooper joined a short retreat led by Jon Kabat-Zinn at Spirit Rock, an Insight Meditation center.[3] Despite the location, a well-known branch of the Buddhist tradition in which Kabat-Zinn trained, no mention was made of the "B" word. However, the camera zoomed in on Kabat-Zinn, who sat cross-legged on a *zafu* cushion in a meditative posture, ringing a Tibetan cymbal, and holding his hands in religious *mudra* gestures. These traditional Buddhist artifacts were on display to convey authenticity, but the science of mindfulness had somehow captured the essence of the dharma, so the need to talk about it vanished. Instead, Cooper went off to a laboratory to get his brain scanned in an fMRI machine, while conversing with white lab-coat neuroscientists. To quote the religious studies scholar Jeff Wilson, these portrayals combined the mystification and medicalization of mindfulness, colonizing Buddhism for promotional purposes:

> The *60 Minutes* piece, basically a commercial for the allegedly de-Buddhified arm of the mindfulness movement, couldn't be any more positive if it were paid by Kabat-Zinn himself. That's pretty common, but still it's unfortunate. Mindfulness may deliver some of the benefits that promoters tout, but Americans deserve to be informed about the full context of what they're being sold.[4]

Epistemic Violence

Processes of cultural appropriation are not always negative. Buddhism changed as it spread from India to China, Tibet and Southeast Asia. While it is inevitable that it will adapt in its encounter with Western modernity, the nature of such transformations is not predetermined. However, its cultural translation in the West is often being hidden from public discourse, shaped by a complex set of interacting forces involving power relations, networks of interests, and interpretative decisions. Ideally, as well as changing Buddhist teachings and practices, Western cultures would also be changed by contact with them. But so far, the process with mindfulness has only worked one way: by validating meditative practice and "proving" its benefits, science is said to be "liberating" it from religion.

Not all scientists share this perspective, even if their work can be used to support it. "There is a swath in our culture who is not going to listen to someone in monks' robes, but they are paying attention to scientific evidence," says Richard Davidson, a pioneer in the emerging field of contemplative neuroscience.[5] A similar idea is less respectfully expressed on the inside cover of the *New York Times* bestseller *Search Inside Yourself: The Unexpected Path to Achieving Success, Happiness (and World Peace)*, which states that mindfulness "cannot be the domain of bald people in funny robes."[6] The author, Google's former in-house guru Chade-Meng Tan, cites study after study to back up his claims that mindfulness delivers greater happiness, health, career success and wealth, and "everything can be completely secular." His version of mindfulness is a way to have it all with the playful spirit. This sort of prosperity-gospel thinking is often combined with a naïve faith in the authority of science as the sole arbiter of truth, meaning and value.

Early promoters of Buddhist ideas used scientific metaphors to make them sound modern. For example *The Gospel of Buddha*, an 1894 book by Paul Carus, hailed the Buddha as "the first prophet of the Religion of Science"[7] — modern mindfulness echoes this rhetoric. In an interview in 2013 at the New York Academy of Sciences, Kabat-Zinn said: "one could think of the Buddha as more like a great scientist — a Galileo or an Einstein — somebody with very deep insight into the nature of his own experience," whose "laboratory tools" are now used to teach mindfulness.[8]

Buddhist modernism — sometimes known as Protestant Buddhism — offers privatized forms of spirituality easily accommodated to Western culture. However, for mindfulness to gain acceptance in clinical, corporate and government settings, and in public schools, even a hint of Buddhism sounds too much. So despite the roots of MBSR in Theravada insight meditation, it is presented as a wholly secular intervention. Observing this sleight-of-hand, the religious studies scholar Candy Gunther-Brown says proponents of mindfulness rarely define what they mean by either "secular" or "religion," which helps them engage in what she calls "code-switching."[9]

The Buddhist switch is off when addressing public-sector funding agencies, which require secularity, but flipped back on for those more welcoming of Buddhism. In the company of Buddhists, promoters of the practice declare themselves purveyors of "skillful means," using mindfulness as a "Trojan horse" for teaching the dharma. For example, in an interview on the *Buddhist Geeks* podcast, the secular mindfulness teacher Tracy Goodman could be heard giggling and joking with the hosts that mindfulness was essentially "stealth Buddhism."[10]

The Dalai Lama's long-time interpreter, Thupten Jinpa, is not impressed. He finds "code-switching" misleading, and discourages promoters of mindfulness from saying one thing onstage and another backstage:

> I've often told them, you know, you cannot have it both ways. It is either secular, or you want to say it's the essence of Buddhism, therefore it's a Buddhist practice. You cannot have it both ways.[11]

The underlying problem is a form of discomfort with foreign ideas. As the religious studies scholar Richard King explains, Western culture operates with intellectual border guards, effectively demanding that other systems of knowledge "declare" hidden beliefs that make them religious, while Western dogma gets a pass:

> Before being allowed to enter the public space of western intellectual discourse, such systems of thought must either give up much of their foreign goods (that is, render themselves amenable to assimilation according to western intellectual paradigms), or enter as an object of rather than as a subject engaged in debate.[12]

The Janus-faced habits of mindfulness discourse are part of this process of epistemic violence. To admit to being "Buddhist" becomes something to be wary of, or even embarrassed about, because it is saddled with "cultural" or "religious" baggage. The symbolic cachet of Buddhism can still be flaunted for commercial convenience, but only if the dharma is purged of its "foreignness" (though not its exoticness, which sells) by assimilating it under a scientific paradigm. The shameful history of Western imperialism and its violent crimes should really be declared as cultural baggage. Unless it is brought to attention, its underlying thought patterns influence mindfulness, which aspires to be a new scientific lineage of the dharma.[13]

Contemporary advocates of mindfulness seem unconcerned. Their rhetoric uses "on and off" Buddhist branding, apparently oblivious to its harmful consequences, which changes public perception of what Buddhism actually is.

Now that MBSR has been safely established, Kabat-Zinn is clear he made a conscious decision to conceal the Buddhist basis for his form of "meditation so commonsensical that anyone would be drawn to it." In itself, this wouldn't really be a problem if he didn't also boast that it encapsulates Buddhism, "without ever mentioning the word dharma."[14] To substantiate his claim, and allow him to appropriate Buddhist symbols, Kabat-Zinn says MBSR teaches something timeless: a "universal dharma" of "pure awareness," which is everyone's "birthright." As a result, he can call it both secular and the "true essence" of Buddhist meditation.

This dubious universalist outlook is religious, whatever Kabat-Zinn thinks. Not only does it use the word "dharma," a Sanskrit term from ancient Indian religions, it claims to have found the essential "heart" of this body of knowledge, while rejecting anything that doesn't fit its sectarian point of view. "Defining dharma as universal and above or beyond any particular religion is, of course, itself a religious statement about the nature of dharma," notes Jeff Wilson. His comments are worth considering at length:

> Claims about human nature and values are religious, or at least they are philosophical claims that clearly overlap with religious concerns. When you say that something is a birthright, you are talking about essences and natures, the very stuff of religion. And the thing that continually strikes me is just how religious "secular" mindfulness really is.[15]

Kabat-Zinn tends to write off critics as Buddhist fundamentalists, or to dismiss what they say as "reactive backlash" from over-active minds.[16] However, both of these tactics serve the broader strategy of laying proprietary claim to the "universal essence" of a non-religious, non-sectarian "dharma." This sort of rhetoric has been long been a staple of Buddhist modernism. Westerners encountering the dharma have often been quick to proclaim expertise as to its true meaning, making reductive assertions about its natural compatibility with scientific rationalism, which distinguishes them from the traditional religious lineages of Buddhism.

Present Momentism

Despite calling MBSR "a potentially transformative dharma vehicle," Jon Kabat-Zinn also likes to insist it owes nothing to Buddhism.[17] "We are never appealing to authority or tradition," he says, "only to the richness of the present moment held gently in awareness, and the profound and authentic authority of each person's own experience, equally held with kindness in awareness."[18] In MBSR, the present moment is a sacred dimension, teaching what Kabat-Zinn calls a "way of being," just as the Buddhist teacher S.N. Goenka called meditation an "art of living."

Rather than communing directly with God, like a Protestant in prayer, the mindfulness practitioner has unmediated access to the present moment. This is said to transform the mind to a state of "being," stepping out of the "doing" mode that keeps people distracted. Most of the time, they operate on autopilot, ensnared by habitual emotional reactions, deliberation about the past and future, and compulsive demands of non-stop connectivity. For Kabat-Zinn, the miracle of mindfulness is that we can "drop in" (a phrase he is very fond of using) to "being" and simply be present. Dwelling in this non-discursive state is equated to a form of spiritual liberation. MBSR enthusiasts consider this shift to be a countercultural force, as the practice provides a peaceful respite from the relentless pressures and constant distractions of digital capitalism.

Although there is clearly therapeutic value in stepping — however temporarily — out of the stream of what Kabat-Zinn calls "A.D.D.," mindfulness over-romanticizes "being." We are told it appeals to Westerners because we have (supposedly) lost touch with experience; our lives have become too stressful and our concerns too overwhelming to appreciate the simple pleasures of being alive. MBSR can help us to get back in touch with embodied existence, deepening and enriching our sensory experience, while radically accepting whatever arises, including the vicissitudes of modernity.

Newcomers to MBSR are introduced to "being" through the mindful eating of a raisin, first inspecting it, then rolling it around in their mouths before finally chewing it. This exercise reveals rich experience through mindful engagement with simple activities, aware of the sensations and pleasures they evoke, perhaps even appreciating them as a miracle. You will *know* the raisin in a different way because you have brought to life the act of eating it. This is the epistemological aspect of meditation, rooted in experience as a way of knowing. However, there is no fundamental *ontological* shift in being, no radical transformation of the self, or the one who knows. In other words, the experience leaves us eager to deepen it (to bring it back to life), but not to question the nature of what we hold to be true (beyond the idea that slowly chewing raisins might be boring). We are open to appreciating more fully what happens, but not to challenging our understanding of what is really happening. Mindfulness teachers discourage this sort of inquiry, instead just celebrating the act of being fully present to the world as it is — no questions asked.

Comparing his approach to the anti-intellectual strands in Northern Chan (Chinese Zen), Kabat-Zinn says conceptual maps obstruct and "can seriously occlude our ability as a mindfulness-based instructor to see and communicate about the territory in any original and direct way — a direct transmission if you will, outside the formal teachings, and thus an embodiment of the real curriculum."[19] While MBSR teachers are required to attend several traditional Buddhist meditation retreats, and to have a strong personal grounding in Buddhist teachings, the only thing taught in the MBSR classroom is "the *essence* of Buddhism." For Kabat-Zinn and his lineage: "Our job is to take care of the territory of direct experience in the present moment and the learning that comes out of it."[20]

Mindfulness, he tells us repeatedly, is "the awareness that arises from paying attention, on purpose, in the present moment, and non-judgmentally." Kabat-Zinn's operational definition has become the gold standard in clinical literature, with institutional backing from contemplative scientists. The media and even the public have also latched onto it as a definitive concept. However, it conflates awareness of the present moment with mindfulness, making the latter a standalone practice — and an end in itself.

It is hard to not hear the voices of Ram Dass and Eckhart Tolle (authors of *Be Here Now* and *The Power of Now* respectively) in Kabat-Zinn's description — they also sacralize the present. It can certainly be pleasant to "turn off your mind, relax, and float downstream," to quote Timothy Leary via John Lennon. The cliché of simply being present — the holy grail of mindfulness, and the essence of Kabat-Zinn's "essential dharma" — elevates resting in "being" to the functional equivalent of spiritual awakening. But this is not how the Buddha defined liberation. He taught a middle path between the extremes of being and non-being, clinging to neither. Fetishizing present experience runs the risk of reducing mindfulness to a pop philosophy that relishes an *amoral immediacy of being*, undermining critical forethought and ethical awareness of the consequentiality of past and future actions.

There are therapeutic benefits to present-moment awareness, but it can also subtly strengthen the sense of being a separate self, existing independently of other phenomena (a prime cause of suffering, according to Buddhism). This happens because MBSR presupposes a split between the observing subject, who is located "here", and "the present" they are told to pay attention to, which is over "there." In this dualistic schema, the observing subject is separated from the present moment and must make a concerted effort to apprehend and capture it by focusing attention on its apparent location.

One could interpret the injunction to "be here now" as a meditative effort to locate the "here" of the subject and the "there" of the present in one place. However, teachers encourage self-orientation via achievement, reinforcing a separate location. Practitioners of mindfulness are in a constant mode of self-surveillance, checking up on their progress (or lack thereof) towards "being present." This is the ultimate goal in MBSR, yet merely the first step in Buddhist mindfulness teachings based on the *Satipatthana Sutta*. Deeper levels of practice develop clear insight into all constituents of temporal experience as inconstant and unsatisfactory. When seen clearly for what it actually is, the present moment is like any other mental object — a transitory fabrication to be viewed with dispassion rather than fetishized.

Mindfulness and Perennial Transcendentalism

The mystification of a personal experience of "being present" owes more to American religious history than to Buddhism. Some of this is conscious on the part of Kabat-Zinn, whose books make regular references to Henry David Thoreau and other nineteenth-century Transcendentalists. In *Coming to Our Senses*, he quotes Thoreau's back-to-nature classic *Walden; or, Life in the Woods*:

> I went to the woods because I wished to live deliberately, to front only the essential facts of life and see if I could not learn what it had to teach and not, when I came to die, discover that I had not lived.[21]

Kabat-Zinn compares this to his own philosophy of "living in harmony with oneself and with the world," while "cultivating some appreciation for the fullness of each moment we are alive." As he explains: "Thoreau saw the same problem with our ordinary mind state in New England in 1846 and wrote with great passion about its unfortunate consequences."[22]

Retreating to a cabin on land owned by his mentor Ralph Waldo Emerson, Thoreau turned his back on the horrors of industrialization and injustice, focusing instead on a simpler existence and transcending the mundane through contemplation. Kabat-Zinn calls Thoreau's experience "a personal experiment in mindfulness. He chose to put his life on the line in order to revel in the wonder and simplicity of present moments."[23] Like Thoreau and Emerson, Kabat-Zinn reels off reasons to feel disenchanted with modern life, while offering a path to re-enchantment through retreat, if not physically then psychologically — in mindfulness practice.

The Transcendentalist focus on direct experience had Eastern influences. Thoreau read the *Bhagavad Gita* at Walden Pond, drawing on its ideas — like Emerson and Walt Whitman — to see a universal freedom in oneness with nature. Early Western translations of other Asian texts found a captive audience in New England, taking root in the fertile soil of Transcendentalism. "For Emerson," writes the scholar of religion Arthur Versluis, "the significance of Asian religions — of all human history — consists of assimilation into the present, into the here and now."[24] By the end of the nineteenth century, adds Rick Fields, a historian of Buddhism in the US, "the drawing rooms of Boston were awash with mysticism, occult fancies and Eastern religions."[25]

One manifestation of this trend was Theosophy, a mix of Western esotericism and mystical ideas from Hinduism and

Buddhism. Founded in New York in 1875, the Theosophical Society aimed to construct a universal doctrine based on science and experiential insight. Another influential development was New Thought, a "mind cure" whose positive psychology inspires modern cults of "The Law of Attraction."

The general focus on cultivating wellness through mental powers impressed the psychologist William James, who called it a "religion of healthy-mindedness." As he described it in *The Varieties of Religious Experience*: "The greatest discovery of my generation is that man can alter his life simply by altering his attitude of mind."[26] James, like Kabat-Zinn, valorized "the intense interest that life can assume when brought down to the non-thinking level, the level of pure sensorial perception."[27] He thereby laid the foundation for New Age thinkers, who — to borrow a phrase from Emmanuel Lévinas — reduce James' insights to "cheap mysticism."

In *The Varieties of Religious Experience*, James describes direct encounters with a common mystical basis for all religion — like the "universal dharma" of Kabat-Zinnism. This appeal to "perennial philosophy" — a phrase later popularized by Aldous Huxley — strips meditative practice of cultural context. It is said instead to give privileged access to "pure awareness," free from history and sectarian boundaries. James helped to make personal *experience* the primary source of truth and religious authority. This rationalized faith, staking out a private realm for religion beyond scientific measurement. Essentially an anti-authoritarian doctrine, James' radical empiricism shifted power from institutions to individuals. It thus enabled

New Age gurus and meditation teachers to claim authority from first-hand experience, while defending a "universal dharma" from critique.

Perennial philosophy also informed D.T. Suzuki's revisionist Zen, which influenced the Beats and brought Buddhist meditation to public attention in the 1950s. Just as Suzuki claimed that Zen offered access to a pure, unmediated, timeless essence of mystical experience, Kabat-Zinn has done the same for mindfulness, privileging it as the essential core of Buddhism. This unbundles the concept, so an "open-source" practice is more easily appropriated. As David McMahan reflects in *The Making of Buddhist Modernism*, a thread links Transcendentalism, Suzuki's ideas and MBSR:

> The internalization of religion, the attribution of religious significance to the natural world, the emphasis on solitary contemplation of nature, and the view such contemplation as a remedy for the excessive materialism of the modern world all served as essential ingredients in the interpretation of Buddhism in the West, particularly North America.[28]

There is only one drawback. For most of the history of meditative practice, doctrinal context has defined the experience. Its priorities are often very different from our own. "It is not just that advanced meditation practitioners in more traditional Asian settings may not exhibit the kinds of behavior that we associate with mental health," notes the scholar of Buddhism Robert Sharf. "It is not clear that they aspire to our model of mental health in the first place."[29] Meanwhile, the very idea of "pure awareness," the decontextualized basis of perennial philosophy, is contested. Although we can turn down the volume on thoughts, our mental conditioning still runs in the background. "Sense experience never operates in an unmediated fashion," explains Richard Cohen in *Beyond Enlightenment*. "What seems to be direct perception of worldly objects is, in fact, always already an amalgam of sense impressions and intellection."[30] However, stripped of the traditional context that makes it make sense, a "mindfulness-only" approach now defines meditation, potentially producing self-centered adherents.

Meditation Sickness

Conflating mindfulness with present-moment awareness was seen as a hazard in Buddhist traditions with only one practice. Early Chan patriarchs also taught meditation to cultivate "no mind" through intense immersion in the here-and-now, inducing deep tranquility and non-discursive awareness. This "silent illumination" approach became quite prevalent in eighth-century China, promoted to the laity as a practice that promised quick results, with no requirements for doctrinal study or ethical training, like MBSR. However, the Song dynasty Chan master Dahui cautioned that this method could lead to the "malady of meditation," in which consciousness of stillness is mistaken for one's own true nature. Hakuin, a master of Zen, was also critical, fearing that meditators fell prey to "dead sitting," attached to quietude and inactivity, with no concern for the suffering of the world. And the eighth-century Indian master Kamalaśila warned that practitioners who wrongly tried to stop thinking would spend five hundred eons as mindless zombies.

The veneration of "bare attention" to the present moment in MBSR derives from Nyañaponika Thera's classic *The Heart of Buddhist Meditation*, first published in English sixty years ago. Its cover now features an endorsement from Kabat-Zinn: "The book that started it all." Nyañaponika's instructions for beginners suggest: "a bare registering of the facts observed, without reacting to them by deed, speech or by mental comment." However, if "comments arise in one's mind, they themselves are made objects of Bare Attention, and are neither repudiated nor pursued."[31] Mental training in non-elaborative "bare attention" has therapeutic benefits, not just calming the mind but decentering awareness to observe thoughts and feelings as passing events, not the way things are. Yet Nyañaponika never said mindfulness should be translated as "bare attention." His long-time student, Bhikkhu Bodhi, recalls him disapproving of how contemporary *vipassana* teachers misinterpret bare attention. He would sometimes shake his head, saying: "But that's not what I meant at all!"[32]

Modern secular mindfulness precludes discussion of context, or the purpose of practice beyond feeling better. It is regarded as blasphemous to question this, since it is assumed a priori that mindfulness is always beneficial. And since it supposedly offers direct access to the essence of Buddhism, to interrogate its applications or ends would be to refuse "the gift of the dharma." Even when these ends are benign, such as offering mindfulness in a medical or therapeutic context, mindfulness is seen as a means to those ends, which alters and reorients the meaning of the practice itself.

This is legitimized with Kabat-Zinn's essentialist and universalizing rhetoric. It has led many to believe that, as isolated subjects, they have private access to the essence of the "dharma," independent of their own dominant cultural values. Once mindfulness has been decontextualized, and reduced to an instrumentalized technique, it can be applied in any context, without any need for critical questioning of the ends it serves. Whether mindfulness is used by US Marines to optimize battlefield performance in Afghanistan, or — as one senior manager at Google put it — "as an organizational WD-40, a necessary lubricant between driven, ambitious employees and Google's demanding corporate culture," it makes no difference.[33] Mindfulness works and it's a Good Thing.

With this self-congratulatory branding, mindfulness sells well on the spiritual marketplace as a means to success. In *What's Wrong with Mindfulness*, Barry Magid and Robert Rosenbaum call this a "for-gain, workshop approach."[34] Mindfulness is marketed as a goal-oriented tool for self-improvement. It promises consumers a short-term fix in the form of relief, whether from stress, relationship difficulties, chronic illness, lack of focus at work or poor academic performance. "Materialistic, for-gain Buddhism may well be an unavoidable part of Buddhism's transmission to the West," note Magid and Rosenbaum. However, they warn that denying the significance of context means "it adapts to, and is translated into, the deep-rooted individualist, materialist, and secular structures of Western culture —

including the culture of science as itself a technique for achieving control and thus better satisfying needs."[35]

MBSR appeals to modern sensibilities, catering particularly to the "spiritual but not religious." In just eight weeks one can learn a form of meditation without Buddhist trappings, which are replaced by the sanctification of personal experience. This serves to strengthen people's conceptions of themselves as self-contained and autonomous agents, rather than as relational and interdependent — and an individualized practice requires no communal ties, moral commitments, or substantive lifestyle changes. Instead, one can be mindful in any way one likes, while washing the dishes, taking in a sunset, smelling an orange, or having sex or sipping wine.

Like his nineteenth-century forebears — Thoreau, Emerson and James — Kabat-Zinn rejects the authority of social and religious institutions. Instead, he salutes the power of individuals. Appealing to a "do-it-yourself" form of American pragmatism, he asserts: "Each person is already the world authority on him- or herself, or at least could be if they started attending to things mindfully."[36]

chapter six
Mindfulness as Social Amnesia

In case you're wondering, I have tried mindfulness. Let me take you back to my first session of an eight-week course on Mindfulness-Based Stress Reduction (MBSR). The teacher was a stocky, bald man of few words. As with most new group endeavors, the introductory session felt awkward and guarded. I knew from my reading that I would soon be facing the MBSR initiation rite: the slow eating of a raisin, an exercise that I was honestly not looking forward to doing. Being a good sport, I summoned what patience I had, gazed attentively at the raisin for a few seconds (naturally, it was organic) and took a small nibble. I've been to foodie meccas in Italy — Parma, Bologna, Reggio Emilia — so the ritual of eating slowly was not new, but it's hard to be sure I was eating *mindfully*.

Over the next few weeks, I began to gain a much deeper appreciation of how MBSR was responding to a longing in Western culture, and how this method, course, or whatever you want to call it, was serving some unmet needs of late-capitalist society. I felt a little out of place. Of the twenty-five or so participants, most were women. As we went around the room and introduced ourselves, explaining what had brought us there, I felt like I was listening to the walking wounded. Many had lost jobs without warning. Others faced the strains of having to work long hours, sometimes two jobs, while caring for others. For a number of women, this was their second or third round of the course. Divorces, bereavements, stories of chronic pain, and a sense of malaise haunted the room. Nearly half of the participants had been referred by their psychotherapists.

Clearly, MBSR is a saving grace for many people, especially those who might not otherwise encounter meditative practices. Within a few weeks, participants on the course were describing the innumerable benefits they felt from the "body scan" exercise; some even reported that it helped them sleep better. The MBSR teacher was certainly sincere and competent. The course was accomplishing exactly what it was intended to do: teach people how to reduce their stress and anxiety, cope with pain, and live a more mindful life. Then why was I unsettled, and experiencing vague irritation?

Was I restless and bothered because of how mindfulness was being presented, as a simple technique without an ethical framework or social purpose? Not really. As far as I could tell, there were no serial killers among us — or cutthroat twenty-six-year-old Uber executives. I had also taken a few courses at Buddhist Insight Meditation Centers, and ethics were not on their agenda either. That wasn't the issue. I briefly came back to my senses as the MBSR instructor led us in a guided sitting meditation. Minutes into the exercise, I had a flashback, or what the teacher called "mind-wandering" — sort of the opposite of focusing on now. Disregarding the instructions to be in the present moment, I decide to indulge the memory, at least a little.

I am back to being eighteen, working as an industrial electrician at one of the largest manufacturing plants on Chicago's South Side. Suited in overalls, with a beat-up, red hard hat over straggly hair, I am anxiously staring at the time clock with everyone else — a group ritual of silence, waiting for the hand to strike the hour so I can punch out. In front of me are hunched-over workers — a few pipefitters who have punched this time clock for the last thirty years of their lives. But on this day, my gaze shifts from the clock to the faces of alienation in front of me. And wait a minute... These workers' faces are not all that dissimilar to the looks of defeat I saw a few weeks earlier in my MBSR cohort — the vacant stares, the pained faces, the anxious waiting for time to change. This past was the present, appearing differently.

Being a bad MBSR student, I began ruminating further. What about *these* walking wounded I once worked with? Would MBSR have helped them too if it had been around then? Would they have stopped punching the time clock if they practiced mindfulness? Would MBSR have made them more mindful at work, allowing them to appreciate and enjoy the routine and monotony of the assembly line? Could they have even afforded an MBSR course? Perhaps the animosity and strained labor-management relations, along with the militant labor unions, would have all become obsolete if corporate mindfulness training had been available? Would this have been a good thing? Who'd have benefited?

That was a little too much thinking; I brought myself back to the present moment.

Blaming the Victim

After our sitting meditation, the MBSR teacher excitedly passed out photocopies of "The Mindful Revolution" —

the *Time* magazine cover story I discussed in Chapter One, which features a youthful white blonde woman with her eyes blissfully closed. But as I gazed across the room, this iconic image of spiritual perfection didn't jibe with the atmosphere. If this was the face of the so-called revolution, it wasn't happening here. Instead, I had become even more mindful of the expressions of alienation, the forlorn, and the weary, as well as bodies beaten down by the daily grind, and minds numbed by the incessant demands of a digital economy. As the course progressed, my gnawing sense of unease did not abate. In fact, it got worse.

The dominant narrative of MBSR just didn't sit right with me. Although people were clearly getting helpful relief from their stress-related symptoms, the message that was meant to empower them had troubling undertones. If fMRI scans from neuroscience suggested that suffering takes place in the mind, the solution was to tune out of thoughts about the past and the future, attending mindfully to the present moment. However, if misery is self-created in this way, I only have myself to blame for being mindless.

As time went on, I had a hard time determining whether I was being trained in a scientific method or a political ideology. Maybe it was both. The etiological explanation sounded just a little too convenient: the stress people were experiencing supposedly had nothing to do with actual material conditions (e.g. loss of income), nor the unreasonable demands of workaholic corporate cultures. The noxious features of neoliberal capitalism were nowhere to be found on the mindfulness radar. Stress was a private, subjective and interior affair — a problem for individuals to deal with. David Smail calls this philosophy "magical voluntarism," in which relief from distress depends entirely on acts of will (also known as the choice to practice mindfulness), not on changing the causal conditions.[1]

Reflecting on this ethos of self-responsibility, I began to feel a sense of déjà vu. As a young, idealistic under-graduate in Northern California in the late 1970s, I was a student of humanistic psychology, immersed in works by Carl Rogers, Abraham Maslow, and Fritz Perls, along with existentialists, depth psychologists and other human potential gurus. Self-improvement seminars like Werner Erhard's EST were all the rage, and the neoliberal priorities of the Thatcher-Reagan era were taking shape. Feeling self-righteous after jumping ship from a behavioral-ex-perimental "rat" psychology program in the Midwest, I enthusiastically drank the Kool-Aid, believing change, self-actualization, and transformation came from within — all within the power and agency of an autonomous subject. Self-mastery was a heroic journey of the individual.

The promise of humanistic psychology has been reincarnated as the mindfulness movement. Instead of earlier quests for the authentic self in the farthest reaches of human nature, one just has to search inside oneself with "pure awareness." By shifting from the "doing" mode to "being," one can find authenticity by practicing mindfulness. And while it might be hard to hang out in the "being" mode if you have to spend seventy hours each week executing trades on Wall Street, there is always the prospect of taking time out for a short daily mindful process of de-stressing.

I tried to stay in the present moment — really, I did — but this "mind-wandering" seemed to be leading somewhere, connecting dots, yielding "ah-ha" moments. First, like humanistic psychology, mindfulness makes subjectivity sacrosanct. Second, both eschew any need to pay attention to social and historical contexts of distress, to power structures and monetary interests. The therapeutic-mindfulness industry may have created its own conformist psychology — complicit in maintaining the status quo of corporate capitalism and neoliberal government.

Better-Adjusted Cogs

I felt conflicted. Here I was, sitting with a community of strangers, all of whom were suffering in some way from modern vicissitudes. Each week, I was observing and hearing how MBSR was helping them cope, offering them tools so that they could adjust to their less-than-ideal working conditions, even building up their resilience. How could anyone be critical of such beneficence? Doing so would seem to make the perfect the enemy of the good. And much that was happening was good. But at the same time, I knew that in a few weeks the MBSR class would come to an end. These folks would soon be back in the trenches and in the firing line of corporate life, still contending with grueling hours in their cubicles, or for some, pounding pavements in search of employment — basic survival. Yes, hopefully the skills they learned would help them cope a little better. But these observations were fueling the discomfort in my gut: was this "mindful revolution" just about coping, fine-tuning our brains so that we can dutifully perform our roles more efficiently — becoming better-adjusted cogs in the capitalist machinery?

Could it even be that mindfulness had gained mainstream acceptance because it ensured a snug fit between individuals and social institutions? Was it a useful accomplice in maintaining social control by regulating our unruly desires, downgrading thought, and teaching us to accept "what is" while retreating into comfortable depths of subjectivity? Is this non-judgmental flight to direct sensory experience (slowly eating a raisin, taking a deep breath before sending off that difficult e-mail, etc) propagating a sophisticated form of anti-intellectualism, throwing us a few breadcrumbs of stability at the expense of mindlessly accepting injustices, just as they are?

By now, some may think I want to drown the baby, never mind throw it out with the bathwater — I do not. The walking wounded, those with chronic stress — like childhood obesity, black-lung disease, and victims of industrial accidents — still need to be treated, and MBSR admirably serves its intended purpose in this regard. But what is missing in this picture, and from mindfulness discourse, is that chronic stress — like most chronic diseases and occupational accidents — has a social and political content. Such insights are not new. Erich Fromm, who himself launched a critique of the orthodox psychoanalysis of his day, pointed out that our distress and anxieties can never be fully understood nor alleviated if the social origins of suffering are ignored.

One of the main reasons that mindfulness programs have gained widespread acceptance among psychologists, clinicians and administrators is because they resonate so strongly with, and even give stronger credence to, the therapeutic ideology of "magical voluntarism." Historical and material conditions are concealed by therapeutic discourse. Through the reductive explanatory narratives of psychologism or biologism, psychic and mental disturbances are depoliticized. What remains is an individualistic view of human distress, with the underlying premise that those who suffer are dysfunctional. However, working conditions within a corporation, for example, and the socio-economic structures of capitalist society are taken as given — even as normal — and critical inquiry is discouraged.

The anti-capitalist scholar Joel Kovel has gone as far as saying that the US mental health industry has proliferated and grown exponentially because the diagnoses of individual disorders and their treatments are part of the same social process.[2] Writing before the mindfulness boom, Kovel observed that the mental health industry had been handsomely rewarded because of its institutional role in smoothing over and masking the growing contradictions of advanced capitalist societies. This took place despite the lack of much conclusive evidence for treatments, scientific progress or mastery over mental illness and psychological disorders. As Kovel puts it: "A purely psychological view of human difficulties is a handy way of mystifying social reality, and it requires no feat of imagination to comprehend capitalist society would come to reward the psychiatric profession for promoting a special kind of psychological illusion."[3]

Social Amnesia

Back on the MBSR course, the next exercise was "mindful movement," or basic yoga. Being more of a Tai Chi practitioner, I sat this one out until they got to the end, a supine posture on the floor. Relaxing, I couldn't help but think about how mindfulness interventions have a Puritan obsession with controlling emotions, especially anger, that is cloaked in new psychological and neuroscientific garb. The labels for dysfunction change over time — immaturity, hysteria, neurasthenia, nervous breakdowns, lack of emotional intelligence, problems of emotional self-regulation, mindlessness — but the fundamental model stays constant, based on a cult of subjectivity.

Many popular therapeutic movements require a collective form of forgetting, characterized by the intellectual historian Russell Jacoby as "social amnesia".[4] This can only function by maintaining an illusion that social context and its institutional structures are either natural or unchangeable. Mindfully fixating on the present means tuning out of thoughts about the past and the future. Thinking is considered a distraction, detrimental to "being" in the here-and-now. This is ironic, because "mindfulness" derives from a word that means "remembrance" (*sati* in the Pali language used to compile the Buddha's discourses). In its original Buddhist context, mindfulness involves an awareness of what leads to insight, and what to avoid. However, by fetishizing the present moment "non-judgmentally," modern mindfulness accelerates what Jacoby calls "a forgetting and repression of the human and social activity that makes and can remake a society".[5]

One way to think about a fetish is along the lines of Marx's notion of reification: fetishes mask the truth by keeping people fixated on, or fascinated by, unreal objects. According to the *Oxford English Dictionary*, the original meaning of fetish derives from the Portuguese word *feitiço*, connoting a "charm" or "sorcery," and referring to talismans once thought heretical. A broader reference to the worship of objects originated in the anthropological work of Charles de Brosses, whose writings Marx was familiar with.[6] The modern figurative meaning was well established by the nineteenth century, defined by Oxford lexicographers as "something irrationally reverenced."[7]

In this respect, there seems a strong link between the political quietism of the mindfulness movement and its present moment fetish. If practice is reduced to "being present," I could be mindful of my experience, but unaware of the causes and conditions that constructed it. If I am feeling resentful, exploited and stressed-out at work, and I am instructed simply to focus on the present, how will that change the conditions that have helped to produce my agitation? It won't. I'll just retreat into watching the breath, letting go of passing thoughts and emotions, and settle into a non-judgmental attitude. Just pay attention to one thing at a time. The present moment is imbued with a magical power to assuage, heal and tolerate. Inquiry, critical thought, or investigation into the nature of experience yields and surrenders to the personal. It's certainly calming, which might make space for clearer thinking. But this is subtly discouraged. Instead, the focus is the magical present, the subjectivized moment, that banishes thoughts — instilling, as Jacoby puts it, "an immediacy that stills reflection."

The injunction to "rise above" all the turmoil of human experience to a detached perch of objectivity resembles the Stoics' goal of *apatheia* — from which the modern meaning of apathy is derived.[8] No doubt, this prescription offers a nice respite from my boss who is threatening to fire me, or the market logic behind his decision. But this is a little like watching a sleight-of-hand artist: you watch carefully — mindfully — because you don't want to be tricked, but you don't know what to look for, so you get fooled again by the causes of discomfort. And you get more skilled at tuning out as a result.

Once again, Jon Kabat-Zinn is on hand to put a positive gloss on this passive state. He calls it an immersion in a "body-centered field of awareness that doesn't have to have a narrative or doesn't have to believe its own narrative or take it seriously. It's more in what you could call a domain of not-knowing." He then provides an example of how "not-knowing" served him well in his encounter with a homeless person:

> I was walking by somebody who was panhandling, and that happens a lot where I happen to be at the moment, but he wasn't actually panhandling. He didn't say anything. I just passed him by. But there was something about the feeling of moving past him that I felt like I did not want to pass him by. So I went back and put some money in the cup that had there and he said, "Thank you." The way he had said "thank you" had so much dignity in it. I mean, it has so much — I felt so badly for this guy.
>
> I mean, we're in such a bad economic situation that people are out there on the streets in so many different degrees of depravation. And many of the people who panhandle are actually quite aggressive. But

the way this person just said "thank you," it just really moved me. And my impulse was to want to be his friend and give him more money and take him home. None of which I did. But there was that moment where I really saw this guy and it was its own thing. It didn't need another thing to happen. It was just a beautiful exchange.[9]

Yes, quite beautiful. Nothing further needed to happen, and both of them got to feel better about themselves. All Kabat-Zinn had to do was to let the present moment be his guide without passing judgment.

Perhaps the moment can move us to act in other ways, but a little more context might make that more likely. Otherwise, the immediacy of Kabat-Zinn's precious "I-Thou" encounter just teaches a passive sort of humanism, based on the assumption that dispensing with narratives leads to the good. Such "not-knowing," however, is "social amnesia" in action — forgetting that the world we live in *is* a narrative. How it is told, and thus how we live, is contingent on power and special interests, on the social and political environment, and economic structures which have warmly embraced modern mindfulness as a new form of opiate for the masses.

Back in the warm embrace of the "mindful movement" class, I realized that I had drifted off into a pleasant nap. But nobody around me was judgmental, or seemed to care, so I left the room without embarrassment.

chapter seven
Mindfulness' Truthiness Problem

There is a simple explanation for the popularity of mindfulness, and its clinical acceptance — "The reason is the science," says Jon Kabat-Zinn.[1] The scientific enterprise, with its demands for replication and quantifiable outcomes, has produced an avalanche of formulaic studies seeking to prove, in various ways, that "mindfulness works." Reframed as a tool for improving one's health and achieving goals — from workplace efficiency to bedroom performance — mindfulness provides things to measure, and thereby yardsticks for scientization.

However, despite the claims often used to sell mindfulness programs — like the ubiquitous idea that its benefits are proven scientifically — contemplative neuroscientists are more circumspect. Although brain scans show some of the active networks involved in situations where mindfulness helps, the underlying mechanisms that explain *how* it "works" remain unclear. In an unusually forthright statement, a recent review of research by three prominent neuroscientists describes our understanding of brain changes due to meditation as "trivial," with "more methodologically rigorous studies" needed to unravel it.[2] Many of the articles published so far have major flaws, including a lack of replication, a bias toward positive or significant results, the absence of elaborated theories, and post-hoc conclusions, among other drawbacks, the article noted.

The Dalai Lama's interpreter, Thupten Jinpa, is also cautious. An outstanding scholar in his own right — with a PhD from the University of Cambridge, and the highest academic qualification in the Gelugpa tradition of Tibetan Buddhism — Jinpa says: "The scientific study of meditation and its effects is very rudimentary."[3]

As observed by Jenny Eklöf, a researcher at Umeå University in Sweden, public outreach by contemplative neuroscientists can be confusing. Although pronouncements suggest that mindfulness helps promote wellbeing, health and happiness, and even brain fitness, "the cultural and social impact of this field is often taken to be a sign of its prior academic validation," Eklöf warns.[4] In contrast to their conservative tone in journal articles — like the review cited above — more popular communications by scientists claim that their field is making "cutting-edge discoveries," or that they are on the brink of a revolutionary shift that could save our culture.

A notable example is the article "Mindfulness Can Literally Change Your Brain" in the *Harvard Business Review*, which ironically shares a co-author with the skeptical study of other people's studies. Rather than hedging, as careful scientists do, the article makes bold claims:

> The business world is abuzz with mindfulness. But perhaps you haven't heard that the hype is backed by hard science. Recent research provides strong evidence that practicing non-judgmental, present moment awareness (a.k.a mindfulness) changes the brain, and it does so in ways that anyone working in today's complex business environment, and certainly every leader, should know about.[5]

There are many things wrong with the headline and what follows. Both parrot a theme much beloved of mindfulness advocates, and their neuroscience allies, yet their message is empty. It reduces the mind to the brain — despite the lack of evidence for this assumption — while glossing over the fact that almost any repetitive practice has similar effects, from playing the violin to driving a taxi around the streets of London. And as the cognitive neuroscientist Fernando Vidal points out: "since the mind is said to be what the brain does, all that is being claimed is that brain activity changes brain activity."[6]

Mindfulness was recast as science to meet Western needs, and to circumvent cultural resistance to meditative practices borrowed from Buddhism. Putting mindfulness to work, like a well-trained mule carrying someone's burden, reflects the focus on results that dominates mindfulness-related discourse. Rather than reviewing and critiquing the scientific literature on mindfulness, I am more concerned with exposing the assumptions, exaggerated claims, and purported truths produced by the process of scientization.

While proselytizers talk up "the science of mindfulness," it barely exists in the form they imply. Their public presentations have more to do with rhetoric than scientific rigor, subordinating proof to what sounds "science-y." Like the "truthiness" of Stephen Colbert, who satirized "alternative facts" long before the Trump era, what matters is not what's true but how things *feel*, and mindfulness feels very "science-y."

Mind the Hype

The entangling of scientists and advocates generates hype. One example of the risks when the two coexist in a single head is a study of mindfulness-based interventions by Bassam Khoury at McGill University. Khoury practices mindfulness and is an avid proponent — he calls himself a "mindful psychologist" and promotes his own workbook of mindfulness exercises. In his meta-analytic review (a statistical approach that combines results from numerous studies), Khoury and his colleagues concluded that mindfulness-based therapy "is an effective treatment for a variety of psychological problems, and is especially effective for reducing anxiety, depression, and stress."[7]

However, an independent review of Khoury's study by researchers at the University of York — under the auspices of the Centre for Reviews and Dissemination — was less convinced. "The authors' conclusions may be overstated given the poor quality and wide variation between studies," it found." Quality was generally low for controlled studies; it was better for before-and-after studies, but this design is open to several sources of bias. Many studies were uncontrolled, which prevents definitive conclusions."[8]

There is convincing evidence that mindfulness studies suffer from positive reporting bias, suggesting therapies are more effective than they really are. Stephanie Coronado-Montoya and her team in the Department of Psychiatry at McGill University recently found that authors of mindfulness studies tended to downplay negative findings. Given the small sample size and weak statistical power of the pool of mindfulness studies examined, McGill researchers were concerned by the skewed results.[9]

The late Catherine Kerr, who trained at Harvard Medical School and was Director of the Contemplative Neuro-science program at Brown, feared the tendency to overstate mindfulness research could backfire. "If this wave of hype continues," Kerr warned, "the backlash will be too strong." Her concern was simple: if findings don't pan out, "people will lose faith and revert to the other side: mindfulness has *no* value."[10]

We are now witnessing what Joel Best describes in *Flavor of the Month: Why Smart People Fall for Fads*. Best calls this problem "the illusion of diffusion," a mistaken belief that the extent of enthusiasm for mindfulness is evidence of its effectiveness and durability.[11] In many respects, branding mindfulness with scientific jargon is not all that dissimilar to the way a new fitness craze or low-fat diet is promoted. Boosters of exercise and dieting are notorious for cherry-picking studies and appealing to the authority of science to bolster their claims that we can shed extra pounds and improve our lives in just a few weeks. Very few of these miracle solutions are anything more than short-lived fads.

The mindfulness movement enjoys much greater credi-bility, yet this rests in part on the sheer momentum of its methods. Self-congratulatory studies, media hype, books and courses all feed off each other. The main problem of skewed research stems from the academic mindfulness industry, in which millions of dollars of grant money are at stake. Research support is most readily available for "evidence-based" studies that work with randomized-con-trolled trials (RCTs) — in theory, the gold standard of science.

However, the problems with studies on mindfulness are not new. Before they started to receive grant funding in the last decade, there was a similar enthusiasm from government funding agencies for Transcendental Meditation (TM). Between 1992 and 2010, the US National Institutes of Health (NIH) awarded nearly $23 million to Maharishi University, the site for the majority of research on TM. However, by 2010 TM had fallen out of favor, and has since received no grant money. As former TM insider Aryeh Siegel points out in his book *Transcendental Deception*, TM's fall from grace in the research world could be traced to such factors as "poorly designed studies that rarely include a randomized active control group," "a history of exaggerated findings," and biased researchers who were themselves TM practitioners.[12]

It is worth noting that TM's efficacy was also explained in biomedical terms, like MBSR's. Early support came from Herbert Benson, professor of Mind/Body Medicine at Harvard Medical School, and author of the best-selling book *The Relaxation Response*.[13] As Benson described it: "The Relaxation Response is a universal human capacity, and even though it has been evoked in the religions of both East and West for most of recorded history, you don't have to engage in any rites or esoteric practices to bring it forth."[14] His method dispensed with TM's secret mantras, initiations, attempts at levitation, and Hindu influences. People repeated a simple word, phrase, or activity to keep the mind from wandering, along with maintaining a passive and receptive attitude.

Like Kabat-Zinn, Benson used universalizing discourse to distance his work from religious traditions, while making science the means of validation and legitimation. Jeff Wilson argues in *Mindful America* that this jettisoning of religious elements accounts for the popularity of MBSR and its acceptance in medicine, while the demise of TM is due in part to racism. As Wilson observes of TM's guru: "The Maharishi was a brown-skinned Indian man with a big beard and long, somewhat unkempt hair worn forward of the shoulders, who typically appeared in yoga robes with Hindu prayer beads." In contrast: "Jon Kabat-Zinn, the face of MBSR, is a clean-shaven white American doctor with short hair and rimless glasses, who delivers his teachings in business attire."[15]

When TM research dropped off government funding registers, mindfulness-based interventions filled the void. The NIH has so far spent over $100 million on mindfulness research, four times as much as it gave TM in half the time. In 2017 alone, the University of Wisconsin-Madison's Center for Healthy Minds — run by contemplative neuroscientist Richard Davidson — was awarded a whopping $7,637,000.[16]

The Myth of Efficacy

Scientific claims by mindfulness researchers are now being examined with greater scrutiny. In another meta-analytic study published in the *Journal of the American Medical Association (JAMA), Internal Medicine*, Dr Madhav Goyal and his colleagues from John Hopkins University searched databases using a set of key meditation terms.[17] They found 18,753 citations, of which forty-seven matched their inclusion criteria, such as the use of randomized controlled trials. They found that mindfulness was moderately effective in treating a variety of conditions, but not more effective than other active treatments, such as drugs or exercise. Moreover, the fact that only 0.25% of the studies were deemed of high enough quality should give one pause. Hype is the unsurprising outcome of such low standards of methodological rigor, despite the lukewarm findings they conceal.

The US Agency for Healthcare Research and Quality also commissioned meta-analytic studies on the efficacy of mindfulness-based interventions (MBIs), first in 2007 and again in 2014. Both studies were critical of the lack of rigorous standards, noting that the majority of studies did not utilize randomized control groups. The more recent 2014 meta-analysis found that MBIs had lackluster efficacy, ranging from moderate to none whatsoever.[18] What is especially noteworthy was the low reported efficacy of MBIs for reducing stress and improving people's quality of life.

One of the claims made by mindfulness advocates is that the practice in and of itself leads to pro-social conduct, enhancing compassion, altruism and empathy, while reducing aggression and prejudice. This is one of the movement's central tenets, used to justify the absence of any overt discussion of ethics. It is the basis of the utopian promise that a mindful revolution will usher in a more humane society and even world peace.

A recent meta-analytic study on the effects of meditation on pro-social behaviors casts serious doubts on these grandiose claims. A paper published in *Scientific Reports* in 2018 found that moderate increases in compassion occurred only in studies that had the meditation teacher as a co-author, and only when the study used a passive (rather than active) control group.[19] Furthermore, 61% of the studies were methodologically weak. Experimenter allegiance and bias (that is, when the teacher of the meditation intervention also authored the study) accounted for the moderate increase in compassion. Take that condition away, and the results disappeared. In addition, their study found no evidence that meditation had any significant effect on the reduction of aggression and prejudice.

The widespread belief that there is compelling clinical proof that "mindfulness works" is simply not supported by the scientific evidence. Another recent meta-analysis found MBSR was not effective for people suffering from depression.[20] Even using the more specific Mindfulness-Based Cognitive Therapy (MBCT), which is sanctioned for treating depression by the UK's National Institute for Health and Clinical Excellence, the efficacy is only modestly helpful for reducing the likelihood of depression relapse.

Blobology

Colorful pictures of brains are often featured in media reports touting evidence that science has verified the efficacy of mindfulness. They come from neuroscientific studies using functional magnetic resonance imaging (fMRI) of meditators' brain states. Their "before and after" shots are seen as an official stamp of legitimacy, incontrovertible proof of functional and structural changes in the brain —

even if the neuroscientists who produce them are more circumspect about the actual significance of increasing the size of grey matter, shrinking the amygdala, or quieting the default mode network. As Richard Henson at the University of Cambridge wryly comments, "the pictures of blobs on brains seduce one into thinking that we can now directly observe psychological processes."[21] A study has shown the dangers of this thinking. Under the title "The Seductive Allure of Neuroscience Explanations," Deena Weisberg and her colleagues found that even bogus and bad explanations for psychological phenomena are seen as more satisfying by most people when couched in the language and dazzling visual imagery of neuroscience.[22]

There is also the flawed assumption that neural correlates of brain states — shown on colorful fMRI scans — can explain first-person experiences. This rests on the premise that mindfulness is a form of inner observation of a private mental realm inside the brain — resembling a "theatre of the mind." But that imagines an Enlightenment ideal of a truly objective inner observer, while reducing mindfulness to the purely biological, ignoring the influence of contextual factors — social, cultural, economic, and cosmological — on meditative experience. Such a reductionist view perpetuates the ill-conceived notion, as the scholar of Buddhism David McMahan puts it, that "meditation can be isolated from the rest of life for the sake of scientific study."[23]

By suggesting that we can see inside the brain in an unmediated way, fMRI scans impose what Michel Foucault called a "regime of truth." They appear to show clear signs of something significant, but there is actually always activity across the whole brain, even at times of so-called rest. The brighter parts of fMRI images show the most metabolically active regions, which may be only a few percent more active than regions colored gray. The images are actually statistical patterns of brain-wide metabolic activity — and, contrary to what much of the public is led to believe, they don't show actual engagement of specific regions as if they were mental organs in any meaningful sense. Nor are they snapshots of cognitive activity actually taking place in the brain; that occurs at the microscopic level. The use of specific regions is just a way to make analysis tractable.

Brain scans are complex composites of statistical mapping and averaging of multiple data points and subjects. Brain imaging is about indirect measurements of cell activity in huge (by brain standards) aggregates rather than at the cellular level, which is where the brain actually performs its electro-chemical processing. As my colleague David Lewis points out, fMRI images only resolve down to cubes of tissue measuring 1-3mm a side, each with upwards of a million neurons.[24] Lewis provides a useful metaphor for brain-imaging studies, comparing them to trying to deduce the economic and social structure of New York City by observing movements of vehicles and people from an airplane. One can see that Lower Manhattan is active from 8am to 5pm, with a spike in foot traffic around noon, and parts of midtown are buzzing around 8pm and again at 11pm. On that basis one might gain a crude idea what is going on, but any assertions about how the financial and theater industries work would be unreliable guesses.

In effect, fMRI images of brain activity amount to a simulation, which in itself is not problematic. Computer simulations are frequently used for earthquake prediction, or computer modeling that tracks hurricane developments — based on quantitative data that can also be reproduced in dynamic imagery. The problem here with fMRI simulations is that their pictorial representations create a powerful illusion of accurate and direct images of phenomenological mental states, what Nikolas Rose and Joelle Abi-Rached refer to as a "visual imaginary." This is a little like that of phrenologists of the nineteenth century, who mapped and measured the contours of the human skull as a means of assessing character, emotional dispositions and mental states.[25]

There are other conceptual and technological issues that make neuroimaging look deceptive. Evan Thompson, a philosopher at the University of British Columbia, has been an outspoken and lucid critic of contemplative neuroscientists who claim to have mapped the neural correlates of mindfulness. Thompson argues that it is empirically unwarranted to map cognitive functions involved in meditative practice onto localized brain areas or networks. Analysis of large databases of neuroimaging data "demonstrates that there is no one-to-one correspondence between particular brain regions and particular cognitive functions; rather any given region is activated across a wide array of tasks," Thompson says.[26] Even the latest attempts to understand brain regions in terms of networks still fail to show any sort of one-to-one connection. This multiplicity has turned out to be true of every brain region involved in cognition and emotion. Worse, even trying to understand and structure the various precursors for each region has not led to scientific consensus on mental function in terms of regions or sub-regions, though they are clearly different from one another. Theories are hotly debated for each region, but experiments turn up new observations that entail reconsideration, and there is no trend toward convergence.

Cognitive functions are not just in the head, but are embodied, involving an array of affective and bodily skills that are situated in a social environment. To illustrate his point, Thompson uses the analogy of good parenting to understand that we cannot simply deduce what good parenting is by mapping brain regions. As he explains:

> Being a good parent consists in a host of emotional and cognitive skills and putting those skills into play in action. The skills and behaviors based on them clearly depend on the brain — and improving them changes the brain — but they are not private mental states and do not exist inside the brain... Parenting simply is not visible at the level of the brain."[27]

The same is true for mindfulness. Decontextualizing it promotes the myth that it is a private mental state detached from social and cultural contexts. Viewed this way, it can be promoted as a way to "train your brain," and scientific careers can be bankrolled with millions of dollars in government funding for brain-mapping studies.

Measuring Mindfulness?

Another weak link in research on mindfulness is the reliance on dubious methods of self-reporting by practitioners. To date, there are at least nine different psychometric questionnaires, all of which define and measure mindfulness differently. In addition to numerous problems of reliability, construct validity and self-reporting biases, there is a basic underlying assumption that discrete psychological characteristics, which can be measured and quantified, are equivalent to mindfulness. However, the wide variety of definitions can allow for very different conceptions of practice and objectives, with no necessary connection to the teachings that inspired Kabat-Zinn to create MBSR.

There are other problems too. Western psychological interpretations conceive of mindfulness as both a single and multifaceted trait. For example, Brown and Ryan's Mindfulness Attention Awareness Scale (MAAS), perhaps the most widely used tool for measuring mindfulness, assumes that it is single-faceted and based on "present-centered attention." The MAAS relies on the notion that mindfulness can be measured by how individuals *think* they experience lapses of attention — what researchers call "mind-wandering." In contrast, the Five-Facet Mindfulness Questionnaire (FFMQ) views mindfulness as multifaceted. It includes such sub-scales as "describing" measuring the extent to which people believe they can express themselves in words. Non-meditators tend to score similarly to meditators, except on one factor — close observation of experience.

Self-reporting measures also are prone to simplistic language, failing to capture some aspects of mindfulness while also allowing for incompatible interpretations. This has resulted in a number of absurd and questionable findings. One classic example is a study comparing binge-drinking students to experienced meditators after an intensive retreat. Based on results from the Freiburg Mindfulness Inventory (FMI), binge-drinkers scored significantly higher on mindfulness than experienced meditators (normal college students were in the middle).[28] In another twist, these scales do not assume that training in mindfulness is needed, since such self-reports are usually based on ordinary states of awareness without any expectation of engaging in deliberate acts of attention.

Many previous studies, also relying on highly subjective self-report measures, have claimed that mindfulness improves the quality of sleep. However, using a different technique — the more sophisticated and objective polysomnographic (PSG) — Willoughby Britton and her colleagues at Brown University found just the opposite. Subjects in their sleep lab study woke up more often in the night and data showed their sleep was much lighter, yet the same subjects had self-reported sleeping better. According to Britton's write-up in *Psychosomatic Medicine*: "Contrary to predictions that [mindfulness] would improve or deepen objectively measured sleep, several findings from this study suggest that mindfulness training had an arousing effect on PSG sleep profiles."[29]

Even Kabat-Zinn has admitted that mindfulness cannot be measured accurately using surveys. In addition, numerous scholars have taken issue with existing mindfulness questionnaires as potentially misrepresenting and distorting classical conceptualizations of Buddhist mindfulness. This is somewhat ironic, since the scientization of mindfulness is adopting an attitude more like religion — making faith-based pronouncements that are as yet unsupported by empirical evidence.

The gap between rhetoric and facts has become so wide that fifteen researchers — including some prominent boosters of mindfulness — have sought to make amends by co-authoring an article entitled: "Mind the Hype: A Critical Evaluation and Prescriptive Agenda for Research on Mindfulness and Meditation." It outlines problems in defining mindfulness, and thus in delineating suitable studies, as well as flaws in existing research and ways to improve it. The problems are starkly laid out:

> As mindfulness has increasingly pervaded every aspect of contemporary society, so have misunderstandings about what it is, whom it helps, and how it affects the mind and brain. At a practical level, the misinformation and propagation of poor research methodology can potentially lead to people being harmed, cheated disappointed, and/or disaffected.[30]

Scientists "have a considerable amount of work to make meaningful progress," the authors conclude, hoping "to surmount the prior misunderstandings and past harms caused by pervasive mindfulness hype." However, none of them notes their own role in this insidious process. One, Sara Lazar, co-authored the *Harvard Business Review* article cited earlier in this chapter, titled: "Mindfulness Can Literally Change Your Brain." That proclaimed: "Perhaps you haven't heard that the hype is backed by hard science."

chapter eight
Mindful Employees

I am in the grand ballroom among two hundred and fifty people at the Marriott Hotel in downtown San Francisco for the first public workshop offering for Google's corporate mindfulness training, "Search Inside Yourself" (SIY). Marc Lesser is a short, unassuming and soft-spoken man, who looks a little nervous. The former director of San Francisco Zen Center's country retreat Tassajara, Lesser is an ordained Zen Buddhist priest, a seasoned management consultant with an MBA, and the first CEO of Google's non-profit Search Inside Yourself Leadership Institute (SIYLI). "My deep vow is to make accessible the benefits of mindfulness meditation to people working in companies and organizations, knowing that this is how to have the most impact in the world," Lesser proclaims. Access to the two-day workshop is only $950 a person.

Google has become the poster child for corporate mindfulness, largely due to the work of Chade-Meng Tan, a software engineer who helped build the first mobile search engine, before starting the work that earned him the job title "Jolly Good Fellow." As Google employee number 107, he retired in 2015, aged forty-five. "My goal in life is to create the conditions for world peace by making the benefits of mindfulness meditation accessible to humanity," he vows.

Sporting a traditional gold silk Tai Chi outfit, Meng relishes his role as Silicon Valley's mindfulness guru. "I came to this goal of world peace nine years ago back when

I was still an engineer at Google," he tells the crowd in San Francisco. "I suddenly realized what I wanted to do with the rest of my life." As he explains, "we developed Search Inside Yourself, a mindfulness-based emotional intelligence training at Google. Because of this program I became the first engineer at Google to move from engineering to human resources," he quips. "Imagine an engineer teaching emotional intelligence!"

Google's program has received a great deal of media attention. The curriculum is touted as "scientifically grounded" in rigorous research. Drawing heavily from Daniel Goleman's best-selling book *Emotional Intelligence* — itself embraced as a scientific path to success — the premise is that mindfulness increases emotional intelligence (EI).[1] This is valued because empathy, self-control and agreeableness have become the new managerial watchwords, not unlike the message of the immensely popular self-help book *How to Win Friends and Influence People*, which Dale Carnegie penned in 1936.[2]

Before the in-house program was developed, Google offered engineers classes in MBSR. Few of them enrolled — stress is seen as a badge of honor among its youthful engineers, who typically work between sixty and eighty hours a week. Dangling the carrot of success would become the new hook. Once mindfulness was linked with emotional intelligence, with greater prospects of promotion and career advancement, engineers started enrolling in SIY courses in droves.

Philippe Goldin, a clinical neuroscientist at Stanford University and co-facilitator of the San Francisco workshop, is a wiry, gray-haired man. He leads our first exercise. "Turn

132

to someone next to you," he begins. Having taught business students for the last twenty-five years, I know this is a common ice-breaking gimmick. "With your partner, answer this question: What do you love about your work?" I try to keep an open mind. My partner, Ursula, is a Swiss woman in her forties from a large pharmaceutical firm, who looks reciprocally reluctant and skeptical. "This program would never fly at my company," she says. "Emotional intelligence training is passé. These exercises are so sophomoric and painful." By midday, we have endured a few more of them, listened to some simplistic lectures on emotional intelligence, and viewed slick PowerPoint slides of colorful fMRI images, emphasizing how meditation can change our brains.

We break for lunch disappointed. Our path is impeded by Chade-Meng Tan, now a celebrity on the mindfulness circuit, who is swarmed by participants wanting to take selfies with him. I ask Ursula, a vice president of human resources, what she makes of the linking of mindfulness to emotional intelligence. "Where is the scientific evidence for these claims?" she asks. It's a relief to talk someone who hasn't drunk the Kool-Aid. Experts are no more impressed. "Goleman's work does not represent a systematic scientific program of research," writes the Yale psychologist Robert Sternberg, in a foreword to *Emotional Intelligence: Science and Myth*. "There appear to be no refereed published studies where hypotheses are predictively tested against data."[3]

A few years after the SIY program, I met up again with Goldin, the co-facilitator. We were at a "Mindfulness in Society" conference, where he was presenting a pilot study he had conducted of SIY graduates in three Bay Area technology companies. His findings surprised him, with little sign of impact on emotional intelligence. In fact, results showed that SIY mindfulness training was associated with increases in both work exhaustion and disengagement. One could speculate that mindfulness helped employees realize just how exhausted they really were; their response was to disengage from work as a form of relief. During the Q&A session, I asked Goldin whether as a scientist — whose duty is to follow the evidence — he would revise the SIY curriculum in light of his findings. He replied: "Well, I have distanced myself from Google's SIY training and I am no longer involved with it." Google, however, still sells mindfulness and emotional intelligence.

The Disengagement Problem

It is no accident that Google branded its program "Search Inside Yourself." As a tool of self-discipline, mindfulness is the latest capitalist spirituality, unifying a quest for productivity and corporate profits with individual peace and self-fulfillment. By directing attention inward, courses such as Google's deflect wandering minds from questions of power or political economy; external conditions are simply accepted as they are. The solution to our problems is inside us, we are told. As Meng promises: "Mindfulness can increase my happiness without changing anything else."[4]

This therapeutic focus on individual wellbeing obscures the real reasons why corporations embrace mindfulness programs. Capitalism faces an unprecedented crisis. Attempts to control, manipulate or coopt labor have historically been resisted in a variety of ways — strikes, industrial sabotage, unionization, and work slowdowns. However, since organization and outright refusal are no longer viable options in most industries, the most common form of post-industrial resistance is stress, burnout, and apathy. Depression is at epidemic levels, and a broader mental health crisis looms.

The enthusiastic boom in corporate mindfulness coincided with the recession that started with financial meltdown in 2008. With massive lay-offs, the rise of the "precariat" and contingent labor, extension of work hours, stagnation in wages, and other forms of "shock therapy," employees were admonished to "do more with less." The growth in worker discontentment is regarded as a threat, both to the state and to corporations. Such disaffection and alienation — manifesting in stress, psychosomatic illnesses, depression, low motivation, absenteeism, and such — has not only fueled the interest in mindfulness but also spurred a burgeoning wellness and happiness industry.

"Employee disengagement" has become a phenomenon, denting corporate profits, productivity and economic output. It is estimated that, in the US alone, $300 billion has been lost to stress-related absences,[5] with losses due to a lack of engagement nearer $550 billion.[6] The fact that seven out of ten employees report feeling "disengaged" from work has human resources teams alarmed. Even employees who are highly engaged, like the engineers at Google, report high levels of stress. So it is unsurprising that corporations have jumped on the wellness and mindfulness bandwagon.

In some ways, none of this is new. In the 1970s and 1980s, stress management and stress reduction programs were hugely popular in corporations. Even then, critics drew attention to the potential injustices of offering such programs to employees while doing nothing to alter the sources of workplace stress. And in the 1990s, organizational psychologists were promoting the idea of "occupational stress," using similarly scary (and dubious) statistics. In 1994, the Confederation of British Industry estimated that 360 million workdays were lost at a cost to corporations of £8 billion.[7] Again, these accounts linked sickness to stress without supporting evidence.

In *Managing Stress*, Tim Newton shows how such dramatic estimates demonize stress while enhancing its legitimacy as an explanatory concept. Given that, as we saw earlier, stress as a biomedical concept didn't enter public discourse until after World War II, Newton looks at examples from the nineteenth century. Without the discursive legitimation of stress by social and behavioral science research, it is unlikely such industrial workers would have reported feeling "stressed," though they may well have had concerns about conditions. As stress discourse became pervasive, it presented an image of the stressed subject "as someone who is apolitical, individualized, decontextualized," Newton says.[8] Stress is thus naturalized and taken for granted — an unavoidable occupational hazard.

Mentally Fit Employees

Corporate mindfulness interventions are often pitched as ways for employees to develop mental fitness. Our brains are equated to "muscles," and mindfulness requires regular practice — just like going to the gym. "We are confident that your pursuit will be beneficial, because we know from scientific research that mindfulness is a trainable skill that grows stronger as we exercise it," says Richard Fernandez, the CEO of Google's mindfulness spin-off, the SIYLI. The man who created it, Chade-Meng Tan, echoes the parallel. "Just as weight-training makes us physically fit, mindfulness meditation is a way of exercising our brain to achieve mental fitness," he says.

It is not a coincidence that both of these activities are individualistic. The fitness metaphor suggests to employees that their psychological and physical wellbeing — and thus their efficiency and productivity — hinges on their ability to cope effectively with stress. Corporate mindfulness programs aim to train individual employees to manage and regulate difficult emotions, as well as improving concentration and attention. These are valuable economic resources, put in the service of organizational objectives.

Viewed as free agents, or "entrepreneurs of the self," employees are exhorted to take full responsibility for their performance, hacking their brains to be more malleable, adaptive, and flexible. Focused non-judgmental attention, emotional self-regulation and pro-social behaviors are subjective capacities that have become instrumentalized — the central target of capitalist social relations. In this sense, corporate mindfulness programs themselves represent a new form of "mental capital," a programmatic attempt to reshape the subjectivity of the employee as a valuable and essential asset to corporate success.

The bottom-line: mentally fit employees are mindful, effective at coping with stress and keeping their emotions in check. Meanwhile, the mental training provided by mindfulness marginalizes alternative ways of talking about workplace stress, along with challenging questions about power relations, and the ways in which corporations make workers responsible for their responses to working conditions.

Self-Imposed Stress?

David Gelles, a *New York Times* business reporter and the author of *Mindful Work,* is a vociferous cheerleader for corporate mindfulness. Gelles makes a bold claim: "Stress isn't something imposed on us. It's something we impose on ourselves."[9] Really? Failure to cope is often blamed on a dysfunction in one's neural pathways or troublesome thoughts and emotions. His colleagues at the *New York Times* would beg to differ. In an exposé of Amazon's sociopathic work culture, the newspaper quoted a former employee as saying that he saw nearly everyone he worked with cry at their desks.[10] Would Gelles have offered his advice to these Amazon workers, telling them that they were imposing stress on themselves, or that they could have chosen not to cry — and that their lack of emotional self-control could be attributed to being hijacked by their amygdala?

For Gelles, like other mindfulness champions, the causes of stress are located in our heads — and since fMRI images show parts of the brain lighting up due to stress, they confirm that we create our own misery through thoughts and emotions that we fail to let go of. We only have our own mindlessness to blame. This is not to deny that experiences of stress and discomfort are partly to do with habitual behavior, but Gelles goes too far. His victim-blaming philosophy echoes the corporate mindfulness ethos: shift the burden of psychological stress and structural insecurities onto individual employees, frame this as a personal problem, and then offer mindfulness as the panacea.

This masks the social and economic conditions that may have caused the problem. Mindfulness programs pay little attention to the complex dynamics of interacting power relations, networks of interests, and explanatory narratives that shape capitalist culture. Yet as Richard Wilkinson and Kate Pickett point out in *The Spirit Level*, evidence from social epidemiology shows that stress and psychosomatic illnesses are concentrated in highly unequal societies, with strongly materialist, competitive values.[11]

Although the focus of corporate mindfulness is on changing behavior at the level of individuals, mere "lifestyle choices" make little difference. A study by researchers at the Stanford Graduate School of Business, who analyzed 228 other studies, found the top ten stressors derived from poor management practices and overly demanding corporate cultures. The biggest causes of stress were a lack of health insurance, the constant threat of lay-offs, lack of discretion and autonomy in decision-making, long working hours, low levels of organizational justice, and unrealistic demands.[12] Job insecurity accounted for a 50% increase in poor health, and long work hours correlated with a 20% rise in mortality.

But Gelles is undeterred. "Mindfulness can be a source of employer value proposition and may in the long run provide organizations with a valuable tool to manage high burnout levels of employees," he says.[13] In other words, in a corporate context, mindfulness is just another way for managers to maximize extraction of optimal value from human resources. George Mumford, a SIYLI mindfulness teacher, likens mindfulness to a tool for "sharpening the saw" of people's minds. "If you keep sawing without stopping to sharpen the saw," he says, "you won't be as effective." Like workplace wellness, happiness, resilience, and the positive psychology of flourishing, mindfulness sees the minds and bodies of employees as sources of economic value.

Docile Subjects

It's ironic that while Google boasts about its mindful quest to "make the world a better place through the 'technology' of meditation," its managers are, as Nicholas Carr puts it in *The Shallows*, "quite literally in the business of distraction."[14] In some ways, the two are connected. Corporate mindfulness works very subtly to train good employees to serve their employers — and the broader system that supports them. It's not an industrial form of brainwashing, as defensive mindfulness teachers think critics are saying. What it does is deflect attention from collective organizing, or the pursuit of structural changes in corporate culture, instead refocusing employees on productive self-discipline. It works like a sophisticated form of bio-power, binding people's inner lives to corporate success.

As Nikolas Rose points out, echoing Foucault, corporate mindfulness programs "work through, and not against, subjectivity."[15] Foucault himself notes the way in which discourses of autonomy, freedom, health, self-fulfillment, prudence, and self-care are the very channels used for "the conduct of conduct" of human beings. And as Rose observes, such approaches "seek actively to produce subjects of a certain form, to mold, shape, and organize the psyche, to fabricate individuals with particular desires and aspirations."[16]

No mindfulness program is neutral, not even if promoted as a "mental tool for self-improvement," writes the Berkeley professor of Buddhism Richard Payne. "All tools are ideologies," Payne adds. "They exercise the values of their makers and instantiate those values in their users."[17] By appealing to universal values of serving the public, scientific rhetoric is used to mask underlying corporate priorities. The basic message is that employees are responsible for their own wellbeing, but the function is to neutralize dissent. It need not always be this way, but unless corporate cultures can be changed by collective means, providing mindfulness classes is like doling out pharmaceutical drugs in a psychoanalytic setting to avoid having to hear a patient's concerns.

In this respect, mindfulness trainings can limit the potential to speak, investigate, and act in ways that threaten existing power relations. One can think of these regulatory influences as a form of "internalized pacification," promoting a potent form of quietism. If employees are compelled to monitor their inner states, and to self-regulate "destructive emotions" by "being mindful," they become — as Foucault warned — "docile subjects."

Another Corporate Fad

Although corporate mindfulness courses are marketed as radically new, they share many of the goals of earlier management science fads. These programs can be viewed as an evolutionary adaptation of a corporate mythology that began in the early twentieth century with Frederick Winslow Taylor, whose "scientific" principles of management were literally touted as a "mental revolution."[18] Taylor's industrial engineering method stripped workers of their monopoly on the knowledge of production by standardizing and fractionating tasks, thereby maximizing worker efficiency while reducing autonomy and potential subversion. Taylor's revolution — based on time and motion studies — promised to convert immigrant laborers into "first-class men," who were more cooperative with management. Obviously, such promises had enormous appeal to the captains of industry.

Corporate mindfulness programs are a continuation of this trend, aligning each employee's sense of subjectivity to the interests of capital. Taylor's evangelism, like that of Google's Chade-Meng Tan, relied on the claim that his techniques were backed by science. Their exuberance describes how objective methods can uncover the secrets of human subjectivity — allowing technocrats to extract even more from labor.

Social scientists are complicit in this managerial enterprise through motivation studies, counseling, personality and attitude surveys, and many other schemes. Indeed, a lucrative social-science industry gave rise to management consulting firms, corporate trainers, leadership coaches, and a growing market for popular business books. Even the American Psychological Association, in 1962, sided with the interests of capital:

> While the psychologist's most basic interest is human behavior, he can help with management's most basic aim, increasing profitability... Essentially what the industrial psychologist attempts to do is to help the employee come to [a] recognition of how his interests and management's coincide [to] help the employee adjust to the requirements of a successful enterprise.[19]

Industrial psychology and management scholarship have claimed to be neutral, scientific and objective, but business schools have a long tradition of masking ideology as management science. According to a book on the subject by two influential writers for the *Economist*: "Modern management theory is no more reliable than tribal medicine. Witch doctors, after all, often got it right — by luck, by instinct, or by trial and error."[20] Not only has science been invoked to legitimize management interests, the materialistic nature of scientific discourse helps to rationalize the accumulation of wealth. And as the scholar of management Gerard Hanlon notes, the discipline is primarily political, making management the first "neo-liberal science."[21] The nature of its project is to organize life to serve particular interests — historically, those of the elite.

Beginning with the "human relations" movement in the late 1920s, workers were no longer viewed as Taylor conceived of them: as mindless automatons motivated purely by economic interests. Instead, they were increasingly seen as psychologically complex, governed by emotions, anxieties and fears, the management of which required new and sophisticated behavioral science techniques. The human relations approach sought to reshape the attitudes and conscience of the worker, realigning their values with the interests of shareholders. Since then, corporations have tried — within limits — to maintain workplace harmony by providing more participative cultures, engaging employees to make jobs feel more meaningful, and organizing teams to foster a feeling of belonging, ownership, and loyalty to corporate interests. The promotion of a sense of wellbeing is just the latest version of this, offering mindfulness training to stressed managers and employees.

Throughout history, most corporate initiatives have shared the assumption that employee discontent is a subjective condition. The locus of change is the individual, who is expected to adjust to corporate conditions, with occasional concessions. Complaints are sometimes psychologized out of existence. In the 1920s and 1930s, Harvard psychiatrist Elton Mayo was hired by the Western Electric Company to make sense of experimental data at the Hawthorne plant on Chicago's West Side. Mayo interpreted discontent with poor working conditions and low wages as "emotional reactions" that shouldn't be taken seriously, especially when coming from women. In many of Mayo's writings, the worker is viewed as irrational, pathological, and lacking in self-control — but no evidence is given for such scientific claims. Modern social scientists have since dismissed Mayo's studies, calling his pro-management bias "cow-sociology." This alludes to the way that contented cows provide more milk, implying that "happy" employees are more productive.

These attempts to manipulate workers — promoting acceptance of exploitative conditions, suppressing and denying conflict, and obfuscating differences in power and interests — have echoes in corporate mindfulness. In *Manufacturing Knowledge*, Richard Gillespie detects "a persistent tendency in Mayo's work to transform any challenge by workers of managerial control into evidence of psychiatric disturbance."[22] In the 1930s, workers were "irrational," "immature," "hysterical" (especially if one was a woman), or prone to "reveries" on the job; now employees are "stressed," "distracted," and exhibit "poor self-regulation" and "self-control," or are prone to "mind-wandering." Mayo's theory of psychopathology reduced workers' complaints to personal problems and social maladjustment, not to objective, material conditions — just like mindfulness apologists.

Mayo seems to have believed that a managerial elite — not democracy and human rights — would save civilization from industrial unrest. He clearly despised socialism and organized labor. For Mayo, salvation from this "rabble" lay in training managers and supervisors to use sympathetic "human relations" techniques that targeted mental health. His methods helped to legitimize oppression, mystifying it with pseudo-scientific talk about managing the emotions and social maladjustment of assembly-line workers — just as corporate mindfulness targets stress and not structural inequities in power relations, while promoting the most productive exploitation of "human resources."

The Trojan Horse Myth

Mindfulness zealots have utopian ideas about transformation. They speculate that training in mindfulness will slowly bring changes, inspiring managers to promote more ethical corporate policies and practices. We just need to keep the faith and wait. Those who teach such courses truly seem to believe that what they offer is subversive, and that one day their "Trojan horse" will spark an awakening, giving rise to corporate acts of loving-kindness. Needless to say, there is no empirical evidence to support these ideas.

However, the likes of Jeremy Hunter — director of the Executive Mind Leadership Institute at the Peter F. Drucker Graduate School of Management at Claremont — assure us that mindfulness is a "disruptive technology," capable of reforming even the most dysfunctional organizations into something more compassionate and sustainable.[23]

I once sat in on one of Hunter's presentations at the International Symposium for Contemplative Studies in Boston. Clean-cut and well groomed, Hunter impressed me as the quintessential management consultant. He began with the standard formula of a TED talk — an emotional story of a stressed executive who was saved by mindfulness. His story came across as an over-rehearsed — and over-repeated — shtick. "As more people within the organization become more open and inquisitive," he gushed, "they become agents for large-scale change." All by searching inside themselves.

Hunter went on to tell the story of Mirabai Bush, who introduced managers and scientists at Monsanto to mindfulness practice as early as 1996. After a corporate retreat, one top scientist was said to lament: "I realized that we're creating products that kill life. We should be creating products that support life." Having told us a tear-jerking anecdote, Hunter conceded: "It's a long journey from personal insight like that to large-scale change, but at least we can say that mindfulness was starting to serve as a disruptive technology within the company." Perhaps. Or perhaps the scientist quit in despair.

Either way, Monsanto — the producer of Agent Orange — has since been bought by Bayer, whose corporate predecessors made Zyklon B. Meanwhile, Monsanto's promotion of genetically modified crops, patenting of "suicide seeds", and global efforts to dominate the food supply continue. As for becoming a nicer organization, it cancelled its "mindful leadership" program in 2000.

Hunter's argument is basically that meaningful transformation starts from within. If one can change one's own mind to be more peaceful and compassionate — and others do the same — larger-scale changes will naturally follow. However, such injunctions to "be the change you wish to see in the world" (a comment that Gandhi never actually made) are at best wishful thinking. Mindfulness consultants like to use this stance to remain apolitical, which has little impact on the institutional causes of suffering. Hunter's presentation was painful. I walked away even more skeptical.

He is far from alone though. Barry Boyce, editor of the glossy magazine *Mindful*, makes similar claims. "Mindfulness may begin at stress relief but it does not end there," he says. "It naturally leads to inquisitiveness about our own minds and examination of how we are connected to other people, of the causes and effects of our actions." [24] Well, it

147

might stand more chance of doing so if mindfulness trainers drew people's attention to such connections. Boyce's flight of fancy continues: "Who knows what a leader — in workplaces from Ford Motor Company to the Los Angeles Fire Department — might do for the greater good with the aid of a little mindfulness?"[25] *Who knows?* It seems on the face of it a reasonable question, apart from the lack of credible evidence that corporate mindfulness programs result in any such "greater good."

Instead, this sort of logic sounds like the book *The Hundredth Monkey*, in which Japanese scientists observed how macaques learned to wash sweet potatoes. A critical mass was reached when a hundred monkeys did it, and the same learned behavior spread to monkeys on nearby islands, which became known in New Age myth as the "hundredth monkey effect," despite the discrediting of the research behind it.[26] There is also an echo of outlandish claims for the transformative power of Transcendental Meditation, which were put to the test in Washington DC in the 1990s. In an experiment watched by the media, four thousand TM devotees camped out for six weeks reciting mantras to reduce violent crime.[27] They declared success, insisting that the crime rate fell by 23%. In fact, during the experiment, Washington's weekly murder count hit its highest level ever.[28]

Integrity Bubbles

Corporate mindfulness is caught in a paradox: it offers employees relief and personal benefits by reducing stress and improving concentration, yet mindlessly ignores external issues, from structural inequalities to corporate behavior. This creates what the communication professor Kevin Healey calls "integrity bubbles," which offer "glimpses of integrity — enough to enhance employee satisfaction and brand image — even as they undermine the achievement of integrity in the broader context."[29] The managed healthcare company Aetna is a classic example. In *Mindful Work*, David Gelles hails Aetna's supposedly benevolent CEO, Mark Bertolini, for offering mindfulness training to a third of its fifty thousand employees.[30] The program produced annual per capita productivity gains of $3000, while cutting employee healthcare costs by $2000, saving $6.3 million in total. Mindful employees are good for big business.

Meanwhile, the supposedly mindful Aetna lied about its reasons for withdrawing from Obamacare, which had expanded access to medical insurance. While the company said that mounting losses had required it to pull out of Obamacare exchanges in eleven states, the real reason, according to US District Judge John Bates, was "to evade judicial scrutiny over its merger with Humana," a $34 billion deal which had been blocked by the Department of Justice for antitrust reasons one month earlier.[31] Corporate mindfulness programs don't train their participants to challenge business practices — that would require a search *outside* oneself, something modern mindfulness has studiously avoided.

Even so, there might be ways to burst the bubble. Becoming more accepting of oneself, as mindfulness teaches, can be mildly threatening. Ignoring constant corporate messages to seek satisfaction by buying new products is not good for business. And as business scholars have opined in the *New York Times*: "the very notion of motivation — striving to obtain a more desirable future — implies some degree of discontentment with the present, which seems at odds with a psychological exercise that instills equanimity."[32] However, this discovery had a silver lining: more sophisticated methods would need to be found to appeal to employees' inner sense of motivation. As long as people feel like they "flourish" by aligning their efforts with corporate needs, business as usual can continue.

chapter nine
Mindful Merchants

Corporate mindfulness training is an extremely lucrative business for savvy consultants. In 2018, the Global Wellness Institute valued "the wellness economy" at $3.72 trillion. The "fitness & mind-body" sector, of which the mindfulness industry is part, is worth $542 billion.[1] Sounding mindful of conflicts of interest, the editor of *Mindful* magazine, Barry Boyce, says "good teachers" are those who "show a strong measure of independence" from their corporate sponsors.[2] But is such independence really possible? With such large amounts of money at stake, can we really believe that mindfulness programs wouldn't dovetail with corporate priorities? How many trainers want to bite the hand that feeds them?

A trip to the Awakened Leadership conference in Los Angeles only amplified my doubts. It all seemed so predictable, starting with the keynote speaker, Dawa Darchin Phillips. Borrowing Aristotle's tactic of *pathos*, he began with a dramatic tale of cheating death. I felt emotionally manipulated, but tried to be mindful, setting aside my instinctive reactions and allowing myself to hear how he almost drowned. Then peace washed over him. A friend eventually rescued him, and his life was changed forever.

The spiel soon went downhill. "I want to tell you right away, research is boring," Phillips said. "And I am going to show you a lot of research." He wasn't wrong. What he told us *was* boring. The research was the same old "this-is-your-brain-on-mindfulness" propaganda. I also noticed a pattern in his slides. Their full-screen, colorful, emotionally laden photos — a smiling child, an elderly loving couple holding hands, a sunset over the ocean — were indistinguishable from those I'd seen at workshops with Search Inside Yourself and Jeremy Hunter. Despite the tedium, there was something just a little too smooth that turned me off. I Googled Phillips and found a slick website. In grandiose terms, it hawked the "Awakened World Global Pilgrimage." For just $22,500, you could join him on an "ascending journey through the seven chakras of our planet."[3]

Back on planet mindfulness, Phillips droned on about why it was so popular in corporations. Don't tell me — because of employee disengagement? Yep. Out came the same Gallup poll. Did he ask why workers "disengaged"? Was there even an inkling of critical thinking? Nope, just a fat dose of "wow!" Look how bad this problem is. The employees are so disengaged. Businesses are losing tons of money. Mindfulness to the rescue! And don't worry — it's not at all weird — check out this science! That was about the sum of his strategy for persuading potential corporate clients in attendance.

During the follow-up Q&A, the conference sponsor asked: "What is your daily consulting fee for delivering a corporate mindfulness training program?" Phillips got a bit cagey. "Well it depends on whether the client is senior management," he hedged. "And it also depends if we send our senior trainers." That wasn't specific enough for the sponsor, who pressed on: "Well, can you just give us a ballpark idea?" Phillips hesitated. The fee? "$12,000 per day," he muttered. The audience audibly gasped.

Mindfulness as a Language Game

How does one actually sell a corporate mindfulness program? Fortunately there is a workshop on just this topic by Richard Fernandez, CEO of the Search Inside Yourself Leadership Institute, and founder of Wisdom Labs. To go incognito, I removed my name badge and sat near the door to make an early exit if I needed to (I eventually did). "We are all experiencing rapid change in our 24/7 connected world," Fernandez began. This was such an old cliché, and delivered in such vacuous corporate-speak, that I decided to accompany his homily on mindless addiction to devices by checking my iPhone. I got a few dirty looks from the people across from me.

Fernandez's session chronicled the strategy and tactics he used to sell a large-scale mindfulness program to senior managers at the Ford Motor Company. He began by telling the story of a rival. "This vendor's business card has a logo of a Tibetan Buddhist mandala on it and the logo appears on all their PowerPoint slides," he said incredulously. "No! No!" Fernandez stressed. "That's a No! No!" In a scolding tone, he warned the audience: "You don't want to have allergy-causing artifacts." He told us to examine his handout: a blueprint for selling corporate programs. "It's all about having the *right language*!" he explained. Unfortunately, I had a strong allergic reaction to this artifact. It droned on about "translation" — suggesting his work selling mindfulness was equivalent to being a translator of the dharma. "It's about creating a compelling brand!" he said. So that's why he called his startup Wisdom Labs. Sounds pretty cool, doesn't it? Getting some of that sexy, scientifically verified, modern Wisdom! Impressive.

"Mindfulness is not Buddhist," Fernandez went on. His animated manner made it seem like he wanted to add a "Damn it!" but mindfully refrained. Then he backpedaled slightly. "Well, of course, I got to give credit where credit is due... a lot of these ideas and practices came from Buddhism. But what we are doing isn't Buddhist." And in case we still had doubts: "Look, you can find mindfulness in the Vedic, Taoist, Quaker and Christian traditions," he said. "Buddhists don't own mindfulness."

This admonition is a popular talking point among mindfulness teachers. Most Buddhists that I know, myself included, have no issue with the adaptation of mindfulness for secular and clinical purposes. The issue isn't one of intellectual property, but of truth in advertising. I have repeatedly observed mindfulness teachers tell corporate sponsors, especially when trying to sell programs, that what they offer is in no way Buddhist. But in other situations, such as these sorts of conferences, the same teachers wax poetic about how they are translating the whole of the dharma. This seems not only disingenuous, but also contrary to the honesty on which mindfulness traditionally depends.

In some ways, Fernandez is clear about intentions. "It's all about branding and positioning," he told the conference. "Yeah, we have to give credit where credit is due, but we are aiming for a more productive worker, not spiritual awakening." He quickly switched tack, as if alarmed by the implications: "I mean, yeah, I can see how this could become sort of mercenary if the focus is all on product and performance, but this is how we have to position it — to get senior managers' attention. And sometimes we do say that happier workers are more productive."

Ever since I dipped my toe into corporate mindfulness, I have observed how its salesmen promise to add value to the bottom line. When pitching programs, consultants actually downplay the benefits to individual workers, focusing instead on "work-related outcomes," such as better productivity, task performance, and decision-making. "Results-focused mindfulness training for your company," is the tag line for Whil, a market-savvy online provider of "on demand" corporate mindfulness programs.[4] Their website vows to "increase job satisfaction and productivity while decreasing stress." Would it be possible for mindfulness to thrive in companies if the practice dented profits? There seems little danger of that if it is pitched as performance enhancement. Even if accompanied by some woolly implications about change scaling up to make companies mindful, the exclusion of structural critiques of corporate policies undermines this. Utopian rhetoric is rarely translated into meaningful action.

Meanwhile, back at the conference, Fernandez got tied up in knots trying to talk up his brand. "You got to have the right subject matter expert," he told the audience. "We don't even refer to our trainers as mindfulness teachers, but as 'subject matter experts' — that is much easier to hear," he said. Then in the very same breath, he switched tack. "You know, a competent mindfulness teacher needs a lineage." A few minutes ago, he seemed adamant that traditional lineages were irrelevant. Yet here he was trying to use Buddhist branding to sound more "competent." At lunch, Fernandez even revealed that he had a well-known teacher:

the Vietnamese Zen Buddhist monk Thich Nhat Hanh.

Not that Ford would have found this impressive. To clinch that deal, Fernandez didn't try to sell "Buddhism minus the Buddhism," or even just "mindfulness training." Remember, this is all a language game. So what did he call it? "Evidenced-based forms of mental conditioning for resilience, wellbeing and sustainable high performance," he said. You what? I asked him to repeat it (the only time I spoke during the session). He obliged with an impish smile: "Evidenced-based forms of mental conditioning for resilience, wellbeing and sustainable high performance." He paused. "See, this is how we perform a translation function. We know it's the dharma, but they don't."

My hackles had risen as far as they could go. Inhale. Exhale. I tried to calm myself. I'd hidden my badge, but any sort of snide remark might have blown my cover. Fernandez continued: "We don't ever lead with compassion or empathy up front — that would never sell. We sort of Trojan-horse that in and sneak that in later after we get some traction with the program," he said. "And our whole thing is really how do we perform this translation function without losing the integrity of the dharma." I was losing the will to be patient. But at this point his sidekick took over, so I gave him a chance.

Mark Higbie, the Vice President of Corporate Public Relations for Ford, held up his business card, telling the crowd: "My real job title is 'Instigator'." Nowhere near the chutzpah of Google's Jolly Good Fellow, but perhaps at Ford that seemed rebellious. To me, Higbie looked the stereo-typical Fortune 500 corporate mannequin — expensive suit, perfect hair, black shiny shoes.

So why did Ford buy mindfulness? "It was really fear and disengagement that sold it," he said. "Managers were really stressed out." Then he hit us with a corporate phrase I'd never heard before "You got to True Up!" Er, what? True up? "Well, look at the handout," he said. "Do you see how you have to True Up?" This appeared to mean almost the opposite — change the language to match corporate discourse. Make it sound like mindfulness is exactly the thing they've been looking for. "Look," Higbie said, "it's about measurable results! You have to have 'engagement scores' and 'metrics'." My eyes glazed over. It went on, and on, and on. "We even have technology for biometrics. We have an online platform — that was really appealing to Ford. And another thing you got to pay attention to is budget cycles. You got to know the best time to pitch a program."

I'd had my fill and left stage right.

Mindfulness as Corporate Propaganda

If I thought I'd escaped, I was wrong. Fernandez and Higbie accompanied lunch. Higbie led their second session. "Why Ford?" he asked rhetorically, plunging into a story about Bill Ford, Jr, the heir to the empire. Apparently, "it was all about his values." How many times had I heard this stuff? The corporate hierophant who tries to save the world? I braced myself. "For Bill Ford, the Ford Motor Company is about valuing the depth of humanity," Higbie said, making sure people grasped how close he was to Bill, the great grandson of good old Henry, who invented the assembly line. "The purpose of every company, Henry Ford believed, was to make peoples' lives better," Higbie said. Henry Ford believed other things too, including that America was being taken over by a vast "Jewish conspiracy" — he bought his local newspaper and ran an anti-Semitic series of articles, later compiled as a four-volume book, *The International Jew*.

"This training is all about creating new emotional sensibilities," Higbie continued. To illustrate his point, he played us a sentimental corporate video. An all-smiles Ford employee comforted a customer whose mother had cancer. Another empathic colleague listened intently to someone else whose father had died. This almost seemed worthy of Sigmund Freud's nephew, Edward Bernays, considered the father of public relations. In 1928, Bernays published *Propaganda*, which argued for "the engineering of consent," by providing the means to "control and regiment the masses according to our will without their knowing about it."[5] He made his name by persuading women to take up smoking, rebranding cigarettes as feminist "Torches of Freedom."

Saving his best shot for last, Fernandez was eager to tell one more story. "When I was still working at Google," he said, dropping one of the names that made him rich, "I wrote a letter to *my* teacher." Up flashed a slide of Thich Nhat Hanh. There were sounds of impressed recognition in the audience. "And I invited him to come to Silicon Valley to talk to all the prominent CEOs who were interested in mindfulness. And, to my surprise, he came! And here you can see him holding hands with me at the meeting, and he even let me ring his bell!"

I can't but help think of this whole charade as a form of what Sean Feit calls "saffron-washing."[6] Just as "greenwashing" masks environmentally harmful policies with token eco-friendly gestures, saffron-washing helps hip postmodern corporations to present a gentler, kinder, wiser public image.

Ford Motor has plenty to hide. It spent nearly $40 million on scientific research to help it fight asbestos lawsuits from mechanics with mesothelioma, an aggressive form of cancer virtually always linked to asbestos exposure.[7] Ford is also being sued for cheating on diesel emission tests for half a million heavy trucks.[8] If those allegations are found to be true, Ford could be liable for billions of dollars. Meanwhile, there is no sign that Ford will stop making vehicles that burn fossil fuels, regardless of the impact on the climate.

Higbie had other things on his mind. "This mindfulness program was for all the top dealers and managers in Ford Canada," he explained. They were to be enrolled in a twelve-month course. The only question was who would provide it. "We looked at two vendors: Google's SIYLI and Rich at Wisdom Labs. What we liked about Rich's pitch is he focused on the neuroscience, the business case and the practice. Plus, his program was metrics driven." As Higbie's canned talk put it:

> Ford has an evolving business model and we see mindfulness training as helping managers with this transformation. Ford no longer sees itself as merely an automobile company but as a mobility services company. That is the new business model. In the future Ford may never make a car in the US. This is a cultural transformation. This is a great place for mindfulness to step in.

I've heard such things many times over, but I couldn't help but wonder what role mindfulness might play in this situation. If Ford moved all US manufacturing offshore, that would be the end of the United Auto Workers union, plunging Detroit, Michigan further into the black hole of poverty. And social dimensions of suffering are not on the radar of corporate mindfulness. At Ford, like most other companies, managers just see it as a way of reducing stress and improving focus, all in the service of profit-making and increasing shareholder value. And if that requires a massive loss of jobs, then so be it.

"It's all about the consumer experience," Higbie elaborated. "In fact, we see what we are doing as part of the consumer experience movement." I felt glad to have skipped the eating part of lunch. I might have had indigestion. "We see mindfulness as helping Ford create a more empathic organization," he insisted. "Yeah, through mindfulness and compassion training, this is how we address the consumerist piece." Fernandez chimed in: "You know, some people are concerned that mindfulness is becoming entangled with business." Cue ripples of laughter from the audience. "Well, I hope so!"

His advocacy for entangling mindfulness with a corporate quest for profits is not an anomaly. The whole movement is pervaded with this sort of spiritual libertarianism, providing a humanistic rationale for exploitation. Individuals are supposedly empowered, so the fact that corporations do better off the back of them is OK. Besides, it's all in the name of consumer service — the ultimate justification for corporate greed.

Consultants like Fernandez sincerely believe in

"conscious capitalism." Their sincerity makes them mindful missionaries for corporate power. As its servants, they perform an important ideological function: to mystify and uphold capitalist hierarchies with crypto-Buddhist libertarianism (known as "mindfulness"). Addressing greed and corruption would not only be less lucrative, it would undermine their mission: spreading mindfulness, one individual at a time, to unleash a corporate transformation. So far, the main thing they've changed is the meaning of mindfulness, which is now neoliberal.

Mindful Rallies

Using mindfulness to shore up class power requires a great deal of media hype and mass enthusiasm. Jumping on the mindfulness bandwagon gave its early adopters a sense of being part of a change of historic proportions — something big, revolutionary, and exciting. Fernandez is full of such irrational exuberance. Towards the end of his conference keynote, he recalled his enlistment in the "movement." The Salesforce CEO Mark Benioff apparently invited him "to curate" events for Dreamforce III, a global meeting of employees in San Francisco. "I designed a whole day on mindfulness," Fernandez said. "We had such people as Eckhart Tolle and Arianna Huffington. And then, the following year, he invited me back... and I asked him, well last year we did a whole day on mindfulness... what are we going to do this year?" He paused for a beat. "Yeah, you guessed it, a whole day on compassion. This is two hundred thousand employees listening and doing training in compassion! IT'S HAPPENING folks!"

Sure, it's happening, but so are rallies by American neo-Nazis. Hula-hoops were once happening too. Fernandez's euphoria resembles a sports fan convinced of the power of optimistic frenzy to drive his team forward. Combine this with the marketing savvy of Marc Benioff, and the hoopla of mindfulness helps make dollars. It's unsurprising that a capitalist stooge such as Fernandez turns a blind eye to the aims of the stunts in which he enlists. Salesforce has been staging them for years. It once tried to pull one with the Dalai Lama, producing a poster of the Buddhist leader meditating under the slogan: "There is no software on the path to enlightenment."[9] Salesforce was forced to apologize. And of course that made headlines.

The Irony of Mindfulness Apps

I was in New York the day after Donald Trump was elected in 2016, riding the subway up Manhattan. The somber gloominess was palpable. As I gazed up, careful not to look anyone in the eye, I saw an advertising banner for Headspace, the most popular mindfulness app. The ad featured the tagline "I meditate to go full salsa," above an image of a young Latino dancer, holding his hoodie wide open. To his right, the ad continued: "Paul uses Headspace to make his moves even sharper. Download the Headspace app to find out what guided meditation can do for you." Spending over $2 million on this New York campaign alone, Headspace seems to be everywhere.[10]

Founded in 2010 by Andy Puddicombe, a British college dropout who was once a novice Buddhist monk, Headspace says it has thirty-six million users in over 190 countries.[11] The idea took shape in the aftermath of the 2008 financial crisis. Puddicombe had been teaching private and group meditation in London, where he met Rich Pierson, an anxious young advertising executive, who was impressed with Puddicombe's clear instructions. The two teamed up, borrowing $50,000 from Pierson's father to start their business.

Headspace has since raised over $80 million from investors, including a number of flashy celebrities. Richard Branson of Virgin, the basketball star LeBron James, the Academy Award winner Gwyneth Paltrow, and the LinkedIn CEO Jeff Weiner are among its fans. Even the NFL's Seattle Seahawks use the app. *Forbes* estimates Headspace's valuation at $250 million, with annual revenues of over $50 million.[12] Located in glitzy Santa Monica, California, Headspace has expanded to nearly two hundred employees. It recently opened another office in San Francisco.

Unlike many other apps, Headspace has succeeded in selling subscriptions. It costs $12.99 for a month, or $95.88 for a year. The app itself is free with a few guided meditations, but subscribers can access "packs" of many more. Alongside the basics, like coping with stress and falling asleep, there is a "Work and Performance" area with multi-session packs for Prioritization, Focus, Creativity, Balance and Productivity. Others have titles like Brave, with meditations for dealing with anger, regret, change and restlessness. Of course, there is also a Happiness pack, as well as Students and Sports. There is even Headspace for

Kids, targeting children under five. Headspace sells bulk subscriptions to companies such as Google, Genentech and LinkedIn. Seven airlines, including Virgin Atlantic, British Airways, Cathay Pacific, and United, are now brand partners, offering exclusive in-flight channels for weary passengers.

Headspace isn't alone in attracting venture capital: Happify Health has raised $25 million, Grokker $22 million. Numerous other meditation apps, such as Calm, Shine, and Thrive Global (Arianna Huffington's latest venture), have also received seed and early stage funding.[13] This "relaxation industry" is fiercely competitive. Headspace currently hovers around ninth or tenth place in the US download charts for Health and Fitness apps.

Headspace used to brand itself as "a gym membership for the brain" (it recently switched to the tagline "meditation made simple"). The app is full of cute animations — a brain lifting weights, a peanut figure meditating with headphones, and other cartoonish creations smiling and playing. The free version offers one-minute teaser meditations for cooking, eating and running. But it's not just fun and games, because of the *science*. The website is peppered with inflated claims (of the "research shows..." variety), most of which cite studies on long-term meditators, not its one-minute app users. It also adds a disclaimer: "Headspace is not intended to manage, treat, or cure any medical condition."

A recent study in the peer-reviewed journal *Evidence-Based Mental Health* found that most mediation apps suffer from the "frequent lack of an underlying evidence base, a lack of scientific credibility and limited clinical effectiveness."[14] The study's lead author, Simon Leigh, warns that relying on mental health apps can backfire: "If you go through the process of downloading and using an app and there are no benefits, it can compound your anxiety about your mental health problems."[15]

There is a peculiar irony in turning to an app to de-stress from problems that are often made worse by staring at phones. Headspace, like its rivals, has a vested interest in keeping users active. "People Meditating Now" on its homepage shows a real-time count. When I checked, there were 20,996 other people using the app. Why not join in when it's so easy and fun? However, behind the playful cartoons and kid-friendly user interface lie sophisticated data-mining tools. With location services enabled, a user entering the San Francisco International airport will be pinged with a notification, reminding them to "check in" and use a "fear of flying" meditation.

Similar to fitness-tracking apps that count daily steps, Headspace also monitors progress. Users are encouraged to share their progress with friends on social media, and to turn on regular reminders throughout the day to "take a pause." A skeptical reporter for the *Financial Times* got quite annoyed by the digital prodding. "Miss your scheduled dose of micro-meditation and mindfulness apps do not, of course, do blame or make recriminations," the *FT*'s Hattie Garlick writes:

> The passive aggression they can level at you is infinitely more powerful. 'We haven't seen you in a while,' they might say, when you finally lock yourself in the loo to secure the requisite few minutes. It is the karmic equivalent of: 'I'm not cross, just disappointed'.[16]

Headspace vows to simplify meditation, as do its peers. Their bite-sized programs help to standardize mindfulness for ease of consumption and "scaling up" revenues. This process follows George Ritzer's sociological theory of "McDonaldization."[17] The first mark of commoditization is efficiency, which allows for mass production and delivery. The second is calculability, quantifying offerings and measuring outcomes — as seen in "tracking" features on mindfulness apps and new wearable products like Muse, a "brain sensing headband" that helps access calm (with the tagline "meditation made easy"). The third step, predictability, is essential. Provision of service has to meet expectations. The fourth aspect, control, helps ensure this, responding to feedback so products are honed.

The classic model for this, of course, is the Big Mac. Ritzer argues that when everyday experiences are McDonaldized, the results can be irrational. The commoditization of "McMindfulness" has sought to make meditation more efficient, calculable, predictable, and controlled. But this has led to the opposite outcome, creating an uncontrollable consumer commodity that devalues mindfulness. Downloading an app as a digital detox is irrational. Mindful merchants don't care. They seem to be proud of creating a global branded product, accessible to anyone, anywhere — like a Big Mac.

chapter ten
Mindful Elites

Mindfulness made its debut at Davos in 2013. The annual meeting of the World Economic Forum (WEF), a week of parties and panel discussions in a sleepy Swiss ski resort, is a schmooze-fest for the global economic elite. The WEF attracts CEOs, fund managers, venture capitalists, heads of state and politicians, economists, representatives of NGOs, and a handful of token artists and celebrities. The 2013 gathering included such luminaries as the German Chancellor Angela Merkel, the former British Prime Ministers Tony Blair and David Cameron, the Chairman of J. P. Morgan Chase, Jacob Frenkel, and "William H. Gates III," the former CEO of Microsoft. Billing itself as a quest for ways of "restructuring economies and companies so that they grow sustainably and responsibly," the 2013 program had the overarching theme of "Resilient Dynamism."

On the forum's first morning, Janice Marturano, a former lawyer for General Mills, led an oversubscribed workshop on "The Mindful Leadership Experience." This drew on her own experience of discovering mindfulness and learning to teach it to fellow executives, as she instructed world leaders and stewards of capital to take "purposeful pauses" and cultivate "presence." Naturally, she assured them that mindfulness was grounded in science, and neither New Age nor religious. To assuage any doubts, her teaching partner had impeccable scientific and scholarly credentials: Professor Mark Williams from the Oxford Mindfulness Centre.

Mindful leaders, Marturano explained, need to master emotional self-regulation. Pure emotions are generally forbidden in the workplace; they threaten order, stability and the smooth operation of corporate machines. Their raw dimensions — such as anger, rage, resentment and contempt — are labeled "destructive," and the balm of mindfulness is offered as an antidote. Its non-judgmental acceptance helps to smother dissent, so the straight and narrow path of corporate etiquette can be trodden more mindfully. As well as increasing productivity at work, it is also a tool for maintaining unequal power relations. And if ever there were a captive audience for such ideas, it would be the WEF in Davos.

Marturano was certainly impressed. "Nowhere is the desire to see the big picture and to influence it in a positive way more apparent than at the World Economic Forum," she reflects in her book, *Finding a Space to Lead*.[1] Since her appearance in 2013, the global elite has latched onto mindfulness. Its purveyors in these rarefied settings work like corporate takeover specialists, stripping acquisitions of assets that might prevent a sale to the highest bidder. As a result, the new mindful jet-set reassure their overlords that what they are getting is a "science-based program" that delivers results, unbundled from unwanted detritus like teachings on ethics. However, the language of spiritual tradition can be subtly reframed to build a brand. At least in the context of the WEF, and related events, a "business mindfulness guru" is not an oxymoron.

So-called "Mindful Leaders" become anointed with pseudo-spiritual authority, acquiring the rhetoric of wisdom, compassion and empathy that helps secure complicity with corporate objectives. Mindful leadership depends on these narratives to cloak and humanize coercion, persuading managers to fulfill a noble mission of reducing suffering in the workplace. Employees can then be induced to consume standardized mindfulness programs, appealing to their sense of autonomy while shaping their experience in ways that are helpful to corporate goals. An echo of liberating doctrine helps legitimize this.

Mindful Courtiers

High on her own PR, Marturano believes that sharing mindfulness with the elite will create a "very big ripple effect" in the world.[2] As she blogged from Davos: "Imagine the possibilities!!!"[3] However, her workshop was typically bland. The usual themes were covered: the stresses of constant distraction, the inadequacies of multitasking, and the general malaise of having too much to do and too little time. However, there was no serious systemic inquiry into the causes of these symptoms. Instead, the diagnosis was simple: personal failure to be mindful and fully present while performing tasks.

As Marturano's book puts it: "We know that working very hard without really paying attention fully to what we are doing, and who we are doing it with, simply leaves us feeling empty."[4] Whatever the merits of this stoic injunction to be more mindful in all one's chores, blaming individuals deflects attention from the political economy of stress, and the structural dysfunctions that sustain it. This neoliberal ju-jitsu is similar to how victims of predatory subprime mortgage lending were demonized for taking on too much risk. Corporate moral failings are externalized and personalized. Employees are at fault if they fail to manage stress, not the system that caused it.

Another Davos acolyte, the MIT management theorist Otto Scharmer, runs an organization called The Presencing Institute, providing cover for elites: "The root cause of our current economic and civilizational crisis is not Wall Street," he says, "not infinite growth [and] not Big Business or Big Government."[5] No, the root cause, according to Scharmer is "between our ears." He was one of the courtiers at the 2014 WEF, chatting about how to be mindful like Nelson Mandela.[6] Following the lead of Marturano, there has been a steady procession of mindfulness teachers, Buddhist monks, neuroscientists, and celebrities spreading the postmodern prosperity gospel. At the 2014 annual meeting, the actress Goldie Hawn promoted her MindUP™ program for children, leading a session on how mindfulness training and social-emotional learning can change the world. While she spoke, the main hall was in thrall to President Hassan Rouhani of Iran, leader of one of the most repressive regimes in the world. Hawn's talk was preceded by a meditation led by Matthieu Ricard, a French-born Tibetan monk who occasionally translates for the Dalai Lama. Ricard has been labeled "the happiest man in the world," on account of the scans of his meditating brain by neuroscientists.

The following year at Davos reached peak mindfulness. The inventor of MBSR, Jon Kabat-Zinn, made a cameo appearance, leading daily early morning meditations. The *Harvard Business Review* even hosted a "mindfulness dinner." At a two-hour panel on "Leading Mindfully," Kabat-Zinn made some trademark wisecracks: "The first thing we notice when we practice mindfulness is how mindless we are," he told the packed room. Alongside him, Arianna Huffington trotted out other standard lines. "Modern science is validating ancient wisdom," she said. "We are living through a major tipping point."[7]

Getting down to business, fellow panelist William George — a senior fellow at the Harvard Business School who sits on several executive boards and once ran Medtronic — underlined the benefits. "The main business case for mindfulness is that if you're more focused on the job, you'll become a better leader," he said. "Even Goldman Sachs is doing it." It remains unclear how this has changed an investment bank once likened to "a great vampire squid wrapped around the face of humanity, relentlessly jamming its blood funnel into anything that smells like money."[8] George is a director of Goldman Sachs.

A few years earlier, the Buddhist scholar and teacher David Loy challenged George's advocacy of mindfulness to managers. Loy wrote an open letter, asking George if his meditative practice had any impact on corporate social responsibility, or his role in demanding it from fellow board members at Novartis, ExxonMobil and Goldman Sachs.[9] Loy's letter included a list of the unethical practices of these companies. "I would like to learn how, in light of your meditation practice, you understand the relationship between one's own personal transformation and the kind of economic and social transformation that appears to be necessary today, if we are to survive and thrive," Loy wrote.

George never replied, despite several follow-ups. His silence speaks louder than words. As observed by Daniel

Anderson, a cultural studies scholar, owning up to the contradictions between his rhetoric and actions would expose the charade of "mindful leadership," which amounts to "the remaking of class power moment-by-moment."[10] For mindful capitalism to succeed, such inconsistencies must be concealed. Matthieu Ricard was also present for the 2015 Davos meeting. His bright red Tibetan monastic robes were quite conspicuous, a contrast to George's embodiment of capitalist power. Ricard serves as a helpfully "aspirational image," Anderson writes, "the 'Oriental Monk' revealed in MRI scans to have singularly-developed brain structures." What better way to brand our subservience to capital than with scientifically sanctioned Buddhist symbols?

The invocation of science at Davos 2015 included a dialogue between Richard Davidson — the neuroscientist who studied Ricard's brain — and Tom Insel, who runs the National Institute of Mental Health, a federal agency that funds research on meditation. Again, Davidson's inclusion was strategic. As the pioneer of contemplative neuroscience, he had colorful anecdotes of his encounters with Buddhist adepts, and how this inspired him not only to study meditation, but also to practice it himself. This process started in 1992, when he met the Dalai Lama at the Mind & Life Institute. Davidson had spent most of his career studying the neural mechanisms of anxiety, fear and depression. The Dalai Lama challenged him to investigate positive qualities, which led to brain scans of monks.

The cultural currency of neuroscience made the WEF crowd especially receptive to Davidson's message. Their increasing interest in mental health and wellbeing is logical — as we have seen, mindfulness is used to alleviate employee disengagement. And since wellbeing is an economic factor of production, the emerging science of happiness seeks to explain how to bolster resilience. However, it functions via surveillance. Neuroscience offers more sophisticated technologies for measuring and quantifying internal states, and positive moods and feelings can be reproduced through mindfulness training.

Davidson's research into the neural mechanisms behind such states as compassion, empathy, resilience, and gratitude thus has tremendous neoliberal value. The calculated management of life, a quest among utilitarian thinkers dating back to Jeremy Bentham, is made possible by mindfulness, with its intent of producing contented employees. Going beyond mere disciplinary power, the findings of neuroscience help develop subtler ways to shape the mind — what Byung-Chul Han calls "neoliberal psycho-politics."[11]

Corporate Mind Control with a Happy Face

Corporate mindfulness programs perpetuate the myth that individuals are simply "free to choose" between stress and misery or wellness and happiness. The seductive lure of libertarian "freedom" is precisely why these new forms of thought-control are different from covert brainwashing. They enlist the supposedly autonomous individual subject in self-discipline, instilling neoliberal assumptions in the name of liberation. As such, note Jeremy Carrette and Richard King in *Selling Spirituality*, "psycho-physical techniques described in terms of 'personal development' seek to pacify feelings of anxiety and disquiet at the individual level rather than seeking to challenge the social, political and economic inequalities that cause such distress."[12]

Instead of paying attention to what our thoughts and feelings may be trying to tell us about our experience — including questionable corporate practices — Jon Kabat-Zinn instructs us to "drop into the being mode," to let go of our "mental chatter." And rather than listening to internal voices of dissent, or our reasons for frustration with bad bosses, social injustices or pointless tasks, we are taught to self-monitor internal states so we become more skilled at riding the waves of competitive enterprise.

"It's best to think of happiness as a skill," Richard Davidson tells us, something not dependent on external circumstances, but on our ability to face them as they are. One can learn to endure all sorts of horrors, but it's a strangely defeatist form of freedom. It also ignores the important role of external factors in being comfortable enough for such views — from socio-economic status, to access to healthcare and stable employment. Presenting mindfulness as a skill — particularly one leading to happiness — helps to rationalize the neoliberal need for autonomous selves, while discouraging them from resisting the status quo. Sam Binkley sums up the problem in *Happiness as Enterprise*: "Happiness has been rendered a depthless physiological response without moral referent, a biological potential of the individual that makes no recourse to psychic interiority, biography, or social relationships of any kind, however sublimated."[13]

The Davos crowd, already well versed in managing assets, tends to view human behavior in terms of economic motivations. Mindfulness framed as a skill just becomes a new way to invest in human capital. The entrepreneurial self is encouraged to make this wise investment so as to gain a competitive edge as an economic actor. This reduces the self to a "collection of assets that must be continually invested in, nurtured, managed and developed," warns Wendy Brown in *Undoing the Demos*, making resistance far less likely.[14] It can be hard to see out of the box if the system that builds it is reinforced by mindfulness, suggesting we can thrive if we only let go of awkward questions.

Let Me Know If I Fuck Up

One frigid November morning in Boston, I ran my own conference workshop, titled "Search Inside (and Outside) Yourself." Just a few seconds into my presentation, after showing a slide with a *Wall Street Journal* photo of Chade-Meng Tan, the man himself took a seat at the back of the room. Afterwards, Google's Jolly Good Fellow — as he was still titled at the time — approached the podium. He looked very serious. "I agree with you that the track record for effecting large-scale organizational transformation is dismal," Meng said. "But that's because the executives weren't trained in mindfulness."

A couple of my colleagues began to eavesdrop. Meng continued: "I fully agree with my good friend Tony Hsieh, CEO of Zappos that the pursuit of mindfulness and the pursuit of corporate profit are completely compatible." Becoming more animated, he reached for my hand. "I am going to tell you a secret that I often don't share," he said.

"My mission in life is to democratize enlightenment and bring one million people to stream-entry before I die." My colleagues gawped in disbelief. "If commercial success ever gets in the way of mindfulness, I'll let go of commercial success."

This seems unlikely. Meng goes out of his way to feel the pain of millionaires. "Fundamentally, I think it comes down to the compassion in recognizing that even the rich suffer," he once told an interviewer:

> Their suffering causes more suffering to the people around them precisely because they have wealth and power. By addressing that population, I can limit the damage it does to the world. If a poor guy suffers, he suffers and maybe his wife does, too. If a rich guy suffers, everyone around him suffers: his butler, his employees, his thousand people.[15]

A few years after our encounter in Boston, Meng retired from Google, aged forty-five. Did he leave because commercial success had impeded mindfulness? He certainly left a very wealthy man. Towards the end of our conversation, Meng conceded that corporate mindfulness had neglected compassion and social justice. As we parted, he said sincerely: "Let me know if I fuck up."

Arrogance 2.0

The year before he retired, Meng was part of a major fuck-up in San Francisco. The Wisdom 2.0 conference is an annual gathering of elites from Silicon Valley, tech hipsters who work for them, and a bazaar of hucksters hawking apps, executive coaching, and brain-stimulation gadgets. Oh, and corporate mindfulness teachers — such outmoded traditions as Buddhism clearly need upgrading from Wisdom 1.0. The general mood is a mix of libertarianism and New Age spirituality. Each year's line-up combines celebrities with the usual suspects from the mindfulness industry — Jon Kabat-Zinn, Jack Kornfield, Sharon Salzberg, Joan Halifax, Eckhart Tolle, Anderson Cooper, Arianna Huffington, Goldie Hawn and the mindful Congressman Tim Ryan, to name just a few. Corporate sponsors have included Google, Facebook, Yahoo, and MailChimp. The conference is the brainchild of Soren Gordhamer, a tall thin man who looks like he runs marathons. With five stages and five thousand mindfulness fans, Wisdom 2.0 is a festival of spiritual capitalism.

The weekend-long event claims to bring "wisdom, purpose, and meaning" to social media and technology corporations. Integrating wisdom is "not a nice extra," say the organizers, "but an absolute necessity to a vibrant and sustainable society." They define wisdom as "learning to focus, to truly connect, to empathize," a hazy definition that anyone can, quite literally, buy into — through the distraction-providing sponsors.

On the morning of Saturday 15 February 2014, at the start of a panel on "3 Steps to Build Corporate Mindfulness the Google Way," a group of activists, called Heart of the City, took the stage. They unfurled a banner that read: "Eviction Free San Francisco," alluding to the city's housing crisis. The leader of the protest, Amanda Ream, distributed bright-yellow flyers to attendees, saying: "Thank you for your practice. We invite you to consider the truth behind Google and the tech industry's impact on San Francisco." Another protestor, Erin McElroy, used a bullhorn, chanting "Wisdom means stop displacement! Wisdom means stop surveillance!"

Ream, a member of the Buddhist Peace Fellowship, was effectively teaching "Wisdom 101." The tech elite has colonized San Francisco, driving up rents and inflating a property bubble that entices landlords to evict low-rent tenants. Add to that the issue of commuting — many tech employees like to live in the city but work in the duller confines of Silicon Valley — and corporate shuttle buses were being physically attacked as proxies for this exploitative relationship. Ream was asking Google and other corporations to look at the problems and address them, by paying for the impact on housing and infrastructure. Heart of the City's demands included funding for affordable housing, public transit, and eviction defense support, as well as an end to for-profit surveillance of the sort exposed by Edward Snowden. What was the response from the wise, empathic, compassionate, mindful sages onstage? Meng sat cross-legged in his Tai Chi costume.

Bill Duane, the senior manager of Google's Wellbeing and Sustainable High Performance Development programs, jumped in with an impromptu meditation. He instructed the audience to — you've guessed it — search inside themselves: "check in with your body," he said, and "feel what it's like to be in conflict with people with heartfelt ideas," while security forced the protesters off the stage.[16] A beefy guard engaged in an embarrassing tug-of-war with one activist banner-holder, who won. As Heart of the City said: "Google and conference leaders proceeded to talk about 'wisdom and mindfulness' but failed to address the grievances of Bay Area communities or the company's own hypocrisy in purporting to be 'mindful'." One could actually argue that it showed very clearly what mindfulness means in corporate terms. The interruption was a mere passing thought, to be observed and let go without judgment — mindfully rising above conflict, or sources of discomfort in the outside world, while taking care to pacify *our* world.[17]

Wisdom 2.0 later congratulated Google for its mindful "leadership" in handling the protest "with incredible grace and compassion," allowing others to express their views, and being comfortable with hearing disagreement.[18] As long as we don't have to consider what they're actually saying, or that it might feel uncomfortable because it's demanding something just, while our pseudo-wise views might be mistaken. According to Wisdom 2.0, "Google demonstrated (not just talked) about how important it is to develop your own practice, then bring that sense of wisdom and compassion out into the world." A Google manager also talked about developing practice in the workplace, saying meetings now started with two-minute meditations. Apparently, one staffer who had started out skeptical was now converted, saying: "I don't know about the rest of you, but I'm a better person for those two minutes. So I'm all for it."[19] Self-improvement in two minutes — just think of the possibilities! Of course, Google already has. For them, "a better person" is someone who buys into the corporate culture — and feels good about it.

The condescending meditation at Wisdom 2.0 was effectively used as a form of censorship. The protesters and their message were mindfully managed out of meaningful existence. If we just breathe and keep calm and centered in the present moment, they will all go away and we can return to business as usual. However, mindfulness is not merely a passive and nonjudgmental acceptance of the status quo. When infused with wisdom, it's used to inquire whether wholesome states of mind are being developed — in other words, compassion and empathy need to be more than ways to feel better about oneself.

The Google emissaries showed corporate mindfulness is a privatized spirituality, encouraging passivity and dissociation. Techie hipsters like Google's Bill Duane think the early embrace of meditation by anti-establishment types is simply "woo-woo" hippie bullshit. Their replacement is "neural hacking" and present moment escapism. Wisdom 2.0's Gordhamer has swallowed the "here-and-now" philosophy wholesale. He defines stress as "fighting or non-accepting what is true in a given moment" and says: "stress relief, then, is accepting and allowing our experience, no matter what it is."[20] Radical acceptance, without judgment, can easily be turned into "Don't Fight The Man" — at Google, he pays pretty well, and that helps soothe stress.

Ironically, Wisdom 2.0 participants should have been prepared for some critical questions about their role in social suffering. The previous year, one of the presenters — Marianne Williamson — peppered her talk with some scathing critique. She asked why a spiritual teacher should "come here and be a dancing monkey to help a bunch of rich capitalists talk about the fact that they can have a more compassionate workplace" while ignoring the poverty outside it, to which they contribute. "Only in modern America could we come up with some ersatz version of spirituality that gives us a pass on addressing the unnecessary human suffering in our midst," Williamson said.[21] She went on to quote Martin Luther King: "Our lives begin to end the day we become silent about things that matter." For now, it seems Google and Wisdom 2.0 prefer keeping silent.

Five years on from Williamson's tirade, little has changed. At the start of the 2018 conference, Wisdom 2.0 attendees were warned about homeless people outside the venue. "Not that they are dangerous," the moderator said, but "to ensure your safety we have security personnel visible in stations both inside and outside the hotel." He wasn't done. "If you are heading towards Union Square just be mindful of your personal belongings. Should you choose to go into the Tenderloin for theatres, restaurants, or galleries it does have a quirky, vibrant community" — pause for giggles from the audience — "you may want to take a cab, Lyft or Uber back to the hotel."[22] Basking in white privilege, Wisdom 2.0 is like a gated community where smug elites spew feel-good sound bites. Meanwhile, the technologies of distraction and addiction they produce cause widespread suffering, while their companies contribute to widening inequality.

For all his talk about compassion and acceptance, Soren Gordhamer still bears grudges. In 2012, the journalist Richard Eskow published a critique of Wisdom 2.0 in the Buddhist magazine *Tricycle*, under the headline "Buying

Wisdom."[23] Furious with the lampooning of his event, Gordhamer tried to discredit the story. He demanded corrections to minor errors — which were amended at once — complaining: "we have never witnessed such little regard for accuracy and basic common decency in journalism." Eskow's reply is insightful: "Mr. Gordhamer also expresses anger that I accepted 'free' admission and then made critical remarks. If he thinks a press pass guarantees favorable coverage, we really do have different views of journalistic ethics."[24]

Many in the mindfulness and Buddhist communities seem to be seduced by what Google and the Wisdom 2.0 crowd are doing. After all, it's mindfulness, so it might make people kinder, and corporations could even act nicer. However, mindfulness has been cut loose from moral moorings. Without a principled anchor, it is a renegade technology that helps people rationalize unethical conduct. The conspicuous absence of an explicit ethical component to corporate mindfulness programs reflects the fraught relationship that these businesses already have to social and environmental responsibilities.

chapter eleven
Mindful Schools

With its promise to reduce mental health problems while improving emotional self-discipline, concentration, and "executive brain function," mindfulness is popular in schools. Although the materials used are different, the framing of the programs is the same as elsewhere, touting support from neuroscience and distancing the practice from religion. Instead, there is a general focus on results — particularly raising test scores and easing the stress caused by constant pressure to achieve. There are also claims that mindfulness can help the disadvantaged to become more resilient in the midst of poverty, crime and racial violence. However, these external conditions are not discussed. As usual, the emphasis is on individuals looking inside themselves, instilling a neoliberal mindset in young people.

The missionary zeal — and humanistic rhetoric — with which the benefits of mindfulness are promoted in schools masks an underlying authoritarian tone. Popular images of students sitting calmly in the classroom, focusing tamely on the task at hand, suggest they have been saved from distracting emotions and unruly impulses. However, they are also regarded as victims — fragile, vulnerable, dysfunctional, and "at risk."

Although there is some truth to this — with apparently increasing rates of anxiety, depression, and self-harm — schools teach children to handle problems by self-pacifying. The issue is how they react, not the conditions to which they react. This therapeutic approach is conservative, directing attention away from the outside world. Mindfulness could be an empowering and emancipatory practice, exploring ways to change social conditions and priorities. Instead, it maintains the status quo. Students are taught to meditate away their anger and accept their frustrations (non-judgmentally, of course). This might help them focus on work, but unless they also learn about the causes of stress in social, economic and institutional structures, links between education and democracy are severed.

Meanwhile, a political orthodoxy has emerged around the idea of a mental health crisis, despite many ambiguities in how "emotional disorders" and "mental ill health" are defined. Mindfulness in schools could not have become as popular as it has without the cultural norms of a therapeutic culture, effectively telling us we need help — which we'll get, whether we like it or not, along with training in obedience.

Consider the Mindfulness in Schools Project (MiSP) in the United Kingdom, which has trained over 4,500 teachers, aiming to bring "face-to-face quality mindfulness" to one million children within the next five years.[1] The MiSP curriculum, dubbed "dot-b" — which is shorthand for "Stop, Breathe and Be!" — was conceived by two educators, Richard Burnett and Chris Cullen (now at Oxford). It likens mindfulness for students to disciplining pets. "Attention is like a puppy," says the scripted syllabus, "It doesn't stay where you want it to."[2] It also "brings back things you didn't ask for [and] sometimes it makes a real mess." Therefore, "in training our minds we have to use the same qualities of FIRM, PATIENT, KIND REPETITION that are needed in order to train a puppy."

Mindfulness to the Rescue

In the United States, mindfulness in education comes with government funding and media attention. The Mindful Schools non-profit organization in Oakland, California, runs trainings for teachers who are said to have "impacted" two million students.[3] Their programs came to national prominence via the documentary *Room to Breathe*, aired on PBS with enthusiastic media coverage. Raving about the film, the *Washington Post* called mindfulness "the fastest-growing technique in classrooms for teaching self-control."[4]

Room to Breathe follows Megan Cowan, the co-founder of Mindful Schools, as she spends several months teaching mindfulness to "troubled kids" at Marina Middle School in San Francisco, known for its high rate of disciplinary suspensions.[5] The trailer shows students — primarily of color — shouting, pushing and hitting each other. The words LOUD, CHAOTIC, and OUT OF CONTROL flash onscreen before cutting to Cowan striking a Tibetan singing bowl in the classroom, and suddenly... all is... calm.

The film itself has a fairly predictable savior narrative. Despite being confronted at first by defiance, Cowan's devotedly selfless service wins students over. After learning mindfulness techniques, they report the usual benefits: feeling calmer and better able to concentrate — which, on the face of it, is surely a good thing. But, as noted by the activist scholar Jennifer Cannon, *Room to Breathe* "reinscribes a racialized discourse about 'troubled' youth of color and introduces a white mindfulness instructor as the teacher-hero."[6]

Gentle, benevolent, and patient, Cowan plays the part effortlessly. She tells the students that mindfulness is unqualifiedly good for them; as a form of self-discipline, it will help them succeed in school and work. As with most programs in schools, we do not see anything in the curriculum that turns mindful attention and critical inquiry to social and economic context. Could their behavioral problems, poor academic performance and stress be related to living in impoverished and crime-ridden neighborhoods, or being the victims of institutional racism? Evidently not, from the mindful teacher's point of view.

This is part of the problem. School mindfulness programs mostly shy away from what David Forbes, a Professor of Educational Counseling at Brooklyn College, calls "the critical cultivation of awareness, appreciation, and employment of the cultural context and cultural capital of both students and educators."[7] In other words, there is a glaring absence of the sort of liberating critical pedagogy that might educate people out of oppression. That omission, Forbes explains, contributes in itself to reinforcing "racist systems within education that in turn reproduces racism in the larger social structure."

At one point in *Room to Breathe*, Cowan's inner authoritarian is revealed. She seems ill-equipped to handle disruptive students in a class of thirty who show no interest in mindfulness. As Cowan says to the camera: "If there were five of them that weren't in there, then the majority of them would be trying, would be participating." One of those is Diego, a Latino who tells her "it's boring." Losing her patience, she orders four students to leave her class. "It's like hitting a brick wall," she says. "I just am

frustrated, and kind of hopeless. The defiance is so deliberate and I don't know if I can work with that in this large
a group." Following this incident, Cowan consults with the
Assistant Principal, who gently admonishes her, reminding
her that "this is a public school, and we take everyone.
Excluding students, that's a paradigm I don't want to set
up." However, it seems that she stuck to her decision — the
disruptive students do not appear again.

Instead, the wisdom of the mindfulness teacher is
valorized, along with her status as disciplinarian. Rather
than exploring the strengths and talents of the young
participants in her class, the film mostly highlights their
defects, until Cowan transforms them into a room full of
docile meditators. The audience gets a warm glow, and can
feel optimistic about the potential for improving urban
education — perhaps even making a donation to Mindful
Schools. However, without also making radical investments in social change, all this does is focus attention on
individuals, reforming students and not the system that
trains them, let alone the broader social problems it reflects.

Much of the rhetoric in Mindful Schools' literature
depicts students of color and those from poor working-class
communities as dependent on welfare, and lacking agency
and power — and therefore in need of saving. Thankfully,
the civilized mindfulness teacher — most often white and
affluent — has the agency, cultural capital, and goodness
of heart to instruct the benighted in emotional etiquette.
Parallels with Christian missionaries are not accidental —
a sentimental "do-gooding" mentality is deeply ingrained
among the privileged, whose blindness to the causes of
injustice stems in part from how they benefit.

"The white savior supports brutal policies in the morning, founds charities in the afternoon, and receives awards in the evening," writes Teju Cole in *The Atlantic*. "The White Savior Industrial Complex is not about justice. It is about having a big emotional experience that validates privilege."[8] The sincerity of well-meaning efforts makes it hard to critique their general naïveté, but unless outsiders are seeking to learn from the people they "help" — particularly about systemic solutions to their problems — then they may well make things worse by applying the calming balm of mindfulness.

There is an unspoken taboo in the mindfulness movement regarding such criticism. It is tantamount to blasphemy to question the impact of teachers and their programs, since they all believe so evangelically in their goodness. And since mindfulness seems to bring relief, it is thought to be pointlessly "negative" to start picking holes in what teachers are doing, or the motives behind it. Those teaching mindfulness in schools are not usually afflicted by the socio-economic inequalities driving the problems they address. Sure, their hearts may be in the right place, but we can't say the same for their critical thinking skills.

Cognitive Capitalism

Mindful school advocates seem to be especially oblivious to how their programs serve the prevailing social order. Mindfulness doesn't exist in a political vacuum; it's shaped by neoliberal ideas, which influence us all unless we consciously resist. Children are schooled to prepare them for roles in an increasingly competitive capitalist system. Mindfulness is therefore a way to boost resilience, producing young subjects who can manage their emotions and deal with the stress of a market-based world. Since schools are increasingly subject to market forces — think privatized charter schools and voucher schemes in the US and academization in the UK — they seek to prove their performance with measurable outcomes. Mindfulness helps improve test scores and student behavior, both of which make managers look good.

"The mindful, 'happy' person emanating from the school system is grist to the cognitive capitalist mill," warns the skeptical scholar James Reveley.[9] Neoliberal logic requires self-promoting and self-disciplined subjects, in charge of their own wellbeing and success, whatever disadvantages they might have to overcome. From a neoliberal perspective, society doesn't exist — everything comes down to individual choices and responsibilities. As Reveley observes: "It is a tall order to ask young people to reject these ideals at the same time as they are being taught to embrace them through a self-technology that stresses self-responsibility."[10]

However, none of the providers of mindfulness in schools discusses this problem, or the need to address it. Focusing instead on achievement-oriented passivity, their programs indoctrinate students to see themselves as vulnerable. In order to be successful in school and life, they learn to "manage" their emotions with therapeutic mindfulness. Feelings should be accepted non-judgmentally, without distinguishing between "good" and "bad" ones, or what they tell us. What happens if a vulnerable student experiences a strong and difficult feeling due to prior trauma? Teachers rarely have the psychological training for such situations, and research on the adverse effects of mindfulness is often ignored. Indiscriminately teaching it to all children could be irresponsible, given the paucity of rigorous studies that show clear benefits beyond pacification.

By pathologizing strong feelings, and teaching children "emotional literacy," the curricula of mindfulness in schools instill a strong sense of "correct" behavior, along with the implication that anything else is "incompetent" or "illiterate." In *The Dangerous Rise of Therapeutic Education*, Kathryn Ecclestone and Dennis Hayes warn that this mentality "erodes the idea of humans as conscious agents who realize their potential for individual and social change through projects to transform themselves and their world and replaces it with a narrow, introspective view of what it means to be human."[11]

Some programs have tweaked their curricula to add other messages. In the US, Mindful Schools now talks about "The Development of Heartfulness," which it describes as "intentional nurturing of positive mind states such as kindness and compassion."[12] Yet the general emphasis is on awareness of the present moment, which means tuning out of feelings and thoughts. "At its most basic level," says the UK's Mindfulness in Schools Project, "mindfulness helps train your attention to be more aware of what is actually happening, rather than worrying about what has happened or might happen."[13]

Although this sounds like engagement with "now," it teaches quietism. Especially in the early years of education, much of the focus is on "school readiness," conditioning students to comply with rules, norms and behavioral demands. Mindfulness is part of this package when taught to young children — this has worrying implications. "The emphasis on sublimating strong emotions such as anger could send unintended messages about not speaking up in the face of injustice," says Natalie Flores, "dissuading children's later participation in social activism."[14] Others say programs should explicitly focus on social justice, especially when offered in low-income areas. Rather than using mindfulness "to make calm test takers," explains Funie Hsu, a progressive approach would include critical analysis of systems of power, "to enliven our students' hearts so that they are stirred to creating the world that they deserve."[15]

Hsu cites one of the pioneers of socially engaged Buddhism, Thich Nhat Hanh, who describes the need to combine mindfulness with action. "When bombs begin to fall on people, you cannot stay in the meditation hall all of the time," Hanh says. "You have to learn how to help a wounded child while still practicing mindful breathing."[16]

This is rarely the message of mindfulness in schools, which encourages passivity instead of engagement. Students are told to focus on themselves, while schools promote high-stakes standardized tests, micromanagement, and surveillance, all adding to stress and serving the needs of neoliberalism. This is often unconscious, but if acknowledged could be counteracted. Instead, Hsu says, mindfulness curricula "discipline students both through neoliberal self-regulation and through a racial conditioning of white superiority as common, and calm, sense."[17] Such power imbalances are not often considered, which only perpetuates colonialist attitudes among white mindfulness trainers assigned to teach students of color. If they are unaware of the racist implications of failing to acknowledge structural racism, it is hardly surprising that mindfulness is so rarely taught as part of a framework of critical thinking and social justice.

Mindful Camouflage

Another major issue for mindfulness in schools is the unresolved question of whether what they teach has religious dimensions. "Silence and contemplation play an important role in the world's great faiths," says the UK's Mindfulness in Schools Project, "but the MiSP curricula remain strictly secular."[18] It is rarely this simple, since many of the advocates of mindful schools are either Buddhist practitioners or have attended retreats in traditional settings. Besides, notes the religious studies scholar Candy Gunther Brown, "The fact that there exist secular benefits to mindfulness does not make the practice secular," especially not when teachers still like to imply that Buddhism's insights are included. One of the founders of the MiSP wrote an academic article for a Buddhist journal positioning his work in "the as yet undefined middle-ground between mindfulness as clinical application and mindfulness as spiritual practice."[19]

A good example of this switch between secular and spiritual is the way Goldie Hawn's pre-high-school MindUp curriculum is marketed. Hawn admits to having written a "script" to smuggle Buddhist meditation "into the classroom under a different name because obviously people that say 'oh meditation' they think oh this is 'Buddhist'."[20] Addressing insiders at the Heart-Mind Conference of The Dalai Lama Center for Peace Education, Hawn switched to Buddhist mode: she said MindUP "all started" with "His Holiness" (who "gave me my mantra") and the Dalai Lama Center ("it's karma").[21] The MindUP script replaces the terms "Buddhism" with "neuroscience" and "meditation" with "Core Practice."[22] Mindful of laws separating church and state, Hawn's aim is to spread MindUP to as many schools as possible, by getting it "absolutely mandated in every state... that's our mission".[23]

As we have seen so far, appealing to science is the standard way of presenting mindfulness. However, Professor Brown disputes that this makes the practice secular. She argues that there is also abundant scientific research on the physical and mental benefits of prayer, but it is unconstitutional to offer a program of prayer in schools. Noting this discrepancy, Brown observes: "In the end, appeals to science can't simply speak religion away."[24]

A number of school districts offering mindfulness have faced legal challenges, accusing them of providing covert religious indoctrination. The mindfulness program at Warstler Elementary School in Plain Township, Ohio was shut down after six weeks.[25] Parents raised strong objections to the undisclosed fact that mindfulness is derived from Buddhism. Citing the constitution's Establishment Clause, which prohibits the imposition of religious beliefs or any form of worship in public institutions, courts have banned such practices as posting the Ten Commandments in classrooms. Even observing a moment of silence has been challenged. Why then should mindfulness trainers be free to use Tibetan Buddhist singing bowls, or tell students to sit cross-legged in a meditative posture?

Some find such things troubling. The National Center for Law and Policy has represented evangelical Christians in litigation against public schools teaching yoga and meditation. In one such case in Massachusetts, it sent a memorandum on behalf of parents to the Superintendent of the Dennis-Yarmouth Regional School District, objecting to a mindfulness program called Calmer Choice. The protest was forthright, arguing:

> Mindfulness is without question a Buddhist religious practice. In a spirit quite frankly smacking of philosophical and spiritual "insiderism" or elitism, promoters of mindfulness claim special "new" insights into the universal causes and the universal solutions of being human. The prescription of mindfulness as a universal, non-sectarian cure for nearly all that ails us in modern life is precisely a religious attitude![26]

Calmer Choice is an adaptation of Jon Kabat-Zinn's MBSR, marketed to schools as Mindfulness-Based Inner Reliance Training. However, the ties to MBSR are undeniable, and Kabat-Zinn even serves as an honorary member of the Calmer Choice board. What are parents to think when he openly claims that MBSR is a "place-holder for the entire dharma" and that it is co-extensive with, and an expression of, the heart of Buddhism?

The legal memorandum cites various research studies that have found a strong association between MBSR training and increased religiosity. One attributed the mental health benefits of MBSR to a deepening of "daily spiritual experiences."[27] Another found that British males took meditation courses to improve wellbeing, but became interested in Buddhism.[28] In a separate randomized study, participants in an MBSR course reported statistically "higher scores in a measure of spiritual experiences."[29] This paper also noted that MBSR is rooted in Buddhist "meditation techniques which were not originally conceived as stress reduction exercises but rather as contemplative practices specifically designed to foster spiritual growth and understanding."[30] Such facts can make uncomfortable reading for people with different religious beliefs.

These concerns echo earlier challenges. In a high-profile case from the 1970s, *Malnak v Yogi*, a New Jersey court ruled that teaching Transcendental Meditation (TM) in public high schools violated the Establishment Clause.[31] Promoters of TM now claim to offer something secular, avoiding religious vocabulary and touting scientific research. TM's Quiet Time school program is backed by the filmmaker David Lynch's Foundation for Consciousness-Based Education and World Peace, which describes its mission as "promoting widespread implementation of the evidence-based Transcendental Meditation (TM) program in order to improve their health, cognitive capabilities and performance in life."[32] Lynch himself has been an avid TM proselytizer since 1973. Like mindfulness programs, Quiet Time flies under the radar, cloaked in the garb of pseudoscience.

Six public schools in San Francisco adopted Quiet Time, but objections arose. This was despite locating the programs in low-income communities, where the majority of families are minorities and non-native English speakers, which might have limited the chances of them questioning authority. Nonetheless, one mother protested, starting a Facebook group "SF Parents Against TM in Public Schools."[33] She became suspicious when her son brought home a permission slip, which lacked the usual Spanish translation for Hispanic parents. Reading around, she found TM used secret mantras and religious ideas. There was even a form of altar at the school. As she wrote on Facebook, none of this had been mentioned on the permission slip. "Isn't Omission a form of Deception?" she said. "Can anyone explain how this constitutes INFORMED CONSENT?[34]

After confronting the high school principal, she received a "cease and desist" letter from a high-powered attorney, allegedly representing the Quiet Time program. The letter insinuated that she was accusing the program of religious indoctrination, requiring her to seek her own legal representation. This does not seem atypical. John Knapp, a TM defector, runs a website called the *TM-Free Blog: Skeptical Views of Transcendental Meditation and Maharishi Mahesh Yogi.*[35] Knapp once planned an online symposium titled: "Tell TM: Hands Off Our Schools!" However, as reported by *Church & State Magazine*, he cancelled it after a threatening letter from William Goldstein, general counsel for the David Lynch Foundation. Goldstein's letter states:

> The listed presenters at your event appear all to have a similar negative mission [...] Therefore, I wished to give you the courtesy of an advisal that we intend to review the global web presentation of the event carefully for

any false, defamatory, tortious, breachful, malicious or otherwise unlawful statements or materials made or published by you or the presenters.[36]

Among those scheduled to speak had been Barry Markovsky, a University of South Carolina sociology professor, who casts doubt on TM's scientific claims.

Back in San Francisco, the Quiet Time program was discontinued after three months, costing taxpayers $110,000. Only one of the original six schools — Visitation Valley Middle School — has persisted with it — it has three full-time instructors funded by the David Lynch Foundation, and receives approving media coverage.[37]

Mindful Guinea Pigs

Critics of teaching mindfulness in schools often highlight the risks, pointing to a scarcity of methodologically rigorous scientific studies supporting the practice. "Right now the promised benefits far exceed the actual findings," warns Mark Greenberg, a psychologist at Penn State University.[38] There is even a skeptical tone at *Mindfulness*, an academic journal to which Kabat-Zinn contributes. In a special edition on "Mindfulness-Based Interventions in School Settings," the introduction noted: "Mindfulness research has often been described as being in its infancy and if this is the case, then the study of mindfulness with youth and schools is in the prenatal stage of development."[39]

Reviewing three recent meta-analytic studies of mindfulness in schools, it's clear that the effects are very small and that general findings are inconclusive. There is still a very limited pool of studies — compared to a similar meta-analytic study of adult mindfulness, in which researchers drew from over eighteen thousand articles, the combined number for children in all three reviews was 111. Even those studies that were included were of questionable quality. In one of the reviews, eleven of the papers had not even been published in peer-reviewed journals; in another, which only looked at fifteen studies, some included TM; and in the third, only thirty-five of the seventy-two studies used randomized controls.

David Klingbeil, a school psychologist at the University of Wisconsin who led the third review, reflects: "The first thing that came to me is just the wide variety of things called mindfulness-based interventions."[40] One study researched the effects on children of coloring for fifteen minutes. Others include a grab bag of activities, says Harold Walach, a co-author on the second review — mindful breathing, listening to bell sounds, group discussions, and so on.[41] With such a disparate collection of activities, it's hard to know how mindfulness is defined and operationalized, or what the actual mechanism is that would account for any positive changes. As Walach puts it: "What is not answered is whether the true contribution is the mindfulness practice itself."[42]

Positive effects could simply be attributed to having some downtime during the school day, or feeling heard in discussion. There is also the risk of "social desirability bias," since children know they have been chosen as subjects in a study with expected improvements. Then there is the issue of publication bias, where only positive findings are published. A recent study by a group of psychologists at McGill University found that of the 124 randomized control studies they reviewed, 90% reported positive results.[43] Such a number is quite high given the small sample sizes; a normal, non-biased threshold for this same sample size should be no more than 65%.

Is it irresponsible to teach mindfulness in marginalized communities when the science is so thin? What about to traumatized children? There is significant research that mindfulness-based interventions are contraindicated for trauma sufferers.[44] There are also general indications that this practice is not for everyone. As noted in "Dark Night of the Soul," a 2014 article by one of the experts in this field, Willoughby Britton, "no one has been asking if there are any potential difficulties or adverse effects, and whether there are some practices that may be better or worse-suited [for] some people over others."[45] This is starting to change. A paper in the *International Journal of Psychotherapy* reviewed seventy-five studies that reported negative outcomes from mindfulness meditation.[46] The researchers observed such effects as relaxation-induced anxiety and panic, paradoxical increases in tension, impaired reality testing, and mild dissociation, to name just a few. Britton is also concerned that mindful school programs do not adequately screen children for psychiatric disorders, nor are they cognizant of criteria for exclusion, which for adults include depression, social anxiety, psychosis, PTSD, and suicidal tendencies.

Given the lack of robust research, what remains as a scientific selling point for mindfulness in schools? Programs tend to fall back on neuroscience, and suggestions of neuro-plasticity: look at how mindfulness changes the brain!

What more evidence do we need? Unfortunately the hype around brain imaging is even more pronounced when it comes to young people. This is ironic as there have so far been no neuroscientific studies on how mindfulness affects the brains of children or adolescents. Moreover, it is well known that brain development isn't complete until twenty-five years of age, so the effects of mindfulness on children's brains could be different from those on adults.[47]

However mindfulness programs routinely teach neurological vocabulary, asking children to conceptualize emotions in these terms. A well-trained child might say: "my amygdala hijacked me," with the implication that being "more mindful" might have helped. The import of "folk neurology" into public and educational discourse locates all experiences inside the brain, foreclosing other ways of looking at them. There are also secular objections. A British Royal Society report on "Neuroscience: Implications for Education and Lifelong Learning" is not a ringing endorsement:

> There is great public interest in neuroscience, yet accessible high quality information is scarce. We urge caution in the rush to apply so-called brain-based methods, many of which do not yet have a sound basis in science. There are inspiring developments in basic science although practical applications are still some way off.[48]

Teaching neurological narratives to children is a form of discipline, through which their development can be molded. Having learned the language of neuroscience, they become more obedient to what it transmits. They do so voluntarily, focusing inward on emotional self-regulation, while also internalizing the norms of authority. Should this be in any doubt, consider what might happen if the language were used in other ways — no teacher would accept the excuse "but my amygdala made me do it!"

In this respect, mindfulness in schools is part of a broader social structure forming neoliberal subjects. Students are taught to see themselves as entrepreneurial individuals, who can administer therapy to help them "flourish" at work. Although this is sold as an important skill, it makes children responsible for adapting to circumstances, not trying to change them. Can moments of mindfulness really mitigate the traumas of poverty, pending unemployment, a school-to-prison pipeline, racial profiling and police brutality, gang violence, and institutional racism? Is the problem just a matter of students being unable to "self-regulate" emotions? Framing it as such creates a moral panic, casting teachers of mindfulness as saviors. It's sad that those who have so little are blamed for so much, and merely told to work on their "deficiencies." Instead they could be taught about the underlying problems in society, and ways to address these as part of a broader civic mindfulness. Mindful school advocates present their curricula as being apolitical, non-ideological, and evidence-based, but such claims are illusory.

chapter twelve
Mindful Warriors

In 1966, my uncle returned from his second tour of duty in Vietnam. He told me that on his next tour he would cut off an "ear from a gook" and send it home to me as a souvenir of the war. Disgusted at the time by this grotesque promise, looking back I feel compassion for what he must have endured. My uncle was already suffering from post-traumatic stress disorder (PTSD) due to the horrors he faced as a US Army Vietnamese interpreter, serving on the frontline of an extremely violent and unjust war.

Up to a third of US soldiers now suffer from stress, trauma, and unimaginable pain from repeated service in Iraq and Afghanistan.[1] I believe every effort should be made to ensure that soldiers, reservists and veterans receive the best available medical and psychological treatments for PTSD, including meditative practices. However, the military also uses these methods to "optimize warrior performance" prior to combat deployment.[2] I have strong objections to the use of mindfulness to train better killers.

As described in a statement on the latest research: "The US military has explored offering mindfulness training to soldiers as a low-cost tool to optimize soldiers' cognitive performance and wellbeing."[3] The underlying study tracked one hundred and twenty elite Special Operations Forces troops, who were given a stripped-down eight-hour course in Mindfulness-Based Attention Training (MBAT), a modification of MBSR, like other courses used by the military. Stressing the combat relevance of developing "Sustained Attention Response" skills, the study says: "simulated small-arms engagements involve similar speed-accuracy compensation."[4] In other words, soldiers shoot straighter.

The lead author of this study was Amishi Jha, co-director of the University of Miami's Mindfulness Research and Practice Initiative. According to Jha, a worldwide authority on teaching mindfulness to soldiers, pre-deployment training acts as a form of "mental armor," protecting against combat stress.[5] This strikes me as another example of the military's fondness for Orwellian doublespeak, or what Professor William Lutz calls "language that avoids or shifts responsibility, language that is at variance with its real or purported meaning."[6] It discourages thought, like the euphemistic vagueness of such obfuscating jargon as "surgical strikes" (which often misfire), "collateral damage" (the foreseeable killing of civilians), or "laying down a carpet" (saturation bombing). Telling us that mindfulness is a prophylactic against "the stressors of deployment" is nothing but a smokescreen for the mission of killing.

Let us not forget that the death toll in Iraq since the US-led invasion in 2003 is conservatively estimated at five hundred thousand. Nearly five thousand US soldiers have been killed, and the cost of the unjust wars in Iraq and Afghanistan — with no end to either in sight — had reached $2.4 trillion by 2017, according to the Congressional Budget Office. Civilian casualties in Afghanistan hit a record high in early 2018, averaging about ten deaths a day.

Amoral Maze

Back in 2009, Jha presented findings on military applications of mindfulness to the Dalai Lama. Describing herself as "very conflicted" as to whether her "science might be used for good or evil," she sought approval, saying: "It seems to me that there's a trust in these practices, assuming they're taught properly, that is corrective, that the qualities that might be developed could lead to greater good." Getting no answer, she followed this up by requesting advice. The response was curt. The Dalai Lama said: "Zero!" After a pause in which onlookers laughed, he added: "I appreciate your work. That's all."[7]

Jha defends what she does as harm reduction. "Noncombatant or friendly fire injuries frequently occur when shooters misidentify their target or fail to appropriately inhibit pre-potent responses resulting in unintentional harm to noncombatants or allies," her latest study says. "The chance to intervene against even a single attentional lapse or cognitive failure would be consequential if that failure contributed to unnecessary loss of life or the loss of critical mission objectives."[8]

Surely there are better ways to prevent loss of life than assisting the military with its objectives? The prospects of mindfulness being "taught properly" in this context are highly debatable, especially as programs scale up, while mainly teaching concentration. Jha has received more than $7 million in grants from the US Army and Department of Defense for her research, with a further $1 million from the Henry Jackson Society, a thinktank that promotes an interventionist foreign policy.[9]

The military is spending heavily on mindfulness. The US Army alone has invested over $125 million in researching resilience as part of its "Comprehensive Soldier Fitness" (CSF) initiative.[10] This controversial program awarded Martin Seligman at the University of Pennsylvania a $31 million no-bid contract to teach positive psychology to 1.1 million US soldiers.[11] The CSF program offers training in emotional self-regulation skills, including mindfulness. And the Army Research Laboratory has given Valerie Rice nearly $1 million for related work on "Expeditious Resiliency."

Discussion of the context requiring resilience is taboo. The clinical psychologist John Dyckman recalls attending a meeting with CSF soldiers and civilian personnel. "As a ground rule for our discussion," he says, "they insisted that we not engage in any discussion of the ethics of the 'missions' — i.e. the wars of dubious morality — that they were sent to." When he objected, Dyckman was reminded that elected officials control the armed forces. As he was told: "It is with the government — and the people who elect it — that the moral burden lies."[12]

Meanwhile, scientists build amoral frameworks to militarize mindfulness. The original model — based on MBSR — was called Mindfulness-Based Mind Fitness Training, shortened to MMFT, or "M-Fit." Offered to soldiers before combat deployment, it was based on "real-world examples from the counterinsurgency environment that show how mind fitness skills can enhance performance," according to a study by Jha and Elizabeth Stanley, who created MMFT.[13]

Early experiments with MMFT by the Naval Health Research Center's Warfighter Performance Lab included the creation of a mock Afghan village near San Diego, where platoons of Marines were confronted by blasts and screaming actors to generate stress. "We're giving you these emotions now so when it happens for real, you won't be acting so crazy," First Lieutenant Giles Royster told a team with minimal combat experience. "You'll be able to calm yourself down."[14] The Marines dismissed the idea that they were misappropriating mindfulness: "Some people might say these are Eastern-based religious practices but this goes way beyond that," said Jeffery Bearor at the Marine Corps training and education command in Quantico, Virginia. "This is not tied to any religious practice. This is about mental preparation to better handle stress."[15]

For MMFT's purposes: "Mindfulness is a mental mode characterized by full attention to present-moment experience without judgment, elaboration, or emotional reactivity."[16] This is a paraphrasing of MBSR's operational definition by Jon Kabat-Zinn, who has long been involved with teaching mindfulness to soldiers, still serving Jha as an advisor.[17] In an interview from 2014, as quoted by Elizabeth Stanley, he briefly mentions opposing the war in Vietnam, before reflecting at length on recent hobnobbing with the military, including "a number of generals who were interested in at least talking about the value of greater mindfulness in their commands." Meanwhile, Kabat-Zinn says:

Col Brumage [an Army physician] invited me to come out to Oahu and conduct a two-day mindfulness retreat. Liz Stanley and I led it together for about two hundred people. It felt like we were probably doing more good than harm sowing these seeds. And those explorations continued with the Surgeon General of the Army, and with senior officers in the Navy and Air Force.[18]

Whether or not this little trip to Hawaii was paid for by taxpayers, Kabat-Zinn's collusion with military top brass raises ethical issues. His dislocation of mindfulness from its traditional framework makes it ethically neutral, whatever he "felt like" about "doing more good than harm." The technocratic descriptions of MMFT as "attentional control training" or "stress inoculation" would not have been possible without Kabat-Zinn's reduction of mindfulness to "bare attention," leaving it vulnerable to decontextualized applications. Had the ethical aspects of mindfulness not been removed, such forms of training would not be compatible with the mission of the military, whose soldiers are indoctrinated from boot camp to inflict harm and pain on the enemy.

Kabat-Zinn likes to imagine that mindfulness will somehow undo this, making warriors kinder. "Even if mindfulness is used by the banker or the soldier to improve their professional skills," he once told Oprah Winfrey, "it will also nurture the innate compassion of their humanity."[19] There is really no evidence for this fluffy idea. The US military would surely have stopped investing in mindfulness if it turned trained killers into models of compassion, refusing to follow orders when their consciences objected. It seems that MBAT and MMFT simply do what they advertise: help soldiers to focus and deal with stress. If this stops them shooting frantically at innocents, I suppose that's better than another My Lai, but it does very little to stop the mass killing that war entails.

MMFT's creator, Elizabeth Stanley, is more plainspoken. A former Military Intelligence officer, she comes from, as she puts it, "a long warrior lineage, with Stanleys having served in the US Army every generation since the Revolutionary War."[20] Her description of MMFT makes it clear that killing remains the soldier's core objective:

> A true warrior must be able to still her body and mind to call forth strength; exhibit endurance during harsh environmental conditions; have awareness of herself, others and the wider environment so she can make discerning choices; access compassion for herself, her compatriots, her adversary and the locals where she is deployed; and show self-control during provocation so that she doesn't overreact. And yet, if the moment demands, she must also have the capacity to kill, cleanly, without hesitation and without remorse.[21]

As she reflects elsewhere, the basic teaching of MMFT — "paying attention to what's happening" — is by no means new. "Warriors have been using these techniques for millennia before they go to battle," she says. "Meditation may become as standard in the military as rifle practice, another way of making troops more effective and resilient."[22] She is not mistaken. When Buddhism has been closely allied with the state, it has also been used as an instrument of militarization. This is particularly likely when its ethical moorings are removed, as happened with Japanese Zen in World War II.

Zen and the Art of the M-16

In his book *Zen at War*, Brian Victoria exposes how both the Soto and Rinzai sects of Japanese Buddhism supported military imperialism.[23] At the start of the twentieth century, Japan had won a famous victory over Russia — the first time an Asian power had defeated Europeans. Many apologists for the war attributed Japan's fierce fighting spirit to the ancient code of Bushido, the Way of the Warrior. Warped interpretations of ideas such as "emptiness" (*ku*) and "no mind" (*mu*) fed a non-dual theory that acts of killing had no karmic effect. Takuan, a seventeenth-century Zen master, assured his samurai disciples: "The uplifted sword has no will of its own, it is all of emptiness. The man who is about to be struck down is also of emptiness, and so is the one who wields the sword."

This line was quoted by the influential scholar D.T. Suzuki's *Zen and Japanese Culture*, first published in 1938. Better known in the West as an inspiring teacher in the 1950s, he also helped to rationalize death during World War II. The imperialist version of Zen revised Buddhist doctrines, and coopted meditation for the war effort. Incredible as it might sound, war was seen as an expression of compassion. Fighting, and even dying in battle, was a way to repay a debt of gratitude to the emperor, and Japanese warriors were considered "bodhisattvas," fearlessly offering their lives to save the state.

"The sword is generally associated with killing, and most of us wonder how it can come into connection with Zen, which is a school of Buddhism teaching the gospel of love and mercy," Suzuki wrote in *Zen and Japanese Culture*.

"The fact is that the art of swordsmanship distinguishes between the sword that kills and the sword that gives life." As he sought to explain, "one who is compelled to lift the sword" has a higher calling than mere killing. Should he ever wield it mortally, "it is as though the sword performs automatically its function of justice, which is the function of mercy."[24]

This unity of Zen and the sword played a fundamental role in indoctrinating troops. Another widely cited teacher was Suzuki Shosan, whose seventeenth-century teachings had stressed the importance of *samadhi*, a Sanskrit term often translated as "meditative absorption." The single-minded concentration of samurai warriors was the source of their power, Shosan explained. "The military arts in particular can't be executed with a slack mind," he said. "This energy of Zen *samadhi* is everything. The man of arms, however, is in Zen *samadhi* while he applies his skill."[25]

In particular, Shosan emphasized the need to practice *tokinokoe zazen*, or Zen meditation "in the midst of war cries." This sounds rather like the modernized version of military mindfulness, with screaming actors drilling Marines to face battlefield stress. Consider Shoshan's admonition to a warrior:

It's best to practice *zazen* from the start amid hustle and bustle. A warrior, in particular, absolutely must practice *zazen* that works amid war cries. Gunfire crackles, spears clash down the line, a roar goes up and the fray is on: and that's where, firmly disposed, he puts meditation into action. At a time like that, what use could he have for a *zazen* that prefers quiet? However fond of Buddhism a warrior may be, he'd better throw it out if it doesn't work amid war cries.[26]

As Brian Victoria's book explains, in World War II "cross-legged meditation (*zazen*) was the fountainhead of the mental power derived from *samadhi*, a power that was available to modern Japanese soldiers as it had once been to *samurai* warriors."[27] A similar one-pointed focus inspired special attack units of *kamikaze* ("divine wind") pilots. The Soto Zen priest Masunaga Reiho even said their suicidal spirit was a "conversion of mind as the achievement of complete enlightenment."[28]

Contrary to these claims — as well as the modern idea that mindfulness is merely paying attention — traditional Buddhist teachings place a clear prohibition on intentionally killing living beings. This cardinal precept is found in many forms in Buddhist doctrine, but they all share a basic commitment to non-violence, non-harming of others and the cultivation of good will towards all sentient beings.

When separated from these ideas — or allied to political doctrines like militarist Zen, or the demonization of minority Muslims in modern Myanmar — spiritual practices such as mindfulness are easily perverted to justify violence. Because Elizabeth Stanley thinks MMFT is a just a way to enhance concentration, she sees no problem with using it to train mindful killers. In a chapter in *Bio-Inspired Innovation and National Security*, Stanley writes:

The military already incorporates mindfulness training — although it does not call it this — into perhaps *the* most fundamental solider skill, firing a weapon. Soldiers learning how to fire the M-16 rifle are taught to pay attention to their breath and synchronize the breathing process to the trigger finger's movement, "squeezing" off the round while exhaling.[29]

The unity of mindfulness with firing a weapon is remarkably similar to Suzuki's propaganda on Zen and the sword.

Mindful Terrorists

Japanese assassins used Zen *samadhi* power in the 1930s, killing the former finance minister, among others. As one of the killers explained when brought to trial:

After starting my practice of *zazen*, I entered a state of *samadhi* the likes of which I had never experienced before. I felt my spirit become unified, really unified, and when I opened my eyes from their half-closed meditative position I noticed the smoke from the incense curling up and touching the ceiling. At this point it suddenly came to me — I would be able to carry out [the killing] that night.[30]

A more contemporary example of something similar is the Norwegian far-right extremist and mass murderer Anders Behring Breivik. In 2011, Breivik detonated a car bomb in downtown Oslo, killing eight people. He then went on a shooting spree, killing sixty-nine others at a summer camp. As well as identifying as a fascist, a worshipper of Odin and a Nazi, Breivik compared himself to a Japanese *banzai* warrior seeking enlightenment. In a psychiatric evaluation, Breivik described how he used meditation to "numb the full spectrum of human emotion — happiness to sorrow, despair, hopelessness and fear."[31] Yet this taught him no empathy for his victims. A court psychiatric expert wrote in his report:

> He shows no emotion in relation to the act he is charged with, and explains his desensitized state as a result of meditation (*Bushido* = meditation to be able to show contempt of death), like other 'Warriors' for example Afghanistan soldiers and others who must do what they do (take lives).[32]

These examples illustrate the dangers of viewing meditation as simply a method for training attention. Decontextualizing mindfulness makes it more available to terrorists and killers. Yet whenever Kabat-Zinn is asked to address these important concerns about militarized practice, he responds with trademark flowery vagueness:

> Woven into mindfulness is an orientation towards non-harming and seeing deeply into the nature of things, which in some way implies, or at least invites, seeing the interconnectedness between the seer and the seen, the object and the subject. It is a non-dual perspective from the very beginning, resting on an ethical foundation.[33]

He compounds this by claiming that mindfulness, as he imparts it, involves the cultivation of "affectionate attention," and that it is therefore inherently wholesome.[34]

The idea of a solider showing "affectionate attention" towards an Afghan while pulling the trigger on his M-16 seems absurd. How exactly does training combat troops result in "non-harming" and "seeing the interconnectedness" between Marines and their targets? It seems very difficult to integrate ethics into military mindfulness, not least on account of the dubious nature of US missions and political objectives.

As noted by Matthieu Ricard, a French Buddhist monk, "there can be mindful snipers and mindful psychopaths who maintain a calm and stable mind. But there cannot be caring snipers and caring psychopaths."[35] Training soldiers to care while killing seems unlikely to change much, however sincerely people try. Rejecting the rationalizations of Kabat-Zinn, John Dyckman suggests learning from Japanese Zen Buddhism, which is still suffering from its enthusiastic collaboration with militarism. "We need to be very careful in separating the 'techniques' of Buddhist practice from the context of non-violence lest we repeat the same shameful history," Dyckman warns.[36]

Proponents of military mindfulness call it a form of "harm reduction." They say it improves working memory capacity and emotional self-regulation, preventing soldiers in war zones from overreacting. These are not empty statements, and it is obviously better to distinguish combatants from children. However, focusing on such benefits shifts attention away from the broader ethics and politics of using mindfulness to make trained killers more effective. "Attention control" for soldiers needs to be differentiated from Buddhist *right mindfulness* — where the aim is not improvements in marksmanship, but to develop compassion, wholesome mental states, and skillful (non-harming) behaviors, which are put in the service of all sentient beings, including those perceived as "enemies".[37]

This is far from the objectives of MMFT, MBAT or any other form of military training in concentration skills. A few moving vignettes about soldiers avoiding snap judgments that could have killed civilians does not amount to evidence that these practices have ethical benefits. Perhaps in the circumscribed world of "military ethics," this counts as a breakthrough. But it means very little when the US invades other countries without justification, dismissing the authority of any institution to charge it with war crimes.

The US military is a highly organized system of violence and institutionalized ill will. Killing is its *raison d'être*. It is a little known fact that 75-80% of soldiers did not fire on exposed enemies in World War II, which caused US generals great concern. By the height of the Vietnam War, the firing rate had been increased to nearly 95% as a result of enhanced psychological techniques in boot camp.[38] These are now well established, using desensitization, operational conditioning and the defense mechanism of denial. Recruits are systematically trained to inflict harm when ordered. Mindfulness just makes them more resilient. If that decreases the chances that they return home and kill themselves, or commit violent crimes, then perhaps that counts as harm reduction. But it is really a very far cry from the Hippocratic Oath, and its principle of *starting* by doing no harm, which is the context in which MBSR was originally developed.

There is nothing in the Buddha's discourses to justify the intentional killing of another human being — civilian or

enemy. Scholars such as P.D. Premasiri and Laksiri Jayas-
uriya assure us that the concept of *holy war* — or even
a "just war" — cannot be found in the early Buddhist
canon.[39] [40] Although the Buddha did not deny the inevitable reality of human conflict, he avoided cozying up to
armies and teaching their soldiers to be more resilient.
Instead, he advised kings and generals to avoid violent
means, counseling them to examine the genesis of conflict
and to identify skillful behaviors to resolve them.

If MBSR is, as Kabat-Zinn claims, an expression of the
"universal dharma that is co-extensive, if not identical,
with the teachings of the Buddha," then the mindfulness
community has a clear choice. Either it should state
clearly that military adaptations are not in accordance
with Buddhist teachings, or it should acknowledge its own
complicity in US militarism, confronting ethical dilemmas
with courage and honesty, not platitudes and doublespeak.

chapter thirteen
Mindful Politics

After winning a third term in the swing state of Ohio, Congressman Tim Ryan was stressed. He signed up for a mindfulness retreat with Jon Kabat-Zinn, and had an epiphany. Freed from the pressure in his head, he felt a sudden urge to share the benefits of mindfulness with everyone. "Why didn't anyone teach me this when I was a kid?" he reflects in his book *A Mindful Nation*. "I wanted to teach it to my two-year-old nephew, to my brother, to my mom." Quickly realizing that he'd got "a little carried away," his buttoned-down self took charge. "I decided I would advocate in Congress and on the Appropriations Committee for integrating mindfulness into key aspects of society."[1]

Kabat-Zinn was delighted. "Each one of us could influence the world by taking a degree of personal responsibility for developing our own unique ways to embody mindful awareness," he writes in a foreword to Ryan's book. "That may well be one of the most profound ways we can contribute to the wellbeing of the larger society and the planet itself."[2] This is Kabat-Zinn's revolutionary vision: changing the world, one individual at a time. "The shift in consciousness that mindfulness involves really is a radical act, in the sense of going to the very root of our problems with suffering and its human causes," he says.[3] All we have to do is search inside ourselves, and the world will be transformed. So the only thing we need to do materially is train more mindfulness teachers.

However, what if Ryan had a different mission? When he marveled at his mindful moment with a raisin ("Have you ever just looked at one?"), what if he had seen it from a broader perspective than his self-centered view? Never mind how the raisin looks, feels, smells and tastes to a privileged congressman, what if Ryan had contemplated the farm where the raisin was grown by Hispanic migrants doing back-breaking work in the San Joaquin valley, earning a cent for every two-hundred grapes harvested. Reflection on the raisin could call to mind units from US Immigration and Customs Enforcement rounding up workers like cattle and deporting them. Might Ryan be cognizant of the smog where the raisin was grown? What about the water shortages, or the fossil fuels burned to transport raisins from central California to his Catskills retreat? What about the grocery store staff that unloaded, unpacked and stocked raisins on the shelf? Would Ryan be mindful of the fact that the CEOs who run large agribusiness and grocery chains earn hundreds of times as much as store clerks?

Needless to say, his book raises none of these questions. Instead, Ryan hawks a form of "mind cure" that stems from nineteenth-century New Thought, which taught that positive mental training could rid individuals of disease. It is unsurprising that his early inspiration was Deepak Chopra, a purveyor of Hindu mysticism dressed up as science. "I think I listened to the *Seven Spiritual Laws of Success* a million and a half times driving back and forth to law school," Ryan recalls.[4] A former high-school quarterback, he got interested in mindfulness when he learned that Phil Jackson, the legendary NBA coach, had taught Michael Jordan and the Chicago Bulls to meditate. If it helped them compete, it must really be powerful. No wonder Ryan wants to share it with everyone; winning is the name of the game in the neoliberal world in which he thrives. When he was elected in 2002, aged twenty-nine, he was the youngest congressman. Now he thinks mindfulness will help him work better with Donald Trump — and maybe even beat him.[5]

Politics as Therapy

Many of the people whom Ryan represents are far from winning. His district includes the rust belt city of Youngstown, whose decline was immortalized in song by Bruce Springsteen. Once known as Steeltown, Youngstown has lost more than 60% of its population since manufacturing collapsed, depriving it of thousands of well-paying jobs. Plagued by high rates of poverty, unemployment, crime, domestic violence, and mental illness, the city hovers near the bottom of the Gallup Wellbeing index, and in 2014 was officially the most miserable place to live in the United States. How might mindfulness help the survivors in a town that resembles a bombed out war-zone? Will a more positive mental attitude bring back jobs? Are inhabitants to blame for their stress and anxiety? Is there more to being mindful than stoically accepting a dire situation?

Not apparently for Ryan, or Kabat-Zinn. Both men are congenital optimists, seeing the issue as restoring hope by building character. As the subtitle of Ryan's book puts it, mindfulness can "recapture the American spirit." The sky is literally the limit. "The mindfulness movement is not quite as dramatic as the moon shot," Ryan writes, "or the civil rights movement, but I believe in the long run it can have just as great an impact."[6] Exciting stuff! So, what does it consist of? The usual inward focus, of course, letting go of painful thoughts: that way, the downtrodden of Youngstown can "rediscover their American values that lead to a prosperous life."[7]

Kabat-Zinn is more overtly depoliticized, having already reduced mindfulness to an "ideological opiate," to quote Craig Martin's term in *Capitalizing Religion*.[8] Kabat-Zinn's psychologized version tells individuals to reframe their experience, ignoring what caused it — or engaging politically to change those conditions. "Mindfulness is not a matter of left or right, Republican or Democrat, liberal or conservative," he writes in the foreword to Ryan's book. "Ultimately, it is about being human, pure and simple."[9] He seems to be suggesting that this pure human nature arises from nowhere, so anyone can be freed of their social conditioning, as long as they are mindful enough to tune out of it. And if that means accepting that the odds are stacked against them, then so be it.

This hyper-individual religion has policy outcomes. Ryan sits on both the House Appropriations Committee and the House Budget Committee — two powerful arbiters of federal expenditures. Ryan's vision of mindfulness does not involve changing economic priorities to make society less brutally competitive and unequal. Instead, he aims to help people cope with these painful conditions by improving access to privatized mindfulness training in schools, corporations, government and the military.

Although Ryan is a Democrat, his idea of a "mindful nation" is conservative, making individuals responsible for their own welfare. Self-help rhetoric cloaks the realm of political struggle — undermining solidarity and quests for social and economic justice. Everything else is subordinate to personal efforts to be more mindful. "We don't need to move to the left or to the right," Ryan writes. "We all need to go a little deeper."[10] This well-intentioned "politics of depth," with its hope for a kinder, more compassionate world, stands little chance against the daily realities of neoliberal culture.

Like organic food and commodified yoga, mindfulness has wide appeal but no political affiliation. Moreover, argues Matthew Moore, a professor of political science: "Because mindfulness seems unlikely to change people's fundamental values or beliefs, wider practice of mindfulness would not be likely to bring otherwise unsympathetic Americans closer to the left."[11]

This is a missed opportunity. Stress is demonstrably linked to social hierarchies, and researchers such as Nancy Adler at the University of California San Francisco have shown that perceived socioeconomic status is a robust predictor of a range of ailments, including cardiovascular disease, hypertension, diabetes, arthritis, stress and depression.[12] Meanwhile, the quality of social relations depends on adequate material foundations. In *The Spirit Level*, Richard Wilkinson and Kate Pickett observe that "the scale of inequality provides a powerful policy lever on the psychological wellbeing of all of us."[13]

None of this is mentioned in *A Mindful Nation*. Instead, Ryan claims that the issues afflicting society are caused by our distraction from our authentic inner selves. His diagnosis is flawed and misguided. He might even use it to run for the presidency. In the summer of 2018, he was said to be targeting "yoga voters." James Gimian, a friend of Ryan's who publishes *Mindful* magazine, calls this constituency "the kind of folks who realize that while they grew up with their mom saying 'Pay attention,' nobody trained them in how to pay attention and use their mind to focus on what's important."[14]

What's important for Ryan is turning inwards. He started a "Quiet Time Caucus" on Capitol Hill, gathering a handful of Democratic staffers and members of Congress for a meditative time out. The benefits seem to boil down to being less judgmental. If we are more mindful, "we may be just a little less critical of others, and of ourselves," he says. "We may more easily forgive the people who have hurt us. We may sit down and have civil political conversations with those who strongly disagree with us."[15] Or we may just tune out, like the Google executives confronted by protestors at Wisdom 2.0. Either way, his revolutionary slogan seems no more inspiring than "can't we all just get along?"

This is unsurprising, since he borrows so heavily from Kabat-Zinn. Ever the guru, Kabat-Zinn prefers mystical waffle to taking a stand that might narrow his audience. His goal is to make people mindful. If enough of us practice, a critical mass could be attained. If politicians join us, they might become kinder, and engage more fruitfully. Perhaps they can even lead us to the promised land of milk and honey. But the last thing we need right now is a political agenda, as Kabat-Zinn tells us in *Coming to Our Senses*:

Cultivating greater mindfulness in our lives does not imply that we would fall into one set of ideological views and opinions or another, but that we might see more freshly for ourselves, with eyes of wholeness, moment by moment. But what mindfulness can do for us, and it is a very important function, is reveal our opinions, and all opinions, *as opinions*, so that we will know them for what they are and perhaps not be so caught by them and blinded by them, whatever their content.[16]

Perhaps. This is one of Kabat-Zinn's favorite disclaimers. His hopeful assertions are littered with qualifiers like "might" and "may," but he asks us to take them on faith. When pushed for supporting evidence, he effectively shrugs and says: "who knows?" As he puts it himself in a scholarly article: "I love the whole notion that it may be too early to tell."[17]

Make America Mindful Again

Ryan and Kabat-Zinn seem to confuse their advocacy of being fully present in the moment with particular forms of political consciousness. Being present is not a guarantee of being just. There is a naïve assumption that spiritual practice develops a "progressive" point of view, so examples of practitioners with different perspectives are dismissed with the claim that they must have practiced wrongly. Yet Heinrich Himmler, the head of the Nazi SS and master architect of the Holocaust, was a fan of yoga and meditation

— he even planned retreats for elite SS members at a medieval castle.[18] He thought yogic practice could internally arm soldiers for battle and help death camp guards to process stress.[19]

Unconvinced by Kabat-Zinn's conjectures, the political scientist and Buddhist scholar Matthew Moore argues that mindfulness might even harden our opinions:

> If through my mindfulness practice I notice that many of my beliefs and dispositions are variable and unstable, but two or three beliefs are consistent and ever-present, I may conclude that those beliefs are not merely central to my experience but true. To the extent that this happens, mindfulness may have the effect, contrary to the hopes of Ryan and Kabat-Zinn, of making me less humble, less flexible, less tolerant, and less willing to engage with people who believe different things.[20]

Ryan seems unwilling to engage more fully with workers' interests. Even though one of his districts swung Republican in 2016 after losing nineteen thousand manufacturing jobs, he is wary of speaking the language of class struggle. "You're not going to make me hate somebody just because they're rich," Ryan told moderate Democrats in 2018, distancing himself from socialists like Bernie Sanders. "I want to be rich!"[21] If he were to run for president, Ryan would prefer to speak to yoga practitioners, who are estimated to number tens of millions. He might find this turns workers off. For now, he's trying to sell himself to both. "I think once you meet me, you realize I'm not necessarily some soft yoga guy," he says. "I've been in the union halls. I'll drink a Miller Lite with you."[22]

Perhaps, as Kabat-Zinn might say — but it doesn't stop Ryan's agenda furthering priorities that disempower workers. Under the prevailing neoliberal consensus, economic policy serves the interests of capital. Individuals bear the brunt of the consequences, and are told to treat their wounds with the practice of mindfulness. The practice also teaches self-discipline, so they mindfully learn to compete for opportunities. This is presented as freedom, and social solidarity is framed as a burden. As Sam Binkley notes in *Happiness as Enterprise*, the whole neoliberal project, supported by mindfulness, is "a privatization of workplace angst and the suppression of its collectivizing potential."[23]

Ryan is clearly sincere and enthusiastic. He seems optimistic that mindfulness can transform failing public schools and dysfunctional healthcare systems, and even catalyze a different economy. The exaggerated promises and heightened expectations — combined with media and scientific interest, and commercial pressures — are generating hype. This has made mindfulness more than a simple passing fad — it's become institutionalized. But so were other fads that came and went. Just because mindfulness is everywhere doesn't mean it's everything that everyone needs. However, Ryan is caught up in the buzz, and seems unable to see past buzzwords.

The subtext throughout his book is that the elixir of mindfulness can salvage society. "We don't need a new set of values," Ryan writes. "I really believe we can reinvigorate our traditional, commonly held American values — such as self-reliance, perseverance, pragmatism, and taking care of each other — by adding a little more mindfulness to our lives."[24] We don't even need new ideas. We just need to make America great again. As usual, this comes straight from Kabat-Zinn, who wistfully repackages nineteenth-century Transcendentalism.

Recalling Henry David Thoreau's celebration of nature and aimless strolling, Kabat-Zinn makes it sound like nothing else is needed. "Thoreau was singing a song which needed hearing then as it does now," he writes. "He is, to this day, continually pointing out, for anyone willing to listen, the deep importance of contemplation and of non-attachment to any result other than the sheer enjoyment of being."[25]

Mindful Lobbying

Regardless, Kabat-Zinn seems attached to promoting mindfulness in government. He has had more success in the United Kingdom, where he met members of parliament in 2012, along with Lord Richard Layard — a promoter of "happiness economics" — and the creator of Mindfulness-Based Cognitive Therapy, Mark Williams. In 2013, Williams and Chris Cullen from the Oxford Mindfulness Centre led an eight-week mindfulness course for MPs. Since then, over two hundred parliamentarians and hundreds of staff have taken courses.

Mindfulness in Westminster has been a focus of media attention, with most of the emphasis placed on its power to treat mental health problems. The comedian Ruby Wax, who credits mindfulness with saving her life, has also told MPs it could help them win votes by helping them to focus better on voters.[26] As early as 2004, Williams secured the endorsement of the National Institute for Health and Care Excellence for using MBCT to treat recurrent depression on the state-funded National Health Service (NHS).[27]

In the media, and in formal government briefings, rising rates of depression, anxiety and mental illness are dramatically emphasized. Though its promoters mumble the caveat that mindfulness may not suit everybody, they mostly wax exuberant about its benefits. When mental illness is discussed, it is mysteriously divorced from the social, economic, and political conditions that exacerbate it. Its symptoms are mostly framed as self-contained personal problems that can be treated with "evidenced-based" scientific mindfulness, helping people back to work to be productive. The appeal of mindfulness has increased after a decade of austerity-driven cuts to the NHS and public services. As Madeleine Bunting, a *Guardian* columnist, says, "mindfulness has unlimited applicability to almost every healthcare issue we now face — and it's cheap."[28]

Bunting co-launched an advocacy group in 2013. Founded at the instigation of Labour MP Chris Ruane, The Mindfulness Initiative lobbies politicians and their policy advisors to support the funding and teaching of mindfulness, both in the UK and around the world.[29] It draws on the work of mindfulness research and training centers in Oxford, Exeter, Bangor, and Sussex. And in 2014, it helped to set up the Mindfulness All-Party Parliamentary Group (MAPPG), whose stated purpose is: "To review research evidence, current best practice, extent and success of implementation, and potential developments in the application of mindfulness within a range of policy areas, and to develop policy recommendations for government based on these findings."[30]

The creation of the MAPPG received gushing media coverage, some of it from those personally involved. "It was an arresting occasion partly due to the setting," wrote Ed Halliwell, who was at the time a co-chair of The Mindfulness Initiative, a contributor to *Mindful* magazine, and a prominent mindfulness teacher:

> We are perhaps getting used to meditation happening in health centers, private businesses, even schools — but here it was being practiced and taken seriously in the symbol of the British establishment, by politicians from all three main parties, offered up as a way to approach some of the most pressing social issues of our time.[31]

The MAPPG led a nine-month study, culminating in a 2015 report, *Mindful Nation UK*.[32] This came with a foreword by Kabat-Zinn, declaring that it "may be a singular and defining document" with findings "addressing some of the most pressing problems of society at their very root — at the level of the human mind and heart."[33] The executive summary proposed rolling out mindfulness programs in the healthcare system, schools, workplaces, and prisons. "Our long-term vision," said the authors, who included both Halliwell and Bunting, "is of the UK as a group of mindful nations, an international pioneer of a National Mental Health Service which has, at its heart, a deep understanding of how best to support human flourishing and thereby the prosperity of the country."

A few days prior to the report's publication, Kabat-Zinn wrote a glowing endorsement of his own, deftly sidestepping critics by warning about "opportunistic elements" that seek to cash in on the craze for mindfulness:

Some have expressed concerns that a sort of superficial "McMindfulness" is taking over which ignores the ethical foundations of the meditative practices and traditions from which mindfulness has emerged, and divorces it from its profoundly transformative potential. While this is far from the norm in my experience, these voices argue that for certain opportunistic elements, mindfulness has become a business that can only disappoint the vulnerable consumers who look to it as a panacea.[34]

This also came with an assurance that nothing he endorses could possibly be part of this critique, since he well understands that "a real understanding of the subtlety of mindfulness is required if it is to be taught effectively."[35] However, the problem isn't just bad courses — or auxiliary products such as mindful coloring books, apps, massage oils, or cosmetics. Commercialized mindfulness involves selling specialist expertise in the form of training programs, for which Kabat-Zinn wants public money. "Funding is necessary to bring a high-quality evidence base into step with widespread popularity, to establish and disseminate best practice and train teachers, and to identify and properly support those most in need of mindfulness," he writes. "Governments and public bodies have a crucial role to play in improving access to the best evidence-based courses."[36]

Kabat-Zinn seems to suddenly want to get on the right side of history with regards to McMindfulness. "This is not McMindfulness by any stretch of the imagination," he told *The Psychologist* a few months earlier.[37] When asked about his role in the commercialized McMindfulness craze, he is predictably dismissive. "First of all, that term first came out of one person's mouth or one person's mind. When you say it is popping up, of course, every term like that tends to just go viral on the web, but it just came out of one person's mind."[38] Yes, the term came out of my mind (and also my co-author's, David Loy, making that two minds) when we published our viral article "Beyond McMindfulness." Defending his MBSR brand, Kabat-Zinn claims, "It's about the teachings of the Buddha." Which sums up the problem: it's Buddhist when it suits him, but not when it doesn't. As for other "opportunistic elements," two of *Mindful Nation UK*'s editors are professional mindfulness teachers. This obstacle to skepticism — with lobbyists preparing a policy document seeking government funds — wasn't addressed with a conflict of interest statement, which is a standard requirement in reputable scientific journals.

Along with Ed Halliwell, the other teacher-cum-editor is a Buddhist, known as Vishvapani. He was given this name by the Triratna Buddhist Order (formerly called the Friends of the Western Buddhist Order), which runs mindfulness courses in most of its centers across the UK, and all over the world.[39] Another Triratna member advises The Mindfulness Initiative, which bills her as follows: "Vidyamala is co-founder and Director of Breathworks — an international mindfulness teacher training and delivery organization specializing in mindfulness for pain, illness and stress."[40] In addition to teaching courses of his own, via a private company, Vishvapani is an associate of Breathworks.[41]

The Triratna organization has itself been criticized. There were numerous allegations of sexual abuse by its leader Sangharakshita (Dennis Lingwood), who died in 2018, aged ninety-three. Lingwood urged heterosexual followers to try homosexuality, allegedly telling one unhappy young man "you need to keep persevering."[42] He later apologized for "all the occasions on which I have hurt, harmed or upset fellow Buddhists."[43]

Caveat Emptor

The commodification of mindfulness has led to teachers being professionalized. Consumers of mindfulness programs are often called "clients" or "service users." This colonization of the teaching process by market logic, with its demands for competition, marketing savvy and entrepreneurship, seems to weigh on Vishvapani, who admits:

> Mindfulness trainers like me can now earn a living from teaching meditation: for a few it is a very good living. But doing so mixes one's practice with drives such as anxiety about money, ambition and the desire for status. Similar issues arise in any vocational pursuit, but we need to be alert to them if our practice is to keep its integrity. My concern about the secular mindfulness movement is not so much that the practice is co-opted and commercialized, as that practitioners are.[44]

Slick presentation is no guarantee of a teacher's competence. *Mindful Nation UK* acknowledges the challenges of upholding standards by regulating teachers. In an article addressing the problem — titled "Has the science of mindfulness lost its mind?" — the researchers Miguel Farias and Catherine Wikholm note: "there is no professional or statutory registration required to teach mindfulness-based interventions such as MBSR and MBCT."[45] Since anyone with minimal training can set up shop, the only mark of a teacher is having students. In the meantime, *Mindful Nation UK* is creating what Kathryn Ecclestone calls an "unaccountable state-sponsored intervention market," in which the vulnerable are not only molded to suit the interests of neoliberalism, but also actively monetized by "new types of therapeutic entrepreneurs."[46]

The UK report says the main obstacle to implementing its ideas is a shortage of teachers. Although it estimates that 2,200 mindfulness teachers had been trained in the previous decade, only seven hundred were deemed clinically qualified to teach MBCT to depressed NHS patients. These seven hundred were thought to be able to treat twenty-five thousand people annually, which equates to "just 4.3% of the 580,000 adults at risk of recurrent depression each year."[47]

However, there are also other aspects to the problem. As Farias and Wikholm warn, since anyone can teach mindfulness without being a therapist, or having formal mental health training, under-qualified teachers could soon fill the vacuum:

For individuals experiencing common difficulties such as stress, anxiety or depression and considering paying for therapy or attending a mindfulness group, the combination of media hype and comparative affordability of a mindfulness group may easily sway them to opt for this, potentially placing their mental health in the hands of someone who may lack adequate training and experience working with psychological difficulties.[48]

Glossing over such issues, the report urges policymakers to invest in training one hundred new MBCT teachers annually over five years, at an estimated total cost of £50 million.[49] The authors cite research by Mark Williams, who created MBCT and introduced it to MPs, suggesting the treatment helps prevent multiple episodes of depression, reducing relapse rates by 43%. However, MBCT is not necessarily this effective. A follow-up study by Williams — not cited in the report — found reductions only applied to those who had experienced three or more depressive relapses, while the rate of relapse for subjects with two or fewer episodes actually increased.[50] The most benefit accrued to the most psychologically vulnerable, who had experienced childhood trauma and abuse. This only adds to concerns about whether mindfulness teachers with no professional training in psychotherapy can be expected to care for such people competently and safely.

Other important findings were ignored. One meta-analytic study by researchers at Johns Hopkins University — well-publicized in 2014 — showed that mindfulness was no more effective than physical exercise or other relaxation techniques. It found moderate improvements in depression, anxiety, and pain, and very small reductions in stress, but there were few other measurable benefits.[51] Another major trial on MBCT — conducted by an advisor to the Mindfulness Initiative, Willem Kuyken — found no evidence that it was more effective at preventing relapses than antidepressant medication.[52] It was not even more cost-effective, despite suggestions to the contrary in *Mindful Nation UK*.

Just Stop and Drop

A core group of about twenty British politicians attends a weekly drop-in mindfulness class at Westminster. Teachers also offer twice-yearly silent practice days. Politicians enthuse about the positive effects on their attention spans, impulse control, kindness, and meta-cognition skills. One Labour member of the House of Lords, Andrew Stone, says being mindful helps him have "different kinds of conversations."[53] A Conservative MP, Tim Loughton, takes hour-long baths and expenses his water bill to taxpayers, saying: "I also reserve a little part of ablution time for some mindfulness."[54] The director of The Mindfulness Initiative, Jamie Bristow, parses such comments in Kabat-Zinn-ese: "This increased familiarity with inner experience in the act of political discourse represents a significant, if not profound shift towards less tangible insights into the human condition, that may offer a key to some of society's most pressing problems."[55]

For now, British politicians are spreading the gospel of mindfulness training, addressing other parliaments around the world. More than a dozen national legislatures are introducing courses. In 2017, MPs and Lords welcomed politicians from fourteen countries to the "Mindfulness in Politics Day" at Westminster. Esther Ouwehand from the Netherlands summed up the benefits from her perspective: "Mindfulness really enables me to stay in touch with what is most important to me: my own values."[56]

Apparently fearing this might be misread, The Mindfulness Initiative's Jamie Bristow — who reported the remark — was quick to stress: "Mindfulness practice is often miscast as a symptom of navel-gazing individualism."[57] As he sees it, what has happened in parliament shows "consideration of mindfulness as helpful to the whole: the whole body politic, the whole of society." Bristow's colleague Willem Kuyken goes further, comparing the significance of Kabat-Zinn's work to that of Darwin and Einstein: "What they did for biology and physics, Jon has done for a new frontier: the science of the human mind and heart."[58]

Before addressing the 2017 summit, Kabat-Zinn told a journalist: "This is not a weirdo lunatic fringe trying to take over the world, but an oxygen line straight into the heart of what is deepest and most beautiful in us as human beings."[59] Also in attendance, "remotely," was Congressman Tim Ryan. He told the same reporter: "Meditation allows me to take a timeout, step back and see issues as interconnected. That kind of big-picture problem-solving is desperately lacking in both US political parties today, and has in many cases been replaced with an almost hyper-partisan kind of hate."[60] In Ryan's view, "we must intentionally try to reduce the influence of these things in our lives so we can think clearly and dispassionately about how we build a better future."[61]

There is obvious merit to this basic idea, but at some point we have to do the actual building. And that takes more than Kabat-Zinn's reheated Transcendentalism, and its unproven claims about a universal goodness accessible to all through "bare attention." Yet he refuses to talk about more than tuning into the moment, which is certainly calming but not a great fount of political wisdom. Unfazed, Kabat-Zinn asserts that turning inward on oneself can fix fake news and overturn the surveillance state, whose requirements it subtly instills through self-regulation:

The mainstreaming of dharma through mindfulness is *prima facie* a positive and healing occurrence and a tremendous opportunity for addressing some of the most fundamental sources of pain and suffering in our world at this moment in time. That would include the Orwellian distortions of truth we are now seeing on a daily basis in the news, and the perpetuation of dystopian "governance" by seemingly elevating greed, hatred, and delusion to new heights, with all its attendant consequences for the fragility of democratic institutions.[62]

But for all this overblown rhetoric about the common good, Kabat-Zinn's emphasis is on individuals and personal fulfillment. The social world — as it seemed to Thoreau, his inspiration — becomes a source of distraction from innocent freedom in the moment. One of Kabat-Zinn's favorite aphorisms is just to "drop in" to this pleasing immediacy.

As he recently put it: "Stop and drop: meaning, drop in to your experience of experiencing, and for even the briefest of moments, simply holding it in awareness as it is."[63]

Meanwhile, his disciples in the corridors of power note "the concept of 'mental capital' has helped leaders and policymakers to see that the cognitive and emotional capacities of individuals determine the health, resilience and future performance of businesses," to quote The Mindfulness Initiative's Jamie Bristow.[64]

Such base concerns are not discussed by Kabat-Zinn. His vision of a mindful politics is that by accessing "pure awareness" — letting go of attachment to "doing" — we will rediscover the innocence of our untrammeled inner nature. He sees mindfulness as the gateway to authenticity, and becoming truly human. Like the mindful nations in the heads of Tim Ryan and UK MPs, no specific prescriptions for collective change need be provided. Simply by stopping and "dropping in," we will be fully autonomous — happy servants of a neoliberal order that they probably imagine they oppose.

conclusion
Liberating Mindfulness

As mindfulness is currently taught, its revolutionary rhetoric is a myth. Even if it helps us feel better, the causes of suffering in the world remain unchanged. To understand why, let's consider Donald Trump. Ever since this clown from reality TV took the global stage, I've been perplexed about the source of his undeniable appeal to millions of voters. I've read many accounts by political pundits, and none are fully persuasive. So I'd like to offer one of my own. Most of us have traits of dishonesty, hypocrisy, arrogance, greed, shortsightedness, racism, hatred, fear, self-centeredness, and stupidity. We are prone to feeling guilty about ourselves as a result, which is part of the endemic low self-esteem in modern culture. Trump not only displays these tendencies without a trace of conscience, he unabashedly flaunts them, encouraging his followers to embrace and celebrate vice as virtue. Denying the dangers of climate change and rampant inequality, he tells the public to focus solely on their personal security, reeling off lists of scapegoats to blame for their problems. Whatever our defects, we want to feel good about ourselves. Trump suggests that we can, while flinging morality to the winds.

Despite the apparent sincerity of his intentions, Jon Kabat-Zinn does something similar. Having secularized mindfulness to help patients face chronic pain, he sells it as a global panacea. We are simply told to focus on the present, ignoring the long-term effects of our behavior. Abstaining from being "judgmental," we are invited to abandon ethical discernment. Just like Trump, the mindfulness movement promotes moral ambiguity to help us feel better. Both reflect the triumph of narcissism in modern American culture.

Wait-and-see-ism

There are traces of this in Kabat-Zinn's analysis, particularly when touting his mindful revolution. "What's the point of not being optimistic?" he tells an interviewer, when asked about the absence of evidence for mass transformation:

> If I fall into despair, you know, and I think it's all going in the direction of greater delusion, and now even mindfulness is falling into the black hole of delusion, well, I might as well kill myself now, do you know what I'm saying? It's like, what is the point? So why not see the beauty in human beings and then create maybe even *laws* that regulate how businesses are done so they don't destroy people in the process, and we have legislators who are trying to do that.[1]

The depth of delusion displayed by such comments is difficult to fathom. Sure, it might help to "create maybe even laws" against corporate excesses, and actually enforce them, but this is not his message when addressing CEOs or politicians, never mind the public, who could conceivably be mobilized for structural change. As for the notion that "we have legislators who are trying to do that" already, the lack of prosecutions of senior bankers for fraud since 2008 speaks for itself.

Instead of combining mindfulness with meaningful steps towards "revolution," Kabat-Zinn prefers to bask in the glow of the present moment, dazzling audiences with fuzzy abstractions like "the beauty in human beings." After all, as he likes to remind us, "it is way too early to tell what the likely fate of humankind will be."[2] This whimsical comment is borrowed from Zhou Enlai, the first Premier of Communist China, who was asked about the impact of the French Revolution (though he thought this meant the protests of 1968). Kabat-Zinn likes to pepper his speech with Asian references, dropping hints at Buddhist wisdom — in the form of Zen koans, or traditional terms such as dharma — to add spiritual cachet to secular mindfulness. By cloaking it in cryptic mystique, he generates interest in his brand. But unless his rhetoric about authenticity is converted into teachings on ethics or interconnection, he might as well be hawking Happy Meals with toys.

In an interview about his promotion of military mindfulness, Kabat-Zinn recalls meeting the Zen master Harada Roshi, who gave him a poster saying: "Never forget the one-thousand-year view."[3] Does it really take that long to grasp that giving soldiers "a kinder, gentler machine gun hand" — as Neil Young puts it — is unlikely to dismantle the military-industrial complex, or end its pursuit of perpetual war? The United States already spends more on weapons than the next ten countries combined.[4]

I'm unconvinced that humans will exist in a thousand years without radical changes. It seems foolhardy to assume that watching one's breath will have any systemic effect on climate change, biodiversity loss, pollution, or mass environmental devastation. As for changing the plutocratic control of government, finance, and the media by corporations — or ending unemployment, inequality, homelessness, substance abuse, or white supremacy — it seems almost mean to suggest that paying attention will wave magic wands.

Ironically, Kabat-Zinn's ideas about future deliverance distract us from what the present most requires of us: political engagement. As the University of Chicago's Lauren Berlant notes: "Optimism is cruel when the object/scene that ignites a sense of possibility actually makes it impossible to attain the expansive transformation for which a person or a people risks striving."[5] Dissent is often stifled by fixation on the moment, letting go of "doing," and thoughts about action. Instead, we are told to retreat to unstable conditions, indulging in what Berlant calls "conventional good-life fantasies." Mindfulness is all very well as a basic coping device, but as a revolutionary strategy it seems empty, tempting its adherents with the comforting impasse of passivity.

A life of mindful moments is one at risk of "cultural infantilization," warns the educational scholar and critic Henry Giroux. "Thoughtlessness has become something that now occupies a privileged, if not celebrated, place in the political landscape and the mainstream cultural apparatuses."[6] Unless it is combined with more liberating teachings, mindfulness just makes oppressive systems work more gently. Echoing the neoliberal message of self-management, Kabat-Zinn shies away from advocating cures, preferring instead the ambiguities of "healing." As he puts it in his magnum opus, *Full Catastrophe Living*: "Healing, as we are using the word here, does not mean 'curing,' although the two words are often used interchangeably." Rather, "healing implies the possibility that we can relate differently to illness," by "coming to terms with things as they are."[7]

Calling this a theory of social change, as Kabat-Zinn does, is not only misleading, it encourages people to bury their heads in the sand. By giving up on action so the present feels bearable, they are "permitting the present to fully colonize the future," writes Eric Cazdyn in *The Already Dead: The New Time of Politics, Culture and Illness*.[8] Of course, no one is mindful all the time, but accepting that it might be desirable is disempowering. It acts as therapy for "realists" who have swallowed the idea that "there is no alternative" to the market logic of Margaret Thatcher. The best we can hope for is palliative care in a neoliberal nightmare, adapting to the brutal forces that afflict us. This is a morally and spiritually bankrupt way to imagine human lives.

Waking Up

Mindfulness could still be revolutionary, but it has to be taught in different ways. Much of this book has effectively shown how not to do it. It has also shown how resistant its leading proponents are to critics. When I draw attention to the flaws of mindfulness programs at conferences, in articles, or online, I'm usually accused of "being negative." For example, Ted Meissner, an MBSR teacher who runs The Secular Buddhist podcast, once asked on Facebook: "Are you going to do anything other than be a crank?"

And Michael Chaskalson, a UK corporate mindfulness consultant, stood up at the end of my presentation at the Bangor mindfulness conference, demanding: "Well, what is it you want us to do differently? What solutions do you have for us?"

It's tempting to say: "You're the ones peddling this crap. Why not stop it?" However, that would be churlish. Besides, unless promoters of mindfulness want to look more critically at what they do, no amount of clarifying is likely to change it. For now, asking challenging questions is important, particularly related to mental conditioning that goes unacknowledged. Perhaps this should even be part of a mindfulness program: sitting with difficult questions, without expecting easy answers. Who or what is privileged when this sort of questioning is shut down? Because most of the time, that's what happens.

In 2015, the veteran activist Angela Davis pressed Kabat-Zinn to confront the limitations of his approach. Teaching individual police officers to be mindful wouldn't stop policing from being a racist institution, she said. "Totally agree," he replied, before throwing it back at her. "If mindfulness can easily be coopted in that way or just kept at a level where it doesn't really change the structural sort of grid or lattice of our institutions because they are self-preserving, then what do you see as an effective alternative?"[9]

Well, one could start by admitting that mindfulness practice alone is insufficient. There is no radical blueprint in paying attention. If the aim is to effect social change, then methods of pursuing it need to be taught. Calming the mind might help these sink in, but it's just a preliminary. By failing to focus on anything but momentary experience, while spouting utopian prophecies of peace and harmony, modern mindfulness is a messianic con trick. The movement's underpinnings are deeply conservative and American: a naïve belief in progress, idealism, and rugged individualism, with all of us free to get lost in a romantic hybrid of Whitmanesque wordplay and ersatz Buddhism.

If promoters of mindfulness are seriously interested in change, they should start by acknowledging the problem: their own complicity in managing systems that naturalize suffering. Instead of channeling people's frustrations into critical questioning of political, cultural, and historical conditions that cause unhappiness, they want to help us endure them. In *The New Prophets of Capital*, Nicole Aschoff explains how calming us down with an optimistic myth serves neoliberal capitalism. For it to endure, she writes, "people must willingly participate in and reproduce its structures and norms," and, especially in times of crisis, "capitalism must draw upon cultural ideas that exist outside of the circuits of profit-making."[10] Mindfulness fits the bill perfectly. Kabat-Zinn is its prophet, joining the ranks of capitalist apologists such as Facebook's Sheryl Sandberg, the media mogul Oprah Winfrey, billionaire Bill Gates, and John Mackey, CEO of Whole Foods.

It is probably no coincidence that Kabat-Zinn — like other mindfulness gurus — traded his activism for meditative quietism fifty years ago. From his comfortable perch, it might make sense to be a passive observer of human afflictions, just "radically accepting" unwholesome conditions. But commoditized impotence is not very helpful to those on the economic precipice, facing a shrinking welfare state, and other disadvantages from xenophobia to cultural trauma. Kabat-Zinn's chief cheerleaders disagree. "Whether you are struggling to put food on the table or you're on top of the world," insists Arianna Huffington, another multi-millionaire, "mindfulness is something that helps you connect you to yourself."[11]

But what do you do after that? If you simply bliss out and accept injustice, how is this different from being a drug addict, sedated into zombified oblivion? Kabat-Zinn likes to talk about "dropping in" to the ever-present wonder of the moment, mindfully enjoying a sunset, washing the dishes, smelling roses, or not missing a baby's smile. This mantra sounds like Timothy Leary's acid catchphrase: "turn on, tune in, drop out." Neoliberal mindfulness wants us to "turn off" critical inquiry, "tune out" of the material world, and "drop in" to a private realm of isolation, reinforcing the cult of the individual. Whatever one might think about psychedelic drugs, at least they dissolve attachment to the self.

Breaking Free

In theory, mindfulness should do something similar — at least in its traditional Buddhist context. As described by Deborah Orr, a York University philosophy professor: "The potential result of this practice is the experiential realization that the self is a construction, we in the modern West would say a social construction, which can foster a delusional self-understanding."[12] The lack of a fixed sense of self is one of Buddhism's core characteristics, along with impermanence, and the dissatisfaction this induces. "Like all those other people and things out there in the world, I, too, am nothing but a mental construct, a phantom's mask covering the reality of change," explains the scholar of Buddhism, C.W. Huntington. "Behind the facade there is no such self, only the ceaseless, ungraspable stream of events that spontaneously emerge and disappear."[13] This revelation can be deeply unsettling unless introduced in a broader context. Our fears and desires tend to make us deny it.

To this extent, some of our suffering stems from personal delusion, and has to be addressed at the individual level. In his final words, the Buddha is said to have urged his disciples: "Strive to attain the goal by diligence."[14] However, the goal includes seeing all things as being connected: the insight of interdependence known as *pratitya-samutpada*. So while some of our delusion is in our heads, tuning out of the conditions that cause us to suffer is also delusional from a political point of view. In Buddhist terms, Huntington notes: "To be somebody — anybody — is to continually suffer." Yet even if we grasp that, we live in a world full of needless suffering, some of which we can alleviate by changing conditions produced by delusion, greed and ill will. These mental poisons are said to be diminished by Buddhist "right" mindfulness, allowing wholesome conduct to prevail. This can also be combined with attempts to do the same at a social level.

When asserting his Buddhist credentials in academic journals, Kabat-Zinn sometimes alludes to these ideas. "The non-trivial question of 'Who am I?' points to wakefulness itself, and non-separation, to the mystery of lived experience and sentience, and the artificial separation inherent in subject/object duality," he pontificates,

> Taking the non-dual perspective into account suggests that it is important to thread the intrinsic complementarity of the instrumental and non-instrumental dimensions of mindfulness together from the beginning both in one's own practice and in one's teaching.[15]

If this means talking about "interbeing" — to use the non-dual language of Thich Nhat Hanh, whom Kabat-Zinn cites — few teachers do. MBSR tells individuals to focus inward on themselves. Yet it is said to impart Buddhist ethics without ever teaching them. "The mainstreaming of mindfulness in the world has always been anchored in the ethical framework that lies at the very heart of the original teachings of the Buddha," Kabat-Zinn says,

> While MBSR does not, nor should it, explicitly address these classical foundations in a clinical context with patients, the Four Noble Truths [of human suffering, its source in desire, and Buddhist teachings that help to remove it] to have always been the soil in which the cultivation of mindfulness via MBSR and other mindfulness-based programs is rooted, and out of which it grows.[16]

What he means is that teachers mean well, so compassion is implied, and nothing needs to be said. This is about as absurd as Kabat-Zinn's suggestions that CEOs might decide to be nice and stop maximizing profits, without being compelled:

> There may be a new way of defining business, so that even banking could rest on an ethical foundation. All sorts of business could actually reexamine what their ethics are, what kind of added value they contribute to the world and then align themselves with that as the absolute foundation for not only any kind of mindfulness programs that they bring into their business but actually the bottom line of how they conduct themselves in the world and what their mission statement is.[17]

His wishful thinking is extreme. If he really wants such things to happen, he needs to begin by liberating mindfulness from its neoliberal shackles. Unless it raises awareness of the social origins of suffering, mindfulness is merely self-management, locating problems in the heads of individuals. This makes the collective solutions we need a lot less likely.

Turning Inside Out

The liberating power of mindfulness is being snuffed out. Experts like Kabat-Zinn impose scientific methods, argues William Davies in *The Happiness Industry*, as "a basis to judge the behavior and mentality of people, rather than the structure of power."[18] We don't have to follow them. Instead of mindfully smothering unhappiness, while ignoring its sources, we should learn to "see things as they are," to

251

quote a meditative truism. "It is often said that depression is 'anger turned inwards'," Davies observes. "In many ways, happiness science is 'critique turned inwards,' despite all of the appeals by positive psychologists to 'notice' the world around us."[19]

Our suffering is often a guide to what needs changing — in the world as well as how we respond. Turning critique back outwards removes the intellectual cover that the mindfulness movement offers capitalism. Privatizing stress as a personal problem, and using science to affirm this agenda, mindfulness turns individuals on themselves. Not only does this blame the victims of cultural dysfunction, it drives a spiral of narcissistic self-absorption. Of course, it's important to feel less stressed, but this has to be combined with empowering insights, not pacification. Truly revolutionary mindfulness is liberating, social, and civic. It depends on critical thinking not non-judgmental disengagement.

Modern mindful elites like Kabat-Zinn reduce social ills to a personal "thinking disease," caused by excessive rumination and outmoded biology from the Stone Age. MBSR draws a simple distinction between being mindful and being mindless, just as neoliberalism divides society into winners and losers. Nowhere is it suggested that our "attention deficit disorder" may have social and political causes, or that connections exist between poverty, lack of adequate housing, and social inequities and the prevalence of mental illness, stress, behavioral problems, and learning disabilities.

This myopic trend may slowly be changing. Two recent letters in *The Lancet Psychiatry*, a prestigious medical journal, call for clinicians and policymakers to classify distress in terms of social factors, not as "disorders" within individuals. The authors, who include a former president of the British Psychological Society, say diagnostic codes should take account of the context of suffering:

> Broadening routine data capture within UK National Health Service records could establish more inclusive, social, systemic, and psychologically comprehensive patterns of difficulties, which could target information regarding established social determinants of mental health problems, such as inequality, poverty, and trauma. Imagine if it were as serious to fail to document extreme poverty as it would be for a clinician to fail to identify severe depression.[20]

They add that the World Health Organization already uses a "non-diagnostic, non-pathologizing, scientific alternative" to document the impact of psychosocial adversity on mental health.

Mindfulness has been undermined by its success. Its radical potential was usurped by elites who have a personal stake in their expert status, through which individuals are pathologized. Seeing things as they really are would reveal such distortions of power and privilege, and the neoliberal framework it helps to sustain. Institutionalized greed, ill will and delusion infest our whole culture, infecting the media, corporations, politics, and the military. This institutionalization makes collective sources of suffering almost invisible, argues Bruce Rogers-Vaughn in *Caring for Souls in a Neoliberal Age*.[21] "Oppressors," he writes, "no longer have faces, even the impersonal 'faces' of the state, the corporation, or the church." If promoters of mindfulness want to stop serving them, they need to limit the biomedical focus on individuals, and develop new explanatory narratives. They need to stop hiding behind their "universal" rhetoric, pleading therapeutic neutrality, or claiming that ethics are somehow "implicit." Instead, they need to take a clear stand.

Rewriting the Rules

It is not only diagnostic models that need changing. Therapeutic methods should also be different, combining practice with critical pedagogies. The causes and conditions of social suffering and oppression should be examined, along with collective experiences of cultural trauma, systemic racism, and other forms of marginalization and displacement that cannot be reduced to psychological maladies. "There is no *Diagnostic and Statistical Manual For Neoliberal Disorders*," notes Rogers-Vaughn, and attempts to address them should not seek to replicate current methods.[22] "I will not be designing a manualized plan for Anti-Neoliberal Therapy (ANT), selling glossy ANT promotional packets, or offering weekend certification programs," he explains. "We simply cannot beat neoliberalism at its own game, or on its own terms."[23] This means that mindfulness curricula should not be confined to internal self-management. A much wider focus is required, using practice to develop an insight into how social experience is embodied.

Not only has suffering been privatized and interiorized, it has also been amplified and marginalized. The result is a level of suffering that cannot be treated at the individual level. Mindfulness offers palliative care for "first-order" suffering: the human existential distress caused by sickness, old age and death, chronic physical pain, conflicts in personal relationships, divorce and loss. When doctors cannot help, this has traditionally been the domain of religious consolation, counseling and therapy. Nowadays, first-order pain is no longer private. It is entangled with social, economic, political, and environmental suffering. Neoliberalism tries to deny this, placing the burden of coping on autonomous individuals, whose bonds of social and collective support have already been weakened. Mindfulness has helped in this process, reinforcing the myth of private suffering.

Human evil leads to second-order suffering, both personally and collectively. Whether individuals are the victims of violence — or whole populations are afflicted by wars, genocide, social injustice, or oppressive conditions — the source of this suffering is identifiable. The third-order suffering caused by neoliberalism is harder to identify, since it is so amorphous, pervasive and systemic. It gets entangled with the first two orders, so the inner and outer worlds become confused. Mindfulness is ineffective at treating this suffering, unless it raises collective awareness of the forces that obscure power relations, class interests, social inequities, and political oppression. Few teachers of mindfulness do this at present, since they themselves are part of the problem. Their form of relief helps to mold individuals into neoliberal subjects, who mindfully accept the status quo like the "cheerful social robots" once described by C. Wright Mills.[24]

Programs modeled on MBSR offer "first-order" therapies of self-management. They were simply not designed for social transformation and collective healing, whatever Kabat-Zinn might like to claim. To become revolutionary, teachers of mindfulness need new practices capable of tackling entangled suffering. They need to develop communal attention, solidarity, and resistance. This requires an understanding of sociopolitical and historical contexts, which are mostly excluded. Take mindfulness in schools. Programs for disadvantaged youth are inept at fostering what Paulo Freire called *concientización*, a critical consciousness that links personal troubles to social situations plagued by violence, poverty, and addiction.[25] Teaching inner-city kids to take a three-minute break to observe their breath just defuses frustration. The conditions producing it are simply ignored.

Part of the problem is a misunderstanding of what people access. Kabat-Zinn's claims about a "universal dharma" assume a false unity in human experience, as if just "dropping in" works the same way for everyone. This is a privileged fantasy, positioning the mostly white mindful elite at the helm of a movement for global salvation. After all, "we're all human," and other such platitudes blinding mindfulness teachers to systemic inequalities. As Robin DiAngelo points out in *White Fragility*:

Whites are taught to see their interests and perspectives as universal [and] they are also taught to value the individual and to see themselves as individuals rather than as part of a racially socialized group. Individualism erases history and hides the ways in which wealth has been distributed and accumulated over generations to benefit whites today. It allows whites to view themselves as unique and original, outside of socialization and unaffected by the relentless racial messages in the culture.[26]

It's obvious that suffering and distress are not universally experienced, nor are they evenly distributed. The universalizing rhetoric of mindfulness is "a discourse of manic defense covering over a complicated situation in which massive numbers of people think otherwise or have serious doubts about business as usual," write Mary Watkins and Helene Shulman in *Toward Psychologies of Liberation*.[27] Cloaking it in science, experts use this ahistorical outlook to talk about what is innate to human nature, while avoiding all the intersecting issues that screw people up.

Mindfulness will not stop the military from lying to justify wars, any more than it will stop corporations from maximizing profits. Mindfulness programs are aligned with the interests of power, not questioning the institutional order. There is never a focus on the exploitation of workers, or the mindless export of suffering as pollution, and other externalities. Mindfulness in politics has not had the slightest impact on global warming, unprecedented inequality, poverty, mass incarceration, racism, sexism, corruption or militarism. Why would it when its aims are so tame and inward-focused?

Psychoanalysis was similarly neutered by being Americanized. Many European psychoanalysts were Marxists and socialists. These neo-Freudians viewed neuroses as a social disease, saying personal troubles could not be divorced from historical and social contexts. As Robert Hattam notes in *Awakening Struggle,* Erich Fromm was dismayed by how "psychoanalysis lost its 'original radicalism' because 'instead of challenging society it conformed to it'."[28] As Fromm himself laments: "The aim of therapy is often that of helping the person to be better adjusted to existing circumstances, to 'reality' as it is frequently called; mental health is often considered to be nothing but this adjustment." As a result, "the psychologists, using the 'right' words from Socrates to Freud, become the priests of industrial society, helping to fulfill its aims by helping the individual to become the perfectly adjusted organization man."[29] Total liberation requires a new praxis, Fromm explains: one that works on the dialectic between self and society, between an interior search for wellbeing *and* changing socioeconomic structures.

We need to revolutionize mindfulness. This requires us to accept the limitations of what is currently taught, and to dispense with the hype surrounding it. The therapeutic functions of mindfulness-based interventions are clearly of value. We don't need to stop using them, but we do need to do much more. Calming the mind can help us engage with social, historical and political realities. We don't need another form of praxis defined in biomedical and universalizing terms. Mindfulness needs to be embedded in the organic histories and local knowledge of communities, empowering them to see how things are.

When we recognize that disaffection, anxiety and stress are not just our own fault, but are connected to structural causes, this becomes fuel for igniting resistance. As Mark Fisher writes in *Capitalist Realism,* "Affective disorders are form of captured discontent; this disaffection can and must be channeled outward, directed towards its real cause, Capital."[30] The liberation of mindfulness depends on building solidarity out of the ruins of McMindfulness, assisting victims of exploitation to resist the inhuman demands of capitalism. Its aim is an individual and collective "conscience explosion," converting exhaustion, depression and burnout into constructive forms of activism.

Beyond McMindfulness

Social mindfulness is not an intervention conducted by experts. It makes no claim to sell "evidence-based" services. Its aims are regenerative, helping to repair solidarities and social bonds that neoliberalism devastates. It does not adopt the outlook of power, and refuses to collude with, or act on behalf of, institutional interests. Instead, it serves community interests, recognizing links between personal, social and ecological liberation. It can therefore be thought of as what Kevin Healey calls "civic mindfulness," restoring collective attention to shared responsibilities.[31]

Instead of despairing at the ravages of capitalism, or clinging to myths about its instant destruction, we can be liberated moment to moment by meaningful action. This is powerful because it reverses our dismembering by neoliberalism, which leaves us divided to fend for ourselves in a cutthroat environment, erasing our collective memory in the process. It is hardly surprising that so many feel hopeless, passive, and cynical. We need to *re-member* — to come back together, to recall what has happened, and to cultivate what Bhikkhu Bodhi calls "conscientious compassion," awakening new visions:

> A collective voice might emerge that could well set in motion the forces needed to articulate and embody a new paradigm rooted in the intrinsic dignity of the person and the interdependence of all life on Earth. Such collaboration could serve to promote the alternative values that offer sane alternatives to our free-market imperatives of corporatism, exploitation, extraction, consumerism, and toxic economic growth.[32]

This approach is the mindful equivalent of liberation theology, allying spiritual practice with radical action. This begins with us bearing witness to shared vulnerabilities, actively acknowledging social suffering, collective trauma and other cultural experiences of oppression. Doing so rebuilds trust and empathy, developing capacities for resistance. Those who suffer together can imagine new futures together. "If our aim is to heal the world rather than to fix it," writes Peter Gabel in *The Desire for Mutual Recognition*, "then we must engage in intuitively-based social-spiritual actions that may redeem our collective being rather than in rationally-based formal changes that we think will bring about social-spiritual effects."[33]

Revolutionary mindfulness neither fetishizes the present moment nor dispenses with judgment. Rather, it embraces the past and the future in conscious pursuit of social change. This communal approach is unapologetically anticapitalist, building on critique to envision the emergence of a new commons. Individual happiness seems hollow unless all human beings are free of oppression, poverty, and violence — as well as free to speak and act in the public sphere. This doesn't mean we have to be miserable in the meantime. We can't help each other if we don't help ourselves. But we have to go further than the smiley face rhetoric of commoditized mindfulness. Dissatisfaction and unhappiness are not impediments to revolution; they are its fuel.

Because liberation is a systemic process, it cannot rely on individual methods. Social mindfulness starts with the widest possible lens, focusing collective attention on the structural causes of suffering. Groups work together to establish shared meanings and common ground, developing a socially engaged motivation before turning inwards. Clearly, this is different to an eight-week program in a boardroom. It goes much deeper and has longer-term objectives, combining resistance with meditative practice. The aim is not to de-stress for more business as usual. It's to overcome alienation by working with others in a common struggle, using inner resources to seek social justice, resisting unjust power both to liberate oppressors and oppressed.

Occasionally, Jon Kabat-Zinn suggests his approach might be mistaken. Despite writing off his critics, he concedes: "There is room for an infinite number of imaginative approaches to healing the human condition." When pushed in a film about *The Mindful Revolution*, he acknowledges that capitalism might stop CEOs from fulfilling his dream. "Well," he laughs awkwardly, "I don't have a problem with the capitalist logic having to change. I mean like everything else it's evolving. The real question is: is it evolving in the direction of greed or is it evolving in the direction of wisdom?"[34]

We don't have time for such indulgent rumination. Liberating mindfulness requires us to face our own delusion. Although this is sometimes a solitary process, it isn't a retreat from the outside world. Instead, it can deepen our sense of connection, provided we see beyond clinging to the illusory separateness of self. If we shed this defensive skin, along with the constant sense of lack that it produces, we face our individual powerlessness. In that insight into the emptiness of self, into the futility of grasping for comfort and control, we find liberating power beyond the isolated "me." Truly revolutionary mindfulness is non-dual: its transformative strength is undivided, owned by no one. By harnessing this together, we can seek the liberation of all sentient beings.

Notes

Chapter One:
What Mindfulness Revolution?

1   http://www.soundstrue.com/podcast/transcripts/jon-ka-bat-zinn.php

2   http://time.com/1556/the-mindful-revolution/

3   Jeff Wilson, *Mindful America*. Oxford University Press, 2014. p.164

4   Jon Kabat-Zinn, *Coming To Our Senses: Healing Ourselves and the World Through Mindfulness*. Hachette Books, 2005. p.143

5   Ibid., p.160.

6   https://www.mentalpraxis.com/zombie-mindfulness.html

7   Wendy Brown, *Undoing the Demos: Neoliberalism's Stealth Revolution*. MIT Press, 2015. p.15

8   Jon Kabat-Zinn, *Mindfulness for Beginners: Reclaiming the Present Moment and Your Life*. Sounds True, 2012.

9   https://greatergood.berkeley.edu/article/item/the_four_keys_to_well_being

10 https://academic.oup.com/jaar/article-abstract/83/3/624/722898?redirectedFrom=fulltext

11 David Forbes, *Mindfulness and Its Discontents*. Fernwood Publishing, 2019, p.34.

12 https://www.youtube.com/watch?v=-kpiqOGpho4

13 https://www.nature.com/articles/nrn3916

14 https://tricycle.org/trikedaily/meditation-nation/

15 http://religiondispatches.org/american-buddhism-beyond-the-search-for-inner-peace/

16 https://www.huffingtonpost.com/ron-purser/beyond-mc-mindfulness_b_3519289.html

17 https://static1.squarespace.com/static/5a8e29ffcd39c3de-866b5e1/t/5b5303d91ae6cf630b641909/1532167130908/McMindfulness.pdf

18 Jeremy R. Carrette and Richard King, *Selling Spirituality: The Silent Takeover of Religion*. Routledge, 2005. p.5

19 Ibid., p. 22

20 Byung-Chul Han, *Psycho-Politics: Neoliberalism and New Technologies of Power*. Verso Books, 2017.

21 https://speculativenonbuddhism.com/2011/07/03/elixir-of-mindfulness/

22 http://theconversation.com/mcmindfulness-buddhism-as-sold-to-you-by-neoliberals-88338

23 Byung-Chul Han, *Psycho-Politics: Neoliberalism and New Technologies of Power*. Verso Books, 2017. p. 30

24 https://www.huffingtonpost.com/ron-purser/beyond-mcmindfulness_b_3519289.html

Chapter Two:
Neoliberal Mindfulness

1 https://www.nytimes.com/2017/03/08/well/mind/how-to-be-mindful-on-the-subway.html

2 Jon Kabat-Zinn, *Wherever You Go, There You Are*. Hachette Books, 2005.

3 https://www.theatlantic.com/business/archive/2015/03/corporations-newest-productivity-hack-meditation/387286/

4   https://medium.com/thrive-global/the-father-of-mind-fulness-on-what-mindfulness-has-become-ad649c8340cf

5   https://www.margaretthatcher.org/document/104475

6   https://mondediplo.com/1998/12/08bourdieu

7   http://www.cabinetmagazine.org/issues/2/western.php

8   https://www.margaretthatcher.org/document/104052

9   Michel Foucault, *The Birth of Biopolitics: Lectures at the College de France, 1978-79*. Translated by G. Burchell. Palgrave Macmillan, 2008.

10 Michel Foucault, *The History of Sexuality Volume 1: An Introduction*. Vintage Books, 1978. p.60

11 Ruth Whippman, *America the Anxious*. St Martin's Press, 2016.

12 https://www.templeton.org/

13 Nikolas Rose, *Inventing Our Selves: Psychology, Power, and Personhood*. Cambridge University Press, 1998. 1999. p.160

14 https://blogs.scientificamerican.com/observations/more-recycling-wont-solve-plastic-pollution/

15 Ibid.

16 Henry A. Giroux, *The Violence of Organized Forgetting: Thinking Beyond America's Disimagination Machine*. City Lights Publishers, 2014.

17 https://rkpayne.wordpress.com/category/buddhism-under-capitalism/

18 Ole Jacob Madsen, *The Therapeutic Turn: How Psychology Altered Western Culture*. Routledge, 2014.

19 Jon Kabat-Zinn, *Full Catastrophe Living*. Bantam Dell, 1990. p.550

20 https://www.mentalpraxis.com/uploads/4/2/5/4/42542199/goto-jones_zombie_mindfulness_manifesto.pdf

21 Julie Wilson, *Neoliberalism*. Routledge, 2017. p.220

22   https://www.uib.no/sites/w3.uib.no/files/attachments/15_
      williams-structures_0.pdf

23   http://digitool.library.mcgill.ca/webclient/StreamGate?fold
      er_id=0&dvs=1547509446906~428

24   Norbert Elias, *The Civilizing Process*. Blackwell, 2000.

25   http://mannersandmindfulness.com/

26   http://www.psow.edu/blog/how-to-be-manners-mindful-
      at-work

27   Jennifer M. Silva, *Coming Up Short: Working-Class Adulthood
      in an Age of Uncertainty*. Oxford University Press, 2015. p.21

28   Lauren Berlant, *Cruel Optimism*. Duke University Press, 2011.

29   Joshua Eisen, *Mindful Calculations: Mindfulness and Neoliberal
      Selfhood in North America and Beyond*. Masters Thesis, McGill
      University, 2014. p.72

30   Lauren Berlant, *Cruel Optimism*. Duke University Press,
      2011. p.1

Chapter Three:
The Mantra of Stress

1   https://www.dailymail.co.uk/health/article-2045309/
      Stress-Top-cause-workplace-sickness-dubbed-Black-
      Death-21st-century.html

2   Jon Kabat-Zinn, *Full Catastrophe Living*. Bantam Dell, 1990.

3   Ibid., xxvii

4   Ibid., p.2

5   Tim Newton, *Managing Stress: Emotion and Power at Work*.
      Sage Publications, 1995.

6   Dana Becker, *One Nation Under Stress: The Trouble with Stress
      As An Idea*. Oxford University Press, 2013. p.18

7   David G. Schuster, *Neurasthenic Nation: America's Search for Health, Happiness, and Comfort, 1869-1920.* Rutgers University Press, 2011.

8   Walter B. Cannon, *The Wisdom of the Body.* W.W. Norton; New York, 1939.

9   Hans Selye, *The Stress of Life.* McGraw-Hill, 1956.

10   https://www.ncbi.nlm.nih.gov/pubmed/3279524

11   Ibid.

12   Dana Becker, *One Nation Under Stress: The Trouble with Stress As An Idea.* Oxford University Press, 2013. p. 37

13   https://www.ncbi.nlm.nih.gov/pmc/articles/PMC3036703/

14   https://www.npr.org/sections/health-shots/2014/07/07/325946892/the-secret-history-behind-the-science-of-stress

15   Ibid.

16   Ibid.

17   Ibid.

18   Dana Becker, *One Nation Under Stress: The Trouble with Stress As An Idea.* Oxford University Press, 2013. p. 40

Chapter Four:
Privatizing Mindfulness

1   https://www.tandfonline.com/doi/full/10.1080/14639947.2011.564844 p.282

2   http://healthland.time.com/2012/01/11/mind-reading-jon-kabat-zinn-talks-about-bringing-mindfulness-meditation-to-medicine/

3   Al Rapaport (ed.), *Buddhism in America.* Tuttle, 1997. p.505

4   Herbert Benson, *The Relaxation Response.* Avon Books, 1976. p.117

5   Richard King, "'Paying Attention' in a Digital Economy: Reflections on the Role of Analysis and Judgement Within Contemporary Discourses of Mindfulness and Comparisons with Classical Buddhist Accounts of *Sati*". In Ronald Purser & David Forbes (eds.), *Handbook of Mindfulness: Culture, Context and Social Engagement*. Springer, 2016. p.38

6   https://www.tandfonline.com/doi/full/10.1080/146399 47.2011.564844

7   Ibid., p.290

8   http://www.integralhealthresources.com/toward-a-mind-ful-society-shambhala-sun-interview-with-jon-kabat-zinn/

9   https://www.facebook.com/rpurser/videos/10154961154191 759/

10   https://symbiosiscollege.edu.in/wp-content/ uploads/2015/03/MBI-An_Emerging_Phenomenon_ Margaret_Cullen.pdf

11   https://www.tandfonline.com/doi/full/10.1080/146399 47.2011.564844

12   https://www.tandfonline.com/doi/abs/10.1080/1463 9940802556560 (p.238)

13   https://www.tandfonline.com/doi/abs/10.1080/0306049 7.2015.1018683

14   https://www.ncbi.nlm.nih.gov/pubmed/24565760

15   https://www.ncbi.nlm.nih.gov/pubmed/24565760

16   Ruth Whippman, *America the Anxious*. St Martin's Press. p.26

17   Carl Cederstrom and Andre Spicer, *The Wellness Syndrome*. Polity Press, 2015.

18   Interview with Jon Kabat-Zinn, *Common Ground*

19   Nomi Morris, 'Fully experiencing the present: a practice for everyone, religious or not', *Los Angeles Times*, 2 October 2010.

Chapter Five:
Colonizing Mindfulness

1   https://bigthink.com/videos/sam-harris-on-secular-med-itation-2

2   https://www.mindful.org/dan-harris-meditation-10-per-cent-happier/

3   https://www.cbs.com/shows/60_minutes/video/V0EAV25FWjaYdEKlbE8w2OgiQAxx8f_T/denied-inside-homs-mindfulness/

4   http://religiondispatches.org/hide-the-religion-feature-the-science-60-minutes-drops-the-ball-on-mindfulness/

5   http://time.com/collection/guide-to-happiness/1556/the-mindful-revolution/

6   Chade Meng Tan, *Search Inside Yourself: The Unexpected Path to Achieving Success, Happiness (and World Peace)*. HarperOne, 2014.

7   Paul Carus, *The Gospel of the Buddha*. (originally published in 1894). Open Court, 1999.

8   http://workplacewellbeing.co/images/davidsonzinn13.pdf, p.95

9   Candy Gunther-Brown, "Can 'Secular' Mindfulness be Separated from Religion", in R. Purser, D. Forbes (eds.), *Handbook of Mindfulness: Culture, Context and Social Engagement*. Springer, 2016. pp. 75-94.

10 Tracy Goodman, Stealth Buddhism. Interview by Vincent & Emily Horn. BG331. www.buddhistgeeks.com/2014/08/bg-331-stealth-buddhism/

11 https://www.mcgill.ca/tcpsych/files/tcpsych/asi_conference_program_2.pdf

12 https://kar.kent.ac.uk/31308/

13   Edwin Ng, Zack Walsh and Ronald Purser, "Mindfulness Is Inherently Political Because Choiceless Exposure To Vulnerability Is a Promise of #MakingRefuge Shared-In-Difference". Unpublished paper.

14   https://www.tandfonline.com/doi/full/10.1080/146399 47.2011.564844

15   Jeff Wilson, "The Religion of Mindfulness." *Tricycle*, Fall, available at https://tricycle.org/magazine/the-reli-gion-mindfulness-essay-jeff-wilson/

16   https://www.ncbi.nlm.nih.gov/pmc/articles/PMC5605584/

17   https://www.ncbi.nlm.nih.gov/pmc/articles/PMC5605584/

18   https://www.tandfonline.com/doi/full/10.1080/146399 47.2011.564844

19   Ibid.

20   Ibid.

21   Jon Kabat-Zinn, *Coming to Our Senses*. Hyperion, 2005, p.9.

22   Jon Kabat-Zinn, *Wherever You Go, There You Are*. Hachette Books, 2009, p.4.

23   Ibid., p.24.

24   Arthur Versluis, *American Transcendentalism and Asian Religions*. Oxford University Press, 2003.

25   Rick Fields, *How the Swans Came to the Lake: A Narrative History of Buddhism in America Shambhal*a, 1992, p.157.

26   William James, "The religion of healthy-mindedness" in *The Varieties of Religious Experience: A Study in Human Nature*. New York, Wayne Proudfoot, 1902/2004. p.95.

27   William James, *Talks to Teachers on Psychology*. Harvard University Press, 1899. p.147.

28   David McMahan, *The Making of Buddhist Modernism*. Oxford University Press, 2008, p.168.

29   http://buddhiststudies.berkeley.edu/people/faculty/sharf/

documents/Sharf%20Is%20Mindfulness%20Buddhist.
pdf, p.479

30   Richard   Cohen,   *Beyond   Enlightenment:
      Buddhism, Religion, Modernity,* 2006.   Routledge.
      p.11.

31   Nyanaponika Thera, *The Heart of Buddhist Meditation.*
      Samuel Weiser, 1973, pp.17-18.

32   https://www.tandfonline.com/doi/abs/10.1080/1463994
      7.2011.564813

33   C. Kelley, "O.K., Google, Take a Deep Breath." http://www.
      nytimes.com/2012/04/29/technology/google-course-asks-
      employees-to-take-a-deep-breath.html

34   Robert Meikyo Rosenbaum and Barry Magid (eds.), *What's
      Wrong with Mindfuln*ess. Wisdom Publications, 2016. pp.
      41-42

35   Ibid., p.42

36   Jon Kabat-Zinn, *Wherever You Go, There You Are.* Hachette
      Books, 2009.

Chapter Six:
Mindfulness as Social Amnesia

1   David Smail, *Power, Interest and Psychology: Elements of a
     Social Materialist Understanding of Distress.* PCCS Books,
     2012. p.7

2   Joel Kovel, The American Mental Health Industry. In D.
     Ingleby (Ed.), *Critical psychiatry: The Politics of Mental Health.*
     Pantheon Books, 1980.

3   Ibid., p.73

4   Russell Jacoby, *Social Amnesia: A Critique of Contemporary*

Psychology. New Brunswick, NJ: Transaction Publishers, 1997.

5   Ibid., p.4

6   W. Pietz, Fetishism and Materialism. In E. Apter and W. Pietz (Eds.), *Fetishism as Cultural Discourse.* Cornell University Press, 1993.

7   T. Dant, Fetishism and the Social Value of Objects. *Sociological Review 44*(3), 1996, p.5

8   Richard Payne, "Modernist Mindfulness." http://rkpayne. wordpress.com/2014/08/22/modernist-mindfulness/

9   http://www.soundstrue.com/podcast/transcripts/jon-kabat-zinn.php?camefromhome=camefromhome

Chapter Seven:
Mindfulness' Truthiness Problem

1   http://time.com/1556/the-mindful-revolution/

2   https://www.ncbi.nlm.nih.gov/pubmed/25783612

3   https://tricycle.org/trikedaily/benefits-mindfulness-hard-prove/

4   https://link.springer.com/chapter/10.1007/978-3-319-44019-4_21

5   https://hbr.org/2015/01/mindfulness-can-literally-change-your-brain

6   https://www.ncbi.nlm.nih.gov/pubmed/19860032

7   https://psicoterapiabilbao.es/wp-content/uploads/2015/12/Khoury_2013_mindfulness-metaanalys.pdf

8   https://www.ncbi.nlm.nih.gov/books/NBK153338/#d1 2013035995.commentary

9   https://journals.plos.org/plosone/article

10 https://tricycle.org/trikedaily/dont-believe-hype/

11 Joel Best, *Flavor of the Month: Why Smart People Fall for Fads*. University of California Press, 2006.

12 Aryeh Siegel, *Transcendental Deception*. Janreg Press, 2018. p.98

13 Herbert Benson, *The Relaxation Response*. HarperTorch, 1976.

14 Ibid., p.140.

15 Jeff Wilson, *Mindful America*. Oxford University Press, 2014. p.80

16 https://projectreporter.nih.gov/reporter_searchresults. cfm

17 https://jamanetwork.com/journals/jamainternalmedicine/ fullarticle/1809754

18 https://effectivehealthcare.ahrq.gov/topics/meditation/ research

19 https://www.nature.com/articles/s41598-018-20299-z

20 https://journals.plos.org/plosone/article

21 https://www.ncbi.nlm.nih.gov/pubmed/15903115

22 https://www.ncbi.nlm.nih.gov/pmc/articles/PMC2778755/

23 David L. McMahan, "How Meditation Works: Theorizing the Role of Cultural Context in Buddhist Contemplative Practice". In D. McMahan & E. Braun (eds.), *Meditation, Buddhism, and Science*. Oxford University Press, 2017.

24 Ronald Purser and David Lewis, "Contemplative Neuroscience's Truthiness Problem." Paper presented at the *Beyond the Hype: Buddhism and Neuroscience in a New Key* conference. Columbia University, 2016.

25 Nikolas Rose and Joelle M. Abi-Rached, *Neuro: The New Brain Sciences and the Management of Mind*. Princeton University Press, 2013.

26 Evan Thompson, "Looping Effects and the Cognitive Science of Meditation." In David L. McMahan & Erik Braun (eds.), *Meditation, Buddhism, and Science*. Oxford University Press, 2017. pp. 47-61

27 Ibid.

28 https://www.ncbi.nlm.nih.gov/pubmed/16022930

29 https://www.ncbi.nlm.nih.gov/pubmed/20467003

30 https://www.ncbi.nlm.nih.gov/pubmed/29016274

Chapter Eight:
Mindful Employees

1   Daniel Goleman, *Emotional Intelligence*. Bantam Books, 1995.

2   Dale Carnegie, *How to Win Friends and Influence People*. Simon & Schuster, 1936.

3   https://pdfs.semanticscholar.org/c5b4/28f63499bd-d3caf39f8bdc28590edce8d8b0.pdf

4   Chade Meng Tan, *Search Inside Yourself: The Unexpected Path to Achieving Success, Happiness (and World Peace)*. HarperOne, 2014. p.134

5   https://www.businessnewsdaily.com/2267-workplace-stress-health-epidemic-perventable-employee-assistance-programs.html

6   https://news.gallup.com/businessjournal/162953/tackle-employees-stagnating-engagement.aspx

7   https://www.researchgate.net/publication/240240954_Stress-management_interventions_in_the_workplace_Stress_counselling_and_stress_audits

8   Tim Newton, *Managing Stress: Emotion and Power at Work*.

Sage Publications, 1995. p. 244

9   David Gelles, *Mindful Work*. Houghton Mifflin Harcourt, 2015.

10 https://www.nytimes.com/2015/08/16/technology/inside-amazon-wrestling-big-ideas-in-a-bruising-workplace.html

11 Richard Wilkinson and Kate Pickett, *The Spirit Level: Why Greater Equality Makes Societies Stronger*. Bloomsbury, 2011.

12 https://www.gsb.stanford.edu/insights/why-your-workplace-might-be-killing-you

13 David Gelles, *Mindful Work*. Houghton Mifflin Harcourt, 2015. p.97

14 Nicholas Carr, *The Shallows: What the Internet is Doing to Our Brain*. W.W. Norton, 2011.

15 http://www.academyanalyticarts.org/rose-power-subjectivity

16 Nikolas Rose, *Inventing Ourselves: Psychology, Power, and Personhood*. Cambridge University Press, 1998. p.114

17 https://rkpayne.wordpress.com/2014/02/18/corporatist-spirituality/

18 Frederwick Winslow Taylor, *Principles of Scientific Management*. Harper & Brothers Publishers, 1915.

19 American Psychological Association, 1962.

20 John Micklethwait and Adrian Wooldridge, *The Witch Doctors: What the Management Gurus are Saying, Why it Matters and How to Make Sense of It*. Mandarin, 1997.

21 https://journals.sagepub.com/doi/abs/10.1177/0038038516655260

22 Richard Gillespie, *Manufacturing Knowledge: A History of the Hawthorne Experiments*. Cambridge University Press, 1993.

23 http://jeremyhunter.net/wp-content/uploads/2013/02/Mindful-Is-Mindfulness-Good-for-Business.pdf

24 https://www.mindful.org/its-not-mcmindfulness/

25 https://www.mindful.org/its-not-mcmindfulness/

26 Ken Keyes, Jr. *The Hundredth Monkey*. Vision Books, 1982.

27 https://link.springer.com/article/10.1023/A:1006978911496

28 Robert L. Park, *Voodoo Science: The Road from Foolishness to Fraud*. Oxford University Press, 2001.

29 http://nomosjournal.org/2013/08/searching-for-integrity/

30 David Gelles, *Mindful Work*. Houghton Mifflin Harcourt, 2015.

31 https://money.cnn.com/2017/01/24/investing/aetna-obamacare-humana-merger/

32 https://www.nytimes.com/2018/06/14/opinion/sunday/meditation-productivity-work-mindfulness.html

Chapter Nine:
Mindful Merchants

1 https://globalwellnessinstitute.org/industry-research/2018-global-wellness-economy-monitor/

2 https://www.mindful.org/its-not-mcmindfulness/

3 https://www.awakenedworldpilgrimage.com/

4 https://www.whil.com/companies

5 Edward L. Bernay, *Propaganda*. Horace Liveright, 1928.

6 https://www.seanfeitoakes.com/mindfulness-the-google-way-well-intentioned-saffron-washing/

7 https://www.publicintegrity.org/2016/02/16/19297/ford-spent-40-million-reshape-asbestos-science

8 https://jalopnik.com/lawsuit-accuses-ford-of-cheating-diesel-emissions-on-50-1821962910

9 https://www.businessinsider.com/marc-benioff-salesforce-

com-chief-has-pulled-some-crazy-stunts-2012-3

10 https://www.fastcompany.com/40433618/not-so-zen-at-headspace-as-layoffs-hit-the-company

11 Headspace factsheet: https://www.dropbox.com/sh/vntkn-lkvkzg98rp/AABIqR-M-IhhCSAcWHXlqQ7na/HS%20Fact%20Sheet?dl=0&preview=Headspace+Fact+Sheet+-+November+2018.pdf&subfolder_nav_tracking=1

12 https://www.forbes.com/sites/kathleenchaykowski/2017/01/08/meet-headspace-the-app-that-made-meditation-a-250-million-business/#713227fc1f1b

13 https://techcrunch.com/2017/09/02/funding-your-bliss-mindfulness-startups-scale-up/

14 https://ebmh.bmj.com/content/18/4/97

15 https://www.wired.co.uk/article/mental-health-apps#_=_

16 https://www.ft.com/content/9b8c0c6e-e805-11e6-967b-c88452263daf

17 George Ritzer, *The McDonaldization of Society*. Sage Publications, 2007.

Chapter Ten:
Mindful Elites

1 Janice Marturano, *Finding the Space to Lead: A Practical Guide to Mindful Leadership*. Bloomsbury Press, 2015.

2 Ibid., p.166.

3 https://www.huffingtonpost.com/janice-l-marturano/mindful-leadership-receiv_b_2543151.html

4 Janice Marturano, *Finding the Space to Lead: A Practical Guide to Mindful Leadership*. Bloomsbury Press, 2015

5 https://www.huffpost.com/entry/collective-mindful-

ness-th_b_4732429

6   https://www.huffingtonpost.com/entry/otto-scharm-
    er-davos_n_4635396

7   https://dealbook.nytimes.com/2015/01/21/amid-the-
    chattering-of-the-global-elite-a-silent-interlude/

8   https://www.rollingstone.com/politics/politics-news/
    the-great-american-bubble-machine-195229/

9   http://www.buddhistpeacefellowship.org/can-mindful-
    ness-change-a-corporation/

10 https://www.academia.edu/25482900/WHAT_IS_
    ENLIGHTENMENT_MINDFULNESS_IN_THE_MOMENT_
    OF_STRESS

11 Byung-Chul Han, *Psycho-Politics: Neoliberalism and New
    Technologies of Power.* Verso Books, 2017.

12 Jeremy Carrette and Richard King, *Selling Spirituality: The
    Silent Takeover of Religion.* Routledge, 2005. p.22

13 Sam Binkley, *Happiness as Enterprise: An Essay on Neoliberal
    Life.* SUNY Press, 2015. p.2

14 Wendy Brown, *Undoing the Demos: Neoliberalism's Stealth
    Revolution.* MIT Press (Zone Books), 2015.

15 http://religiondispatches.org/rich-people-need-inner-
    peace-too-an-interview-with-googles-jolly-good-fellow-
    chade-meng-tan/

16 https://tricycle.org/blog/2014/02/17/protest-
    ers-crash-google-talk-corporate-mindfulness-wis-
    dom-20-conference/

17 https://www.huffingtonpost.com/ron-purser/google-miss-
    es-a-lesson_b_4900285.html

18 http://wisdom2conference.tumblr.com/post/76757167
    725/wisdom-20-2014-google-handles-protesters-with

19 Ibid.,

20 Soren Gordhamer, *Wisdom 2.0: The New Movement Toward Purposeful Engagement in Business and in Life: Ancient Secrets for the Creative and Constantly Connected.* HarperOne, 2009. p.40

21 https://www.youtube.com/watch?v=fFE0GMI9HJ8

22 https://www.youtube.com/watch?v=oTJ9_KM4i4U

23 https://tricycle.org/magazine/buying-wisdom-2/

24 https://tricycle.org/magazine/buying-wisdom/

Chapter Eleven:
Mindful Schools

1 https://mindfulnessinschools.org/

2 https://www.tandfonline.com/doi/abs/10.1080/14639994 7.2017.1301032

3 https://www.mindfulschools.org/

4 https://www.washingtonpost.com/sf/feature/wp/2013/04/11/the-education-issue-believing-self-control-predicts-success-schools-teach-coping/

5 https://www.mindfulschools.org/resources/room-to-breathe/

6 https://link.springer.com/chapter/10.1007/978-3-319-44019-4_26

7 https://link.springer.com/chapter/10.1007/978-3-319-44019-4_23

8 https://www.theatlantic.com/international/archive/2012/03/the-white-savior-industrial-complex/254843/

9 https://journals.sagepub.com/doi/pdf/10.2304/pfie.2013.11.5.538

10 James Reveley, "Neoliberal Meditations: How Mindfulness

Training Medicalizes Education and Responsibilizes Young People." *Policy Futures in Education* 2016, 14 (4) pp. 497–511.

11 Kathryn Ecclestone and Dennis Hayes. *The Dangerous Rise of Therapeutic Education*. Routledge, 2008.

12 https://www.mindfulschools.org/about-mindfulness/mindfulness-in-education/

13 https://mindfulnessinschools.org/mindfulness-in-education/what-is-it/

14 https://link.springer.com/chapter/10.1007/978-3-319-44019-4_29

15 http://www.buddhistpeacefellowship.org/the-heart-of-mindfulness-a-response-to-the-new-york-times/

16 https://www.lionsroar.com/in-engaged-buddhism-peace-begins-with-you/

17 https://link.springer.com/chapter/10.1007/978-3-319-44019-4_24

18 https://mindfulnessinschools.org/mindfulness-in-education/what-is-it/

19 Richard Burnett, "Mindfulness in Secondary Schools: Learning Lessons from the Adults, Secular and Buddhist." *Buddhist Studies Review*, 2011, 28 (1), pp. 79–120.

20 https://www.youtube.com/watch?v=7pLhwGLYvJU

21 Ibid.,

22 https://www.huffingtonpost.com/candy-gunther-brown-phd/mindfulness-meditation-in_b_6276968.html

23 https://www.youtube.com/watch?v=7pLhwGLYvJU

24 https://link.springer.com/chapter/10.1007/978-3-319-44019-4_6

25 https://www.huffingtonpost.com/2013/04/17/warstler-ele-

mentary-school-ohio-mindfulness-program_n_3101741.html

26 http://www.nclplaw.org/wp-content/uploads/2011/12/
DYRSD-Legal-Opinion-Memorandum-2-2-161.pdf

27 https://www.ncbi.nlm.nih.gov/pmc/articles/PMC3151546/

28 http://psycnet.apa.org/buy/2014-14116-001

29 https://www.ncbi.nlm.nih.gov/pubmed/9097338

30 Ibid.

31 https://law.justia.com/cases/federal/district-courts/
FSupp/440/1284/1817490/

32 https://www.davidlynchfoundation.org/

33 https://www.facebook.com/tmfreeblog/photos/pb.137
913942929551.2207520000.1518324891./14424128358
12982/?type=3

34 Ibid.

35 http://tmfree.blogspot.com/

36 https://www.au.org/church-state/june-2009-church-state/
featured/levitating-over-the-church-state-wall

37 https://www.theguardian.com/teacher-network/2015/
nov/24/san-franciscos-toughest-schools-trans-
formed-meditation

38 https://www.theatlantic.com/education/archive/2015/08/
mindfulness-education-schools-meditation/402469/

39 https://link.springer.com/content/pdf/10.1007%2Fs12
671-015-0478-4.pdf

40 https://www.vox.com/science-and-health/2017/5/22/
13768406/mindfulness-meditation-good-for-kids-evidence

41 https://www.ncbi.nlm.nih.gov/pmc/articles/PMC4075476/

42 https://www.vox.com/science-and-
health/2017/5/22/13768406/mindfulness-medita-
tion-good-for-kids-evidence

43 https://journals.plos.org/plosone/article?id=10.1371/

journal.pone.0153220

44 https://tricycle.org/trikedaily/trauma-meditation/

45 https://www.theatlantic.com/health/archive/2014/06/
the-dark-knight-of-the-souls/372766/

46 http://minet.org/www.trancenet.net/
research/2000perezdealbeniz.shtml

47 https://www.researchgate.net/publication/272240728_
Biologising_parenting_Neuroscience_discourse_English_
social_and_public_health_policy_and_understandings_of_
the_child

48 https://royalsociety.org/topics-policy/projects/brain-
waves/education-lifelong-learning/

Chapter Twelve:
Mindful Warriors

1 https://www.ncbi.nlm.nih.gov/pubmed/18157882

2 https://www.army.mil/article/29549/mind_fitness_
improving_operational_effectiveness_and_building_
warrior_resilience

3 https://news.miami.edu/stories/2018/11/ensuring-suc-
cess-in-demanding-roles.html

4 https://doi.org/10.1016/bs.pbr.2018.10.001

5 http://www.amishi.com/lab/wp-content/uploads/Stanley_
Jha-Mind_Fitness-JFQ.pdf

6 William D. Lutz, *The New Doublespeak: Why No One Knows
What Anyone's Saying Anymore.* HarperCollins, 1996.

7 https://www.youtube.com/watch?v=t_WI68yHFqM

8 https://doi.org/10.1016/bs.pbr.2018.10.001

9 http://www.amishi.com/lab/wp-content/uploads/

JhaCV_8.24.17_Web.pdf

10 https://www.psychologytoday.com/us/blog/danger-ous-ideas/201103/the-dark-side-comprehensive-sol-dier-fitness

11 https://thewinnower.com/papers/49-a-critical-examination-of-the-u-s-army-s-comprehensive-soldier-fitness-program

12 http://psycnet.apa.org/doiLanding?doi=10.1037%2Fa00 24932

13 http://www.amishi.com/lab/wp-content/uploads/Stanley_Jha-Mind_Fitness-JFQ.pdf

14 https://psmag.com/social-justice/a-state-mili-tary-mind-42839

15 https://www.theoaklandpress.com/news/marines-study-ing-mindfulness-based-training/article_c4ac9534-d1d9-5eab-91e5-fdec5e4c10c3.html

16 https://www.ncbi.nlm.nih.gov/pubmed/20141302

17 http://www.amishi.com/lab/mbat_project/

18 https://www.inquiringmind.com/article/3002_14_kabat-zinn-interview-with-jon-kabat-zinn-the-thousand-year-view/

19 https://www.youtube.com/watch?v=D5r2sBQM31k

20 https://www.inquiringmind.com/article/3001_16_stanley-cultivating-the-mind-of-a-warrior/

21 Ibid.,

22 https://federalnewsnetwork.com/federal-drive/2013/01/federal-drive-interviews-jan-28-2013/

23 Brian Victoria, *Zen at War*. Rowman & Littlefield, 2006 (second ed.).

24 D. T. Suzuki, *Zen and Japanese Culture*. Princeton University Press, 1938. p.145

25 Brian Victoria, *Zen at War*. Rowman & Littlefield, 2006

(second ed.) p.210

26 https://www.thezensite.com/ZenEssays/CriticalZen/An_
    Ethical_Critique_of_Wartime_Zen.pdf (p.201).

27 Brian Victoria, "Samadhi Power in Imperial Japan."
    Unpublished paper. p.13

28 Brian Victoria, *Zen at War*. Rowman & Littlefield, 2006
    (second ed.) p.139

29 Elizabeth Stanley, "Neuroplasticity, Mind Fitness, and
    Military Effectiveness." In Robert Armstrong & Mark
    Drapeau (eds.), *Bio-Inspired Innovation and National Security*.
    CreateSpace, 2012.

30 Brian Victoria, "Teaching Buddhism and Violence." In
    Brian K. Pennington (ed.), *Teaching Buddhism and Violence*,
    Oxford University Press, 2012. p.89

31 https://www.theguardian.com/commentisfree/
    belief/2012/may/22/anders-behring-breivik-meditation

32 https://sites.google.com/site/breivikreport/documents/
    anders-breivik-psychiatric-report-2012-04-10

33 https://www.inquiringmind.com/article/3002_14_kabat-
    zinn-interview-with-jon-kabat-zinn-the-thousand-
    year-view/

34 https://www.inquiringmind.com/article/2202_4_cullen_
    mindfulness-conversation/

35 http://www.huffingtonpost.com/matthieu-ricard/
    caring-mindfulness_b_7118906.html

36 John Dyckman, "Letter to the Editor". *Inquiring Mind*,
    Fall 2014.

37 http://www.mindfulnesstrainingcourse.org/the-applica-
    tion-of-right-mindfulness--fo

38 Lt Col Dave Grossman, *On Killing: The Psychological Cost of
    Learning to Kill in War and Society*. Back Bay Books, 2009

(revised ed.).

39 http://blogs.dickinson.edu/buddhistethics/files/2010/12/
Premasiri.pdf

40 https://journals.sagepub.com/doi/abs/10.1177/002088
171004600403

Chapter Thirteen:
Mindful Politics

1 Tim Ryan, *A Mindful Nation: How a Simple Practice Can Reduce Stress, Improve Performance, and Recapture the American Spirit.* Hay House, 2012. pp.33-34.

2 Ibid.

3 Ibid.

4 https://www.huffingtonpost.com/one-world-with-deepak-chopra/the-art-of-mindfulness-in_b_5023022.html

5 https://abcnews.go.com/Politics/rep-tim-ryan-meditation-reduces-stress-work-trump/story?id=48378736

6 Tim Ryan, *A Mindful Nation: How a Simple Practice Can Reduce Stress, Improve Performance, and Recapture the American Spirit.* Hay House, 2012.

7 Ibid.

8 Craig Martin, *Capitalizing Religion: Ideology and the Opiate of the Bourgeoisie.* Bloomsbury, 2014.

9 Tim Ryan, *A Mindful Nation: How a Simple Practice Can Reduce Stress, Improve Performance, and Recapture the American Spirit.* Hay House, 2012.

10 https://www.washingtontimes.com/news/2012/jul/11/ohio-democrat-uses-mindfulness-stress-reduction-te/

11 https://www.tandfonline.com/doi/full/10.1080/073931

48.2016.1153195

12 https://www.ncbi.nlm.nih.gov/pubmed/18031225

13 Richard Wilkinson and Kate Pickett, *The Spirit Level: Why Greater Equality Makes Societies Stronger.* Bloomsbury, 2011.

14 https://theintercept.com/2018/07/23/tim-ryan-presidential-run-2020/

15 Tim Ryan, *A Mindful Nation: How a Simple Practice Can Reduce Stress, Improve Performance, and Recapture the American Spirit.* Hay House, 2012. p.167

16 Jon Kabat-Zinn, *Coming To Our Senses: Healing Ourselves and the World Through Mindfulness.* Hachette Books, 2005.

17 https://www.ncbi.nlm.nih.gov/pmc/articles/PMC5605584/

18 https://www.ibtimes.com/heinrich-himmler-nazi-hindu-214444

19 https://www.yogajournal.com/blog/nazi-leaders-fascinated-by-yoga

20 https://www.tandfonline.com/doi/full/10.1080/07393148.2016.1153195

21 https://www.nbcnews.com/politics/elections/sanders-wing-party-terrifies-moderate-dems-here-s-how-they-n893381

22 https://www.politico.com/magazine/story/2018/09/09/tim-ryan-2020-presidential-candidate-yoga-beer-mindfulness-interview-profile-219738

23 Sam Binkley, *Happiness as Enterprise: An Essay on Neoliberal Life.* SUNY Press, 2015.

24 Tim Ryan, *A Mindful Nation: How a Simple Practice Can Reduce Stress, Improve Performance, and Recapture the American Spirit.* Hay House, 2012

25 Jon Kabat-Zinn, *Wherever You Go, There You Are.* Hyperion,

2005

26 https://www.theguardian.com/society/2014/may/07/
politicians-ruby-wax-parliament-mindfulness-meditation

27 https://www.ncbi.nlm.nih.gov/pmc/articles/PMC3964149/

28 https://www.theguardian.com/lifeandstyle/2013/apr/07/
zen-buddhism-nhs

29 https://www.themindfulnessinitiative.org.uk/about/
who-we-are

30 https://www.themindfulnessinitiative.org.uk/about/
mindfulness-appg

31 https://www.mindful.org/can-mindfulness-transform-pol-
itics-2/

32 https://www.themindfulnessinitiative.org.uk/publications/
mindful-nation-uk-report

33 https://themindfulnessinitiative.org.uk/images/reports/
Mindfulness-APPG-Report_Mindful-Nation-UK_Oct2015.pdf

34 https://www.theguardian.com/commentisfree/2015/
oct/20/mindfulness-mental-health-potential-benefits-uk

35 Ibid.

36 Ibid.

37 https://thepsychologist.bps.org.uk/not-mcmindful-
ness-any-stretch-imagination

38 Ibid.

39 https://thebuddhistcentre.com/text/triratna-around-world

40 https://www.themindfulnessinitiative.org.uk/about/
who-we-are

41 https://www.breathworks-mindfulness.org.uk/
meet-our-associates

42 https://www.bbc.co.uk/news/uk-england-hamp-
shire-37432719

43 https://thebuddhistcentre.com/news/statement-ur-

gyen-sangharakshita
44 http://www.wiseattention.org/blog/2012/10/19/secular-mindfulness-buddhism-2-a-wider-view-of-mindfulness/
45 https://www.ncbi.nlm.nih.gov/pmc/articles/PMC5353526/
46 https://eric.ed.gov/?id=EJ1120864
47 https://themindfulnessinitiative.org.uk/images/reports/Mindfulness-APPG-Report_Mindful-Nation-UK_Oct2015.pdf
48 https://eric.ed.gov/?id=EJ1120864
49 https://themindfulnessinitiative.org.uk/images/reports/Mindfulness-APPG-Report_Mindful-Nation-UK_Oct2015.pdf
50 https://www.ncbi.nlm.nih.gov/pubmed/24294837
51 https://www.ncbi.nlm.nih.gov/pubmed/24395196
52 https://www.ncbi.nlm.nih.gov/pubmed/25907157
53 https://www.sciencedirect.com/science/article/pii/S2352250X18301209
54 https://www.conservativehome.com/platform/2018/08/tim-loughton-mindfulness-has-a-crucial-role-to-play-in-tackling-mental-illness.html
55 https://www.sciencedirect.com/science/article/pii/S2352250X18301209
56 Ibid.
57 Ibid.
58 https://www.theguardian.com/lifeandstyle/2017/oct/22/mindfulness-jon-kabat-zinn-depression-trump-grenfell
59 https://www.theguardian.com/lifeandstyle/2017/oct/13/politicians-meditate-commons-mindfulness-event
60 Ibid.
61 https://www.sciencedirect.com/science/article/pii/S2352250X18301209

62   https://www.ncbi.nlm.nih.gov/pmc/articles/PMC5605584/

63   http://www.wbur.org/onpoint/2018/08/14/medita-tion-mindfulness-jon-kabat-zinn

64   https://www.sciencedirect.com/science/article/pii/S2352250X18301209

Conclusion:
Liberating Mindfulness

1   https://vimeo.com/ondemand/themindfulrevolution

2   https://link.springer.com/article/10.1007/s12671-017-0758-2

3   https://www.inquiringmind.com/article/3002_14_kabat-zinn-interview-with-jon-kabat-zinn-the-thousand-year-view/

4   https://www.iiss.org/publications/the-military-balance

5   https://www.dukeupress.edu/cruel-optimism

6   https://truthout.org/articles/domestic-terror-ism-youth-and-the-politics-of-disposability/

7   Jon Kabat-Zinn, *Full Catastrophe Living*. Bantam Dell, 1990. p. 200

8   https://www.dukeupress.edu/the-already-dead/

9   https://www.eventbrite.com/e/video-of-angela-davis-jon-kabat-zinn-east-bay-meditation-center-benefit-tickets-50134682184

10   Nicole Aschoff, *The New Prophets of Capital*. Verso, 2015. p.3

11   http://mindfulnessinamericasummit.com/

12   Deborah Orr, "Ethics, Mindfulness, and Skillfulness," in *Handbook of Ethical Foundations of Mindfulness*, ed. Steven Stanley, Ronald Purser and Nirbhay Singh. Springer, 2018,

pp.137-8.

13 https://tricycle.org/magazine/seeing-things-they-are/

14 Bhikkhu Bodhi, *The Connected Discourses of the Buddha, A Translation of the Samyutta Nikaya*. Wisdom Publications, 2000, p.251.

15 https://www.ncbi.nlm.nih.gov/pmc/articles/PMC5605584/

16 Ibid.

17 https://vimeo.com/ondemand/themindfulrevolution

18 William Davies, *The Happiness Industry: How the Government and Big Business Sold Us Wellbeing*. Verso, 2015. p.251

19 Ibid.

20 https://www.thelancet.com/journals/lanpsy/article/ PIIS2215-0366(18)30394-8/fulltext

21 Bruce Rogers-Vaughn, *Caring for Souls in a Neoliberal Age*. Palgrave Macmillan, 2016. p.126

22 Ibid.

23 Ibid.

24 C. Wright Mills, *The Sociological Imagination*. Grove Press, 1961.

25 Paulo Freire, *Pedagogies of the Oppressed*. Continuum, 2000 (30th Anniversary edition).

26 Robin DiAngelo, *White Fragility: Why It's So Hard for White People to Talk About Racism*. Beacon Press, 2018. p.59.

27 Mary Watkins and Helene Shulman, *Toward Psychologies of Liberation*. Palgrave, 2008. p.29

28 Robert Hattam, *Awakening Struggle: Towards a Buddhist Critical Theory*. University of South Australia Press, 2002. p.228

29 Erich Fromm, *Beyond The Chains of Illusion*, Abacus, 1989. pp.131-132

30 Mark Fisher, *Capitalist Realism*. Zero Books, 2009. p.80

31   http://nomosjournal.org/2013/08/searching-for-integrity/

32   https://tricycle.org/trikedaily/conscientious-compassion/

33   Peter Gabel, *The Desire for Mutual Recognition: Social Movements and the Dissolution of the False Self.* Routledge, 2018. p.210

34   https://vimeo.com/ondemand/themindfulrevolution

Acknowledgements

I would like to give special thanks to my publisher, Tariq Goddard, who took an immediate interest in my book and has been a champion of promoting it. I could have chosen several larger publishing houses, but in the end I chose Repeater because of Tariq's leadership and vision for publishing critical books that challenge the status quo. Etan Ilfeld, owner of Repeater Books and the managing director of Watkins Media, was enthusiastic and supportive of my project from the beginning. I would also like to give a shout out to Josh Turner, Michael Watson and Jonathan Maunder at Repeater for all their help and expertise.

I owe special gratitude to Daniel Simpson, a talented freelance developmental editor, whose expertise and sharp eye helped me enormously in revising the book. Several years before the conception of this book, Daniel and I had many exchanges regarding our mutual suspicion and skepticism towards the mindfulness movement. I would like to express my deepest thanks to friend and mentor, David Loy, who encouraged me to pursue my critique of the mindfulness movement and which led to our viral article "Beyond McMindfulness" in the *Huffington Post*. I have been a fan of David's writings for many years.

Thanks to David Forbes who was an early comrade in establishing a beachhead for the McMindfulness critique. Our collaboration on the Mindful Cranks podcast inspired many of the ideas found here. An earlier version of our account of Google's Wisdom 2.0 debacle appeared in the *Huffington Post*.

I had many conversations with my friend and colleague Andy Cooper, features editor for *Tricycle* on different aspects of the McMindfulness critique. Our mutual concern for the hype and exaggerated scientific claims of the mindfulness movement led us to publish "Mindfulness' Truthiness Problem" on Salon.com.

Thanks also to Edwin Ng, who collaborated with me on a number of social media articles, including "Corporate Mindfulness is Bullsh*t," "White Privilege and the Mindfulness Movement," "Cutting Through the Corporate Mindfulness Hype," "Mindfulness and Self-Care: Why Should I Care." Edwin Ng and I worked on the "Making Refuge" project, which helped me immensely in decoding the discursive habits and rhetorical strategies of the mindfulness movement. Another friend and colleague, Zack Walsh, deserves special thanks. His writings were influential in my critique of neoliberalism and the ideological underlays of the mindfulness discourse. Zack and I continue to collaborate on a number of critical-social mindfulness projects. I am also indebted to David Lewis for his friendship and support since we first met in a lively and controversial Facebook group devoted to critical issues in the mindfulness movement. David educated me on the technical limitations of fMRI brain imaging studies which informed our paper "Contemplative Science's Truthiness Problem," presented at the "Beyond the Hype: "Buddhism and Neuroscience' in a New Key" at Columbia University.

Thank you to many colleagues and friends who supported me along the way, many of whom have made their own unique contributions to a critical mindfulness discourse, including Steven Stanley, Venerable Bhikkhu

Bodhi, Robert Thurman, Christopher Titmuss, Kevin Healey, Glenn Wallis, Richard King, Jeff Wilson, Jack Petranker, Linda Heuman, Hugh Wilmott, Alex Caring-Lobel, Joe Millilo, Deborah Rochelle, Bernard Faure, Tom Yarnall, Richard Payne, Lisa Dale Miller, Shaila Catherine, Alan Senauke, Ilmari Kortelainen, Mushim Patricia Ikeda, Katie Loncke, Dawn Haney, Funie Hsu, Brian Victoria, David Brazier, Manu Bazzano, Gary Gach, Peter Doran, Samuel Stephan, Juan Humberto-Young, Pierce Salgado, David McMahan, C.W. Huntington, Nirb Singh, Antonino Raffone, Massimo Tomassini, Ruth Whippman, William Davies, Willoughby Britton, Paul Grossman, Miguel Farias, Catherine Wikholm, Rabbi Michael Lerner, Justin Whitaker and Josh Baran.

I must also thank James Shaheen, editor of *Tricycle*, who was a generous co-sponsor for "Mindfulness and Compassion: The Art and Science of Contemplative Practice", an international conference which I organized at San Francisco State University. Likewise, I am grateful to Norm Oberstein and the generous financial support the Frederick Lenz Foundation for American Buddhism has provided me for envisioning ways to liberate mindfulness from its current stranglehold under neoliberalism.

I extend special thanks to my friend and mentor B. Alan Wallace, who, from the beginning, shared my concerns regarding the commodification of mindfulness. Alan's supportive presence was behind the scenes throughout the writing. His unwavering source of spiritual and intellectual support was critical to sharpening the critique. I am also deeply indebted to the Ven Dr Jongmae Kenneth Park, former Bishop of the Korean Buddhist Taego Order, whose wisdom, compassion and unbridled energy has been a source of inspiration.

I would like to thank Tom Thomas, my department chair at San Francisco State University, for his tolerance and patience given that I was missing in action from department duties for about a year.

Finally, I wish to thank my lifelong partner, Wendell Hanna, for her initial prodding that I should venture off to become a solo author. She has stood behind me in taking on the mindfulness movement and without her this book would never have made it into print. And, a special thanks to my dog, Nick, who helped me to get the exercise when I needed breaks from the computer.

Repeater Books

is dedicated to the creation of a new reality. The landscape of twenty-first-century arts and letters is faded and inert, riven by fashionable cynicism, egotistical self-reference and a nostalgia for the recent past. Repeater intends to add its voice to those movements that wish to enter history and assert control over its currents, gathering together scattered and isolated voices with those who have already called for an escape from Capitalist Realism. Our desire is to publish in every sphere and genre, combining vigorous dissent and a pragmatic willingness to succeed where messianic abstraction and quiescent co-option have stalled: abstention is not an option: we are alive and we don't agree.